LAND
BEYOND THE NILE

LAND BEYOND THE NILE

MALCOLM FORSBERG

HARPER & BROTHERS
PUBLISHERS NEW YORK

19353

To my sister Ellen

To my wife Ellen

Contents

III. THE SUDAN

. . . the full corn in the ear

A group of illustrations follows page 128

Appreciation

THIS STORY had to be autobiographical. There was no other way to write it. But the story represents the thousands who have labored more than we and whose experiences did not always end in deliverance. And it is the story of our fellow missionaries who have given themselves gladly for Africa. They will recognize themselves, often unnamed, in the pages of this book. If I should name all of them, and place well-deserved crowns on their heads, they would unhesitatingly remove them and cast them at His feet. They are that kind of people.

I am grateful to our Sudan missionary-artist, Charles Guth, also of Wheaton, for setting aside his own important work to make the maps.

His Excellency Dr. Ibrahim Anis, the first ambassador of the Republic of the Sudan to the United States, kindly granted me an interview in New York and brought me up to date on present trends in the Sudan.

His Excellency Mohammed Osman Yassin, Undersecretary for Foreign Affairs in the Sudan government, graciously received me at his hotel in New York. He was there to set up his government's delegation at the United Nations, of which organization the Sudan is now a member. His commentary on the place of the Sudan in world affairs was most helpful.

My appreciation also goes to the following individuals:

Janet Smith, of Tacoma, Washington, who first typed the manuscript.

The many persons who sent me pictures for the book.

The First Presbyterian Church of Tacoma, Washington, for its loyalty and support over many years, and to my pastor there, Dr. Albert J. Lindsey, for giving me an office in which to work.

The Garfield Avenue Baptist Church in Milwaukee, Wisconsin, and its pastor, Dr. William E. Kuhnle. None of our supporters has prayed more earnestly or given more liberally than these.

The First Methodist Church of Santa Barbara, California, and its pastor, the Rev. Frank Matthews, for providing me with a place in which to write.

The First Presbyterian Church in Flushing, New York, and its pastor, the Rev. Louis F. Hutchins. The church has contributed to our support during most of our time in Africa, and while I was in New York City, working on the final draft of the manuscript, the Hutchinses welcomed my family.

Friends and officers of our Mission in our New York headquarters, who put up with me during this time.

Dr. A. D. Helser, General Director, Sudan Interior Mission, the Rev. Guy W. Playfair, General Director Emeritus, and Dr. M. A. Darroch, Home Director, who gave their blessing to my writing.

It is a source of deep satisfaction that I can write of the work of the Sudan Interior Mission with complete confidence and affection. We have carried on our missionary labors in this organization during all our adult lives. Many of our happiest friendships have been formed within its membership. Without the Sudan Interior Mission there would have been no book.

It was while taking a course in nonfiction writing at the Adult Education Center in Santa Barbara, California, in the spring of 1956, that I received my first real indication of where I was going. As part of my homework, I turned in a chapter of this book which was already under way. The instructor, Chet Holcombe, of the Santa Barbara *News-Press*, read it to the class and asked for criticism. The favorable response encouraged me to continue.

Some missionaries go abroad over the protests of their parents. In 1933, my mother said she would mortgage her home if by doing so she could help me go. I hope I have brought some of her loyalty to the Lord into my work and into the writing of this book.

When I launched out on this uncharted literary sea, I needed help. Virginia Matson plotted my course and Muriel Fuller brought me to harbor. I owe a great debt of gratitude to them.

Eleanor Jordan of Harper & Brothers took a personal interest in my manuscript and guided it through the editorial shoals.

Enid and the children, with their courage and devotion, made the writing of the book possible. Without the prayers and support of God's people back home through the years, nothing would have been possible.

MALCOLM FORSBERG

Khartoum
The Sudan
January, 1958

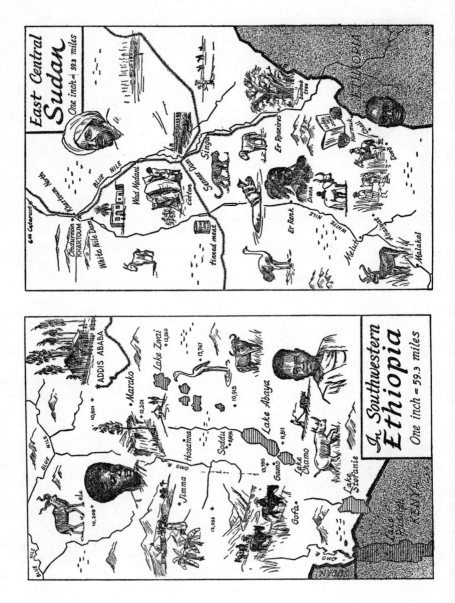

East Central *Sudan*
One inch = 59.3 miles

In Southwestern *Ethiopia*
One inch = 59.3 miles

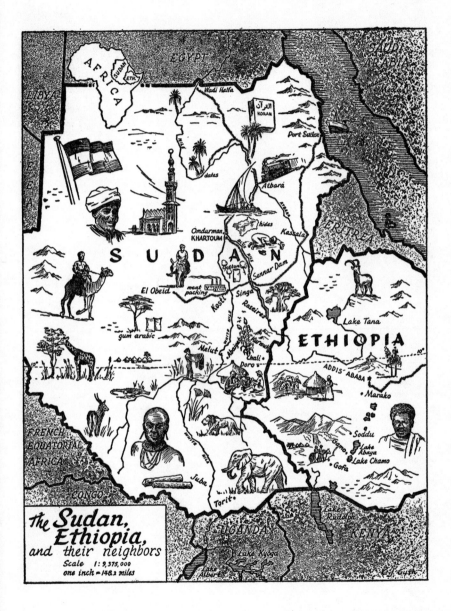

The Sudan, Ethiopia, and their neighbors

Scale   1: 9,375,000
one inch = 148.2 miles

PART I

Ethiopia

First the blade . . .

1

The Evil Eye

IT WAS only seven-thirty but already the sun had risen high and hot over our African home. We were sitting in the living room, our after-breakfast devotions completed, and our daughter Dorothy, blonde, curly-headed, not yet two, had toddled out the door to where her two friends were waiting. They were daughters of native Christian couples and together they disappeared down the path toward the clinic to see what new babies might be there.

Enid, my wife, was preparing for her class when Mona, our first convert in the Uduk tribe, suddenly appeared at the back door.

"The woman has come!" he said. The Uduks do not show excitement easily and Mona was plainly excited. His eyes, trained to conceal rather than to reveal feeling, were alight.

"What woman?" we asked, as we both tried to get through the screen door at the same time.

"The woman has come with her twins," he said.

So certain were the superstitious Uduks that twins brought calamity, that up to the present time none had been allowed to live. The non-Christian Uduk women were killing their twin babies at birth.

We ran down the steps and out into the yard. There, in the shade of a tree, sat Doatgay. Her short hair was matted with red oil and dirt, and although she was still young, wrinkles were forming. Her face was haggard, her eyes pleading. She held her babies but did not press them to her breasts. Since childhood she had been told that twins were not human. Only goats had twins. She knew that even though the babies were destroyed, as the mother of twins she would be considered dangerous to her tribe. In the long years ahead she would always be suspect in any illness, death, hardship, or famine that might come to her people.

We snapped fingers—the Uduk version of a handshake—with Doatgay. I pressed the middle finger of her right hand with the thumb and middle finger of mine and she did the same to me. Then, drawing apart, I pressed hard and the act was completed with a loud snap.

As we beamed at the babies, we realized the significance of this day for us; these were the first Uduk twins we had ever seen. My mind flashed back to our early days at Chali, when we had noticed the conspicuous absence of twins and encountered a frustrating secrecy about multiple birth. "Twins have the evil eye," the people had finally told us, shuddering.

Gradually we had learned that even to talk about twins was taboo. Then the truth was revealed: Twins were buried alive at birth! Thirteen years had passed since our first arrival at Chali. Now, unexpectedly, on this hot morning in 1952, an opportunity such as we had prayed for was being offered.

"We are glad you have brought your twins, Doatgay." Enid measured her words carefully as we stood looking down at the trio. "We will help you take care of them."

Doatgay was the picture of misery. "I wanted to bury them," she said, "but I was afraid of the government. My people said I couldn't stay in the village with the curse on me, so I came to you."

Three years before the birth of Doatgay's babies, a mother and two women helpers had been caught in the act of burying newborn twins alive. The infants had not been saved but the British District Commissioner issued a solemn warning to the Uduks. He held a trial to which he called the elders of all the villages. He asked us to sit with him, for he knew we could be a help in this particular case. The situation called for drastic action.

"You have buried your babies alive," he began, addressing the women. "Why shouldn't I bury you alive?"

The mother of the twins and her two helpers turned their heads slightly. They were sitting sideways. The whites of their eyes showed as they looked up with the faintest trace of surprise.

"In fact," the D. C. continued, "the men will start digging the hole now." He selected several men and showed them where to begin. Then he went on: "It is the job of the government to see that the people of the country behave themselves. Nowhere does the government allow people to be killed, not even twins." He turned to the gravediggers. "How is the hole coming?"

"It's not ready yet," the men replied.

At first the three women had not believed that the government official would actually bury them alive, but as the digging proceeded they slowly turned ash-gray. One of the women called her son to her side, and instructed him about her affairs. "Keep an eye on the red cow which is about to calve," she said. "And don't forget to pay the witch doctors. We owe them a goat."

The D. C. walked over to the grave and inspected it carefully. Then, returning to his seat, he ordered the men to stop digging. He pronounced his verdict.

"I am not going to bury you alive."

The crowd relaxed. The women sighed with relief.

"However," the D. C. said, "the mother will spend one year in prison. The others will get two years each. This is the first time we have had court about a matter like this. If it happens again, the guilty people will be hanged with a rope until they die."

The crowd scattered, leaving the women sitting forlornly on the ground. The D. C. turned to us.

"We have no place to keep women prisoners here," he said. "I'll parole them into your care. They can spend their time grinding grain and cooking food for the school children. I gave the mother only one year because she was the victim of tribal custom. The other two are professionals. They have probably been involved before."

I was thinking of all this as Enid, Mona, and I stood looking down at Doatgay. Mona spoke:

"You don't have to be afraid of the old talk any more, Doatgay. The paper tells us that twins, too, are people. We who believe the paper are not afraid of twins. God will help you and we will help you."

"What have you named the babies?" Enid asked.

"Have twins in our tribe ever lived to have names?" Doatgay countered. "You name them."

Enid looked at me questioningly. Names do not always come easily. We had had a hard enough time naming our own children. "I know," she said at length. "The Lord has heard us in this matter of twins. We'll call them Borgay and Thoiya—Praise and Prayer."

Thus the first twins ever allowed to live in the Uduk tribe were appropriately named. It was by such incidents that we marked our progress in a program that had started a long time ago. Looking back, there was much to remember . . .

2

Our African Home

IN 1952, we had been missionaries in Africa for nearly two decades, first in Ethiopia, then, after Mussolini put us out of that newly conquered dominion, in the Sudan. The official records of the Sudan Interior Mission list us as Malcolm and Enid Forsberg, appointed in 1939 to the Chali Station of our Sudan field. On our arrival, the station had consisted of one house. In 1952, there were several. Our bungalow had three small rooms in a row—a bedroom and a bath on one end and a combination dining room and kitchen on the other, with a living room in the middle. A screened-in veranda, nine feet wide, stretched the length of the house. One end was separated by screening to form a sleeping porch, for it was usually too hot to sleep in the bedroom.

The outer walls of the bungalow were red brick veneer, with an inner layer of mud bricks which were cheaper than the burnt ones and also provided better insulation against the heat. The inner walls were plastered with a mixture of dirt and sand and were whitewashed. A ceiling of aluminum sheets was topped by a roof of corrugated iron over a framework of mahogany timbers.

In the living room we sat in solid, comfortable armchairs made by local Arab carpenters, who had also built the dining-room table of lumber sawed from native trees. The heavy furniture, so out of place in the modern American home, was perfect in our African bungalow. There were pictures on the walls, one a snow scene, and occasional tables, bookcases, and knickknack shelves. The windows had no glass, but there were wooden shutters, open most of the time.

At her desk Enid put the finishing touches to her Bible lesson for class. For several days she had been trying to get the Children of Israel out of Egypt but added detail and application of the lesson to the lives of the Uduk school children had made the march to the Red Sea a slow one. Today she was determined to cross it.

I had sent the mail boys off with their donkeys. They were late starting for it had rained in the night. During the rains, mail came only once every two weeks. Air-mail letters to us reached Khartoum from New York in five days, were then sent to Kurmuk, the end of the government mail line, and delivered to us ten or fifteen days later. Two days would be spent by the mail boys slushing through mud and crossing swollen streams to cover the thirty miles to Kurmuk. Then, after a day's rest, they would start homeward with the heavy mailbags. However late the mail was, we always hunted for the familiar handwriting of our three boys— Leigh, in boarding school in America, and James and Kim in our own Mission school in Addis Ababa.

On this September day, made memorable by the advent of the twins, I looked at the distant mountains of Ethiopia, their heads dark and majestic just across the fields. They always seemed much closer after the rain, and even after eighteen years, they still excited me. The rocky hills scattered about the plain looked like abandoned offspring of the mountains. I walked around to the front of the house. The big baobab tree was in full leaf, with nests of the white-bellied storks forming dark blobs along its branches. The young storks had hatched out in April and flown north in June. Perhaps they were in Europe, getting ready for the return flight, though they would not visit us on the southward journey.

Several years before we had planted neem trees, which are native to India, but they had not grown well in the shallow soil that covered the solid granite of our Chali knoll. Still, they did add greenness and shade during the dry season. Along the edge of the station the grass grew like a wall, eight to ten feet high, stretching away into infinity. The trees in that vast expanse never grow tall, becoming twisted and stunted by the furnacelike fires that sweep through the grass in the dry season.

The Sudan is a land of birds. Perhaps Isaiah meant this land when he wrote of "the land shadowing with wings, which is beyond the rivers of Ethiopia." A sunbird lit on a zinnia blossom nearby and helped itself to the nectar. A blue waxbill scouted along the ground for insect food, while just beyond, a wagtail foraged, tail flipping up and down as it minced along. Overhead a flock of grain-eating finches, myriads of them, wheeled and whirred in perfect, if seemingly erratic, formation. Soon their young would be hatched out in the thousands of woven nests hanging from the tall grass down by the stream just a mile away. Then the Uduks would rob the nests before the young had their feathers, the baby birds eaten almost like candy. The bee eaters were still with us. They flashed crimson and malachite in the sun as they dived and turned and swooped after their prey—bees, moths, and grasshoppers—which they caught in their slender turned-down bills.

As I mused upon these scenes, a single line of Uduks came toward me. Instead of clothing, they were covered with red oil, and held their short-handled hoes. These were men and boys of a Chali clan on their way to the field of one of their number. They would work all morning on their knees, hoeing out the weeds and grass in the sorghum field. By one o'clock the group would return to the home of the owner of the field to spend the rest of the day drinking the beer his wife had brewed in ten-gallon earthenware pots. Dozens of men and women who had not worked in the field would also be there to drink the beer. Unfortunately, this maldistribution of time between working and drinking resulted in small crops and there was never really enough to eat. The grain used to make beer would have gone much further as food.

I returned to the house in time to hear the mothers of Dorothy's playmates call from the back yard. They were looking for their daughters. They stood there in their clean dresses, heads clean shaven, a sharp contrast to the men and boys I had just seen. But it was not only clothing that made the difference. Their pleasant, bright, relaxed expressions set them off from the others. Each of the women held her copy of the Gospel of Mark, in Uduk. I told them I had last seen their daughters going down the path in the direction of the clinic and that by now they would be outside the school, distracting the children with their antics. The mothers laughed and went off to find them.

It was easy then to prepare my Bible lesson for the men's meeting. The contrast between the men in the front yard and the women in the back made our long efforts as missionaries seem worthwhile. It had not been a superficial change. The women believed in Christ in their hearts and the joy they felt was visible in their faces. The power of God was working. A visiting Egyptian anthropologist had once told us that the Uduk people were among the most primitive in Africa. But we believed that eventually some of the people would accept the truth that Christ died for their sins and would become Christians. Then we would teach them to read the Scriptures, which we were to translate into their language.

The Lord had been good to us and to our fellow workers. Once we had but one baptized believer, Mona. Now there were others, living settled Christian lives. A new generation of boys and girls was coming up through the school. They would not follow the old ways of their fathers.

3

Africa Began at Wheaton

IT ALL began in 1928 at Wheaton College in Illinois, twenty-five miles west of Chicago. Back in the First Presbyterian Church in Tacoma, Washington, I had been deeply moved by the magnificent preaching of my pastor, Dr. Clarence W. Weyer, and decided to go to Wheaton to prepare for some kind of active Christian service. Its fame as a Christian college had reached the Pacific coast. Wheaton had been founded in 1860 by a sturdy Vermonter named Jonathan Blanchard, whose purpose was to provide a higher education dedicated to the elimination of the sins of slavery, intoxication, secret societies, and worldliness. I had been attracted to Wheaton by its evangelical precepts and its high moral standards.

The sun was warm and the tree-lined streets beautiful on my first day there. I made my way up the walk to Blanchard Hall, the long limestone building named for the founder and his successor-son, Charles A. Blanchard. It was on top of a small rise known as College Hill, from which a wide expanse of lawn sloped gently, dotted with hardwood trees. I remembered reading in the college catalog that the east wing had been completed the previous year. The building was indeed nicely balanced. Dominating the center of the structure was the Tower, the architectural heart of the college. The annual was called *The Tower*, and I remembered also that the bell in the Tower was rung to announce athletic victories and engagements.

It did not take long to see the whole campus. There were the women's dormitory, the chapel shared with the College Church of Christ, the cracker-box gymnasium, and the Academy building. But Wheaton was growing, and even then enrollment had to be limited, so numerous were the applications from prospective students. As materialism and an agnostic interpretation of science and life increased in secular universities and

23

even in once-Christian colleges, the popularity of Wheaton and colleges like it expanded. In the 1950's Wheaton, with facilities for only fifteen hundred students, would be receiving seven thousand applications a year.

I took my place with the Class of '32. There were six hundred students in the college and a sense of belonging came very quickly. I found I could enter wholeheartedly into every activity. Chapel was daily and compulsory in the same way that it had been compulsory at home to appear at the table three times a day. The services were seldom dull though the student body was critical. The rare speaker who was dull soon found himself looking into a sea of bored faces. The one who had something worthwhile to present could hardly find a more responsive audience.

One day during the first term of my freshman year, a missionary from the Congo was the chapel speaker. He told of representatives of tribes in the Congo coming to him and begging for preachers and teachers to help them. There were never enough. So impressed was I by the lack of opportunity Africans had to hear the gospel compared to the opportunities thrown away in the United States, that I left the service convinced that God wanted me to meet some similar need in Africa. This is a conviction that sometimes takes months or years to mature. My experience, for which I was wholly unprepared, was compressed into minutes. It had never occurred to me before that day that the Lord might want me to serve Him in a foreign land.

Most of my college days still lay ahead of me. I earned much of the money I needed for my college expenses shoveling coal into the furnaces of the college heating plant and raking ashes out. I had time for lectures and student activities, parties and musicals, too. Wheaton was fun and deeply satisfying.

My second year, Enid Miller arrived on the campus from Milwaukee, Wisconsin. She, too, was a Presbyterian. On her father's side she came from the same Pierpont family from which Jonathan Edwards took his wife. Enid's English mother and Yankee father had moved their family to Wisconsin from Waterbury, Connecticut, about the time Enid entered high school. When she was ready for college, she had wanted to go with her high school friends to the University of Wisconsin. However, her mother felt she needed the atmosphere of a Christian college and urged her to consider Wheaton. Enid finally agreed, if she could transfer to Wisconsin at the end of her freshman year.

The fall evangelistic services were held early in the new term. Enid soon realized that she was not a born-again Christian. The visiting minister said there had to be a personal acceptance of Christ as Savior. She decided for Christ and the University of Wisconsin was not mentioned again.

Enid was full of life and ideas so it was quite natural that she should be elected social chairman of the freshman class. I was attracted by her naturally curly brown hair, her ready smile, and the fascinating little wrinkles on her forehead when she was in deep thought. Her head reached to my shoulder (I was about an inch less than six feet) but she made up in drive and zeal what she lacked in height.

She saw a youth with blond hair, a first-generation American, as my parents had both been born in Sweden. I regret to say a shock of hair usually hung down over one eye, and my nose was as high as my Scandinavian cheekbones. My friends frequently remarked on the size and shape of my nose, but I found it provided a firm saddle for the horn-rimmed glasses I wore through college.

It was midwinter before Enid even knew who I was. One night at ten below zero the freshmen were going on a sleigh ride. As social chairman, Enid arranged for the sleigh to be at the Tower entrance at eight o'clock. I heard about the plans and, asserting my privileges as a sophomore, called the livery stable and told them not to send the sleigh. In the furor that followed, I was exposed as the culprit.

That autumn Enid and several friends were subjected to lengthy discipline for a campus prank, and they were sent home for a week to reflect on their conduct. When I overheard two of my friends planning to date Enid and her companions on their return to the campus, I thought it a good idea. I decided to get ahead of the rest by writing her a letter, but when she returned to college, she and her friends were not permitted to attend social or athletic functions for the remaining four months of the term. All I could do was say "Hello." I had to progress the hard way.

At that time I was eating at various boardinghouses around town. When I learned that Enid was working behind the counter of the college cafeteria, I changed my habits and joined the slow-moving line there. I had plenty of time to observe her. She seemed to be the center of the banter behind the counter, with a word and smile for each person. I had complicated matters for her by writing; now she had to face me in line. She blushed slightly as she served me, wrinkling her forehead quizzically, and seemed relieved when I turned away.

Friday nights were sacred to the half-dozen college literary societies, but as these meetings were regarded as social events, Enid and her friends could not go. To fill in that time, the assistant dean of women met with them and told of her former work among the Navajo Indians. This meeting was followed by prayer for missionaries all over the world. Enid's heart was stirred. Missionary speakers from Africa also moved her and by midterm she realized that Africa was looming large on her horizon.

Now I was at least a speck on that horizon. During study periods I began to sit by her in the library and I also walked home with her to her dormitory, a distance of nearly two hundred yards. At least I wasn't losing ground. By the end of my junior year we were seeing each other often. We walked the Wheaton streets until they were familiar. One Sunday night we decided to try the subdivisions. There plots had been divided, but the depression had come and no houses had been built.

The street ended and we stood looking at each other. I blurted out the question and she said "Yes."

Suddenly the restraint was gone and Enid told me about the prayer meetings. "Since then," she added, "I've told the Lord I was willing to go to Africa but I asked Him to give me somebody to go with."

The fact that I also wanted to go struck her as the answer to her prayer. That was Baccalaureate Sunday, June 14, 1931. From then on, things began to happen. We knew nothing about mission boards. I had assumed that since I was a Presbyterian, I would go out under its foreign mission board. But one day the following year a representative came to Wheaton to interview all candidates of that denomination.

"Are you interested more in working with your hands or with your head?" he asked.

I tried to think of things I liked to do. It wasn't easy to answer such a question on the spur of the moment. "I guess I like both," I replied.

I waited for my interviewer to ask me something about my understanding of the gospel and of my spiritual fitness to be in Christian work. The question never came and I left in confusion. For the first time I had misgivings. I thought of the speakers we had had in chapel, especially Sir John Alexander Clark, the Plymouth Brethren missionary who had represented their missions in the Congo, and Dr. Thomas Lambie from the Sudan Interior Mission—a faith mission whose support comes not from any one denomination but from believers everywhere. Both men had told of their pioneer work and of the tribes that were then without a witness.

We learned that James Hudson Taylor, better known merely as

Hudson Taylor, was the father of faith missions. In the 1850's he had gone to China as a medical missionary under the Chinese Evangelization Society. China was then being torn by the Taiping rebellion and foreigners were allowed to live only in Shanghai and in four other coastal Treaty Ports. During his first term, Taylor did medical work and learned the Chinese language. But he was unhappy that the Society was going into debt to pay him his small allowance and he longed for an organization that would be alive to China's need and that would seek to meet that need in utter dependence upon God.

Hudson Taylor's first furlough was spent in acquainting Christians in Britain with the appalling conditions in China. God was moving in his life. He felt he could not fully respond to that moving in his present affiliation, so he determined to start out alone. He made his first bank deposit in the name of the China Inland Mission, announced his need of twenty-four men and women to accompany him back to China, and with these recruits returned to Asia.

His expressions of faith and his compassion for China had stirred thousands to give their support to him and his new organization. He formed a board at home in England to receive the contributions of these people and to send the funds on to China. There would be no public appeals for funds and the board would be under no obligation to send any stated amount to the missionaries who would trust the Lord to supply whatever they needed. Nor would the missionaries in the new organization, who came from many denominations, receive any help officially from these denominations.

But trusting the Lord for money was only one side of faith. The doors to inland China were still closed. Taylor kept up the pressure against these doors by prayer, by faith, and by negotiation with the Chinese. Faith opened the doors not only to the China Inland Mission but through it to dozens of other societies that followed. Eventually Hudson Taylor's missionaries preached the gospel in every province of China.

It was 1893 before West Africa had its Hudson Taylor in the person of Rowland Bingham. Bingham went to the coast with two companions, determined to take the gospel inland. Evangelical missionaries from several denominations eventually joined him and the work of the Sudan Interior Mission began in inland Nigeria. One day John Gunther would refer to our Mission in *Inside Africa* as "one of the most celebrated institutions in Africa." Elsewhere, similar groups were rising and in time formed a loose organization called the Interdenominational Foreign Missions Association.

Meanwhile, the Christian church in Europe and America was becoming deeply concerned with the expanding field of textual criticism of the Bible. Many of its leaders were asserting that the Bible could no longer be taken literally. Part of the church experienced a new theological outlook and consequently lost much of its evangelical fervor. Missionary work found greater expression in educational, medical, and social institutions.

The new self-styled interdenominational missions represented a reaction to this theological and missionary change in the church. They preached the simple evangelical gospel. They built their program on a wide basis of reaching as many people as possible through evangelistic work rather than giving intensive training to a few in institutions, although they gave increasingly of their time to help the church with educational and medical work. The older missions now emphasized an applicant's educational qualifications. Gradually, some missionaries were accepted who were more educated than devout. On the other hand, the new missions made spiritual fitness basic to all other qualifications. In the end, both types of missionary organizations produced their spiritual giants and both had to number their failures.

Enid and I found that our study of the various types of organizations was leading us more and more in the direction of the interdenominational missions, in our time no longer new. Some friends of ours, Wheaton graduates, had been accepted by the Sudan Interior Mission and assigned to Ethopia. Our interest ripened.

"Perhaps it's more than a coincidence that they're going to Ethiopia," I said to Enid when we heard the news. "I was impressed with the message Dr. Lambie gave with his pictures last year. I don't think I'd ever heard of Ethiopia before that."

"I suppose it wouldn't hurt to write the Mission and ask them for information," Enid suggested.

With the information came application forms. By this time our friends had reached Addis Ababa and were writing to us about Ethiopia and the mission board. We would be expected to go out single, but we could marry after spending a year learning the language and getting into the work.

We decided to apply for membership. The papers, along with a written statement of our Christian experience, were mailed to the Mission. Then there followed a six-week period during which we were observed by Mission officials at the Berkshire Bible Fellowship in Massachusetts. We survived this test. At the end of it, we went to Mission headquarters in New York for questioning by the Mission Council. Finally the ordeal was over, and both of us accepted for service in Ethiopia on condition that Enid finish college. I spent that year at home in Tacoma. I needed funds to pay for my outfit and my passage to Ethiopia. The Mission had said I should trust the Lord to provide these funds. It seemed they looked on this provision as the Lord's seal of approval on my call to Africa.

It was not the easiest time to be entering the foreign mission field. Enid's capable engineer father had lost his job. He had found other employment of sorts but he had had to dig into his savings to keep his family clothed and fed. My schoolteacher sisters were being paid in warrants that were not valid for a month or two after receipt. They had to support my mother, as my father had died when I was eight years old. America was in the depths of depression. Few Christians could pay their church pledges in full and fewer still could make extra contributions for sending out a new recruit. I tried to find a job but there was none to be had.

I spoke in several churches, telling the people of my call and of my hopes for the future, helped with the work of my own church, and prayed long hours for the needed funds, believing that the Lord had a purpose in delays as well as in progress. In answer to my prayers many members of my church decided to designate their missionary money for my work. I would soon be able to sail!

Enid and I were to learn that missionary life is marked by frequent separation from loved ones. I said good-by to her in Milwaukee. I was to sail ahead of her and by December, 1933, I was on my way.

Many missionaries had crossed the oceans of the world but not many had landed at Djibouti at the bottom end of the Red Sea. Nor had many made the journey by train from that sea-level town in French Somaliland to Addis Ababa, the capital of Ethiopia, which sits on the plateau at an elevation of eight to nine thousand feet. I disembarked at Djibouti and entrained on the express for Addis Ababa. Early on the morning of the third day we began winding our way through the eucalyptus groves of the highland towns. We watched and smelled intently. This seemed to be the only kind of tree growing there. It covered the hills and filled the valleys around the farms.

I had heard that Ethiopia was beautiful. The previous day I had seen only the black volcanic rocks of the eastern slope. During the night we entered the highlands. As day dawned, we could see mountains in every direction. Meandering streams flowed through the meadows. Newly cut grain was stacked in the fields. There were brown, recently harvested fields, and green fields in which sheep, cattle, horses, mules, and donkeys pastured. The smoke from the many fires in the thatched huts smelled strongly of eucalyptus. Warmly dressed Ethiopians were beginning to move about, their shoulders hunched. The problem here did not seem to be one of staying cool but of keeping warm.

When I arrived in Addis Ababa, Dr. Lambie was away visiting mission stations in the south. He was then Field Director of our Mission and on his return would introduce the new missionaries to the work and give us our orders. The Field Council advised him on all matters.

One of my first concerns was to find out if Enid had sailed yet. I went to the office to inquire. The secretary looked over the schedule of arrivals and departures. "Enid Miller is traveling in Dr. Bingham's party," she informed me.

A month and a half, I thought as I left the office. And she'll be traveling in a party headed by the General Director! We were young and easily awed by Mission officials, especially by Dr. Bingham, its founder. We never did stop being awed by him. He was a great man.

My first task was one that would occupy me for years—language study. I was confronted with the two hundred and fifty-two characters of the Amharic alphabet. Amharic is the official language of Ethiopia. An Ethiopian teacher labored with me over the new sounds. There were the ejected t, k, and ts. There were gutterals. I had to learn how to form letters using down strokes only. The whole process looked hopeless, but soon I could put a few simple sentences together. When the boy who kept our horses understood me, I became optimistic. Perhaps I would one day speak this language after all.

As the day of Enid's arrival approached, my agitation increased and my linguistic interest decreased. The younger men and women at headquarters did everything to me but take my pulse and temperature. A large delegation turned out to welcome the traveling party. I joined the group but for me Dr. Bingham was not the main attraction. I walked far down the platform. As the train approached the station, it slowed down, and Enid leaned out from her car in our prearranged signal. I jumped onto the platform as the train passed. By the time we reached the rest of the crowd, we had finished our greetings and I could meet our General Director.

Missionaries new and old were massed around him. Time had chiseled his face and paid special attention to his nose. There was firmness in the jaw and kindliness in the eye. He greeted us individually.

"I remember you," Dr. Bingham said to each of the new missionaries. He had met very few of us but he remembered us from our candidate papers, which he no doubt studied carefully.

Each morning during the days that followed, Dr. Bingham brought us messages from the life of Abraham. As he illustrated his talks with experiences from his own life of faith, we wondered if he were not another Abraham.

At first Enid and I were considered one of those odd pairs—an engaged couple. We had heard many remarks about young people who embarrassed others by their open display of affection, so we agreed not to offend anyone. But, correct as we seemed to be, we were not so settled in our ways that we didn't long for the time when we could be natural and act as though we were meant for each other. After all, we had been engaged for nearly three years and knew we had at least one more to go.

4

We Go Our Separate Ways

SOON IT was March, 1934, and time to say good-by again. Dr. Lambie had returned from his trek through the country and the Field Council had met. We received our orders. Enid was to stay in Addis Ababa for a few months, studying the Amharic language. I was being sent to Gamo to help open up our new station there, and would travel with Merle and Lillian Anderson, who were going to Gofa.

Before I left Addis Ababa, Dr. Lambie delivered a series of lectures to the younger missionaries. He was a loose-jointed man, of medium height. Many hours in the saddle had given a swinging motion to his walk so that he seemed to be riding instead of walking. His face radiated kindness and concern for us young workers.

Dr. Lambie had started his missionary career with the United Presbyterians in Egypt and in the Sudan near the Ethiopian border. The governor across the border had called him to remove an insect from his ear. Word of the successful operation traveled rapidly and before long Dr. Lambie found himself building a hospital in Addis Ababa. But Dr. Lambie was a pioneer at heart. He could not settle down to hospital routine when millions in Ethiopia were still unaware of what God had wrought through Christ. He felt there would be more opportunity to carry on a widespread ministry in the Sudan Interior Mission. So he joined that organization in America and entered Ethiopia as leader of the work in that field.

Dr. Lambie was a man of wide interests and many of us who began our missionary work under his leadership owe him much. I remember him best for leading me to a love for the old hymns. Whenever I sing one of them, he is not far away. Dr. Lambie's lectures were very helpful. He told us how to travel southward and where we would find water and market places. He told us about Ethiopia and its Emperor, His Majesty Haile Selassie.

After the lectures and the books he suggested we read, we began to piece together some Ethiopian background. We were surprised to learn that the Amharas, who are Christians and who form the top strata of Ethiopian life, do not consider themselves African. They had probably migrated from Arabia to their African home in pre-Moslem times. Streets and market places in Addis Ababa provided evidence enough that the population was made up of more than Semites. There were Moslems, and their mosques were scattered throughout much of the country. There were pagans who needed no buildings for their religious practices. But the Amharas dominated the country politically and their Coptic religion dominated the populace religiously. We felt that, like the churches in England in the time of Wesley, the Ethiopian church needed an awakening.

If Ethiopia and its state church were not thriving it was not the fault of the Emperor. Though small of stature and with fine features he was every inch a king. Some of his ministers towered above him but they bowed low and did his bidding. Under his regal bearing and air of authority he was a kindly man whose heart was burdened for his country's welfare. He called on foreigners to introduce their education, machinery, and medicine. He especially encouraged missionaries to make their contributions to the spiritual and material welfare of his people. But he had to carry the whole country on his frail shoulders and progress was slow.

Roads were almost nonexistent. The Franco-Ethiopian Railway brought manufactured goods to Addis Ababa from the port city of Djibouti and took hides and coffee to the coast for export. Between Addis Ababa and other points almost all goods had to go by mule and camel caravan. It was a slow and costly system. One missionary had two pounds of cement sent to him in each fortnightly mail. He used it to set the stones in his fireplace.

The generation of Ethiopians that we saw was trying to bridge the wide gap between the passing feudal state and the future modern African state. Old-timers in the country said that with each round of change, the modern, the organized, and the stable emerged with substantial gains. Each time a move forward was visible, His Majesty was leading the way.

There was no doubt in the minds of the Ethiopians that their monarch was born to reign. The legend of the origin of the royal line was real history to them. The Queen of Sheba had gone to see the wonders of King Solomon in Jerusalem. Their acquaintance, though fleeting, had been intimate enough to result in the birth of a son who was named Menelik I. His Majesty Haile Selassie had come from this royal line. The Ethiopians had tucked their story between the lines of 2 Chronicles 9:12: "And King Solomon gave to the queen of Sheba all her desire, whatsoever she asked, beside that which she had brought unto the king. So she turned, and went away to her own land, she and her servants."

Dr. Lambie had to acquaint us with Mission affairs, too. He reminded us that we could expect financial difficulties. "When it was proposed to Dr. Bingham," he told us, "that the Sudan Interior Mission begin a new work in Ethiopia in the midst of depression in the home countries he put the matter up to his missionaries. He asked them, 'Shall we go ahead with our program of reaching out to unreached people and perhaps suffer a decrease in our personal allowances or shall we stop expanding?' The missionaries voted for continued expansion, even though it meant hardship for them."

This kind of response to Dr. Bingham's question warmed our hearts. After all, millions of unemployed at home were living on the brink of disaster. It would have seemed strange had the missionaries voted against expansion in the field. Better to follow the Biblical way, "And whether one member suffer, all the members suffer with it." If we had to cut down on our food supplies or hired help or equipment, it would be all right. We had joined the Mission not for what we could get out of it but for what we could put into it.

Enid and I said our real farewells in the evening. Our final one took place the next morning, when the Andersons and I rode out into the great unknown.

Travel in Ethiopia meant mule caravans, head carriers, camp equipment, and riding horses or mules. I had bought a dappled gray horse. He had not come out ahead in any of the missionary gallops we had indulged in across the fields to the weekly inter-mission prayer meetings, but in walking he could outdistance almost any horse. Ethiopian geography was beginning to take some shape in my mind. The route I would travel lay south and slightly to the west. After ten days in the saddle we would reach our central station in the province of the Walamo-speaking people. It was called Soddu (pronounced *so do*). There the Andersons and I would separate. They would go west for another eight days to Gofa, I southeast for three days to Gamo.

The Andersons were older than Enid and I. They had had their own home in America before coming to Ethiopia. Though still in his early thirties, Merle's hair had begun to thin. He was the studious type, the saddle hardly seeming the place for him. He was always interested in something extracurricular. On trek it was bird watching and duck hunting. On the station it was stamp collecting and such specialties as delivering a calf, studying anatomy with the aid of the body of a monkey, and pursuing and killing a twenty-five-foot python.

Lillian was a homebody. Her combed-back hair and pointed nose and chin showed determination. Like Merle she was good-natured if timid. She was accustomed to having places in which to store her household goods and foodstuffs so that she could work efficiently, but she adjusted bravely to the tightly packed trek boxes that replaced her cupboards at home. She soon had the stove—three stones with a circular metal piece resting on top—producing tasty camp meals.

The three of us were greenhorns; we had been in the country a bare few weeks. We could speak and understand a few phrases of Amharic but could not communicate effectively with the mule drivers and carriers, although we had been coached on travel and camping. But we muddled through and eventually reached Soddu.

"Uncle Nick is waiting for you," Harold Street informed me on my arrival. Street was later to join me in Gamo.

"Is that what you call Mr. Simponis?" I asked, referring to the missionary at Gamo.

"Yes," Street replied. "Out here we are all uncles and aunts to the missionary children. But Mr. Simponis seems to be a special uncle. Anyway, you'll soon find out."

The Streets had heard the call to Ethiopia after they and their children were already settled in a pastorate, but they pulled up stakes and went anyway. I learned that Uncle Nick had gone to America from his native Greece when he was about fifteen. He had become a citizen but when he heard Dr. Lambie tell about the many Greek people living in Ethiopia, he decided to go there to give them spiritual help. After making good progress with the Amharic language, he assisted in the increasing work in the provinces, and was now readying the new station at Gamo.

I continued on my journey to Gamo where I met Uncle Nick. He had a large classic Greek head which could have easily been graced by an olive wreath. In the absence of the latter, his black wavy hair was an excellent substitute. Socrates and Plato would have recognized him as one of their own. His shoulders were broad, but from that point his figure tapered down to spindly legs.

America was Nick's homeland, not Greece. He loved his adopted country passionately and treasured his citizenship and passport more than did we who were native born. I detected a trace of a foreign accent in his speech but I was soon unconscious of it. He did have a few peculiarities, such as pronouncing the "p" in "psalms," but he spoke better English than most Europeans.

Nick led me to an unlikely looking building resembling a haystack with a door. "This is our house," he said. "We bought it from some Gamo people as temporary quarters until we build our own."

He opened the door and I entered the haystack. The room inside was about twenty feet in diameter, the size of a modern living-dining room. A partition of woven bamboo, six feet high, divided the hut into two rooms, each with a little square window resembling a porthole and providing the only light and ventilation.

"This is our living room," Nick announced. "And that is our heating plant."

He pointed to a flat fireplace without a chimney which sat on the floor. There was a small table by the window and a few cupboards lined the walls, which were plastered with mud to a height of about six feet. The air blew through freely above that. I looked up. The walls gradually came together until at the peak, some thirty feet above me, there was scarcely room for a bird's nest. Thirty feet, I recalled, was approximately the height of a three-story house.

"The Gamo people build this way in order to have a long-lasting house," Nick explained. "When the termites eat off the bottom or when it rots away, they dig a trench around the house and drop the walls into it. The whole house is lowered by a foot each time they do it. With a house this height, they can lower it many times."

It sounded sensible. The Africans were engineers in their own way in spite of all that I had heard to the contrary.

The building of the station had already begun. The first house was to be for the Street family, who would move from Soddu to Gamo as soon as it was ready. The house had not been started but Street and Nick had erected a unit that would serve as kitchen, pantry, and storeroom for the new house. Each room in the building was about eight by ten. The kitchen was already in use.

"When we start building the main house, I'll have to do most of the dealing with the men on materials and labor. You could help out most by taking over the responsibility for the meals," Nick suggested.

Those were distressing words. I had not thought I would begin my missionary career at such a level. Weren't missionaries supposed to be aided in their work by hired help? I had brought a boy with me from Addis Ababa and Nick had one working for him. They seemed much like ourselves. We needed help for we had a great deal to do and would require many free hours for uninterrupted language study.

I had been given a set of Walamo language notes when I passed through Soddu. It was the language used with variations all through Gofa, Gamo, and Walamo provinces. I was to study Walamo (with a Gamo accent) instead of Amharic. Learning the Amharic alphabet had been helpful, for our missionaries always used it in reducing the tribal languages to writing. Language study would include much time spent visiting our neighbors so I could hear the correct pronunciation of words, the use of idiom, and real native sentence structure. By getting established on a friendly basis with the people, they would be more likely to believe what I said about spiritual matters once I spoke their tongue.

Building the main house would be a full-time job. I would have to snatch what time I could from housebuilding and household duties. In tropical Africa the building of houses for missionaries to live in cannot be avoided. Unlike some parts of the missionary world, there are no houses to rent or buy.

I looked forward to the day when I would be able to speak the language fluently, to the day when there would be no more houses to build. The housekeeping affairs would be Enid's, and together we would start Sunday services and weekday meetings for men and women. There would be an informal school where we would teach the neighborhood children their two hundred and fifty-two characters. As we gained believers, we would give their leaders special instruction in Bible school. The church would be established and we would try from the beginning to make it the church of the people. Each local church would mean a goal achieved.

But these plans were all in the unknown future. I was still in Gamo, scarcely able to converse with my neighbors, and the time I thought might be used in language study was to be spent in the kitchen. We had no stove. For baking, Nick used an uninsulated sheet-iron oven. I did not know how I could produce bread with the little metal box he balanced on one hand as he explained its simple operation. He showed me how to set the bread in the evening. Then, early in the morning, he added the necessary flour and kneaded the dough. I watched with interest but no enthusiasm.

"Now we have to put the bread in a warm place to rise," Nick said.

The mornings were always cold in Gamo's mountains. I was shivering. I could not think of any place warm enough to raise bread but Nick had solved that problem long ago. We carried the pans from the kitchen to the house. Nick threw back the covers of the bed from which he had recently risen, put the pans in, and pulled the covers over them. In about an hour the bread was ready for baking, at least as ready as it would ever be. The bed was not getting any warmer.

Nick had set his oven on four stones out in the yard. The fire was burning brightly under it. Soon it burned down, leaving a bed of coals, some of which Nick placed on top of the oven. When the oven was hot enough—I never did learn how to find that out—we whisked the bread out of the bed, through the door, and into the oven which sat smoking forlornly. Not once in the nine months that I was with Nick did the dough rise in the oven. It always sank to a level nearer the bottom than the top of the pans.

Our so-called Ethiopian cooks could put wood on the fire, boil water, and watch vegetables or meat cooking, but they could not make desserts. I tried to stir up various kinds but inevitably returned to the simplicity of chocolate pudding. We had built a stone fireplace in the kitchen. It was shaped to provide a firebox over which we laid a sheet of iron, already warped out of shape by the heat of previous fires. A sheet-iron pipe served as a chimney but most of the smoke escaped into the room.

When the chocolate pudding was ready to be cooked, I stoked the fire and began stirring. I could not keep my eyes open, the smoke was so thick. I coughed, blew my nose, and occasionally went outside to recover. Eventually the pudding thickened and was ready to be served. According to the cookbook the recipe would serve six people, but Uncle Nick and I divided it and it was just enough.

The most important item in our diet was coffee. With the rain, the fog, and the loneliness, we needed something to lift our spirits. We had coffee for breakfast, in the middle of the morning, for lunch, in the middle of the afternoon, and for supper. Occasionally Nick brought out his Turkish coffee maker and we had some black brew before going to bed.

One day I told Nick that I thought our boys were taking sugar. It was disappearing at an alarming rate. We knew that boys who worked for foreigners were often tempted by the ample supplies of sugar, salt, and cooking oil that had to be on hand. We believed it our duty to keep temptation out of the way of the boys, but a certain amount of food had to be available. While meditating on the problem, I began to consider our own rate of consumption. Two cups of coffee each . . . five times a day . . . that added up to twenty cups. Nick used at least two heaping teaspoons in each cup and I used only a little less. That was where the sugar was going—though I can't remember that we cut down on the coffee drinking.

The boys who helped us were having their problems, too. We missionaries timed our work by our watches, but the food was not always ready when we wanted it. Africans tell time by the sun, moon, and stars, and are usually accurate within an hour. Then we noticed a sudden improvement in the timing. The boys had worked out a system of their own. When the corrugated iron was nailed to the roof, a nail hole had been left. This allowed a thin ray of light to describe an arc on the shaded floor as the sun passed across the heavens.

The boys explained it this way: "When the spot of light is here, we put the vegetable on to cook. Then at this point we put on the meat, and here the potatoes. When the ray hits the middle of the floor, we put the coffee on. Then at this point we wait for you to say 'Bring the food!' "

After I had served half-cooked beans and nearly raw potatoes to Nick and myself a few times, I began to ask questions. Then I recalled that the higher the altitude, the lower the temperature at which water boils. Of course it would take longer to cook the food! After that, the string beans and potatoes went onto the fire right after breakfast. I thought of the ladies in Denver and how they had to regulate their cooking to their mile-high altitude. That of Gamo was eight thousand feet, more than half again as high as Denver. Far away and below us at five thousand feet—still nearly as high as Denver—Lake Chamo and Lake Abaya lay in the floor of the Great Rift Valley which runs from Kenya to Palestine. The dry season haze gave the lakes an otherworldly appearance, perhaps a netherworldly one. As the rainy season came, billows of fog rolled up from the lakes. Other billows descended on us from the tops of the mountains. It was not merely that the weather was bad; at eight thousand feet we were living in the clouds. For weeks on end the sun did not break through. It was no place for a lonely person like me.

Every morning and evening the boys lighted the fire in our open hearth. As we sat reading or studying, the smoke rolled around us. We coughed, sneezed, and rubbed our eyes. The clothes would not dry outside in the rain and fog, so we had to hang them on the lines that crisscrossed our tiny living quarters. We often ate lunch invisible to each other, our heads up among the shirts and trousers.

One day we received a letter from Earl Lewis, in Soddu, saying that he was coming with a gang of workmen to help us build the house. Our two beds left very little space in our half-moon bedroom, but we would squeeze him in somehow. Lewis had taken over the office of District Superintendent from Walter Ohman when the latter went on furlough. As D.S., Lewis was supposed to see that we kept the building job moving.

Lewis was about five feet ten, with a solid frame. He disliked inactivity and a trip to Gamo to spend a few weeks on the building job with a gang of noisy, singing Walamos would be just what he wanted. His presence would make life more interesting for Nick and me. Lewis had learned the Walamo language by spending long hours with the people in their huts, for he could not sit still long enough to study the language notes worked out by his fellow missionaries. It was natural that he should become as fluent in Walamo as he was in English. And he was very fluent in English! He kept the conversation going; all Nick and I had to do was respond now and then. He hustled around the station all day long, bringing his native optimism to every problem. It did not matter how crooked the wood; we could build a house with it. Nor did it matter how wet it was; we could make a fire with it.

We laid out the Mission house to suit our Western mode of living but the manner of construction was Ethiopian. We marked the places where the windows and doors were to be. Then a workman dug holes on either side. The heaviest and straightest cedar poles were selected and set in place, then trenches dug between these openings. Alternate split cedar or eucalyptus and bamboo were set in the trench and tied together with cross pieces lashed with rope.

"It's hard to make a straight wall with this split timber," Lewis observed as we surveyed the completed woodwork.

"When we plaster the walls, we can always put a little more mud in the low places and a little less in the high," Nick commented.

The house looked ghastly with its array of split timbers tied together with ropes, but we were not through yet.

"We'll start on the roof tomorrow," Lewis said one day. We had to get the roof on before mudding the walls. The rains had begun in earnest and the plaster would need protection.

Between periods of supervising the cooking of potatoes and meat, and the baking of bread and stirring chocolate pudding—the coffee came by itself—I helped Lewis with the building of the roof. Nick worked on the ground. It was all he could do to watch us walk around on the slender roof timbers. He suffered from acrophobia.

We built the ridge and then ran the rafters into it, picking out long poles for the hip rafters. Then we stretched lines and hammered down the purlins as straight as possible. Lastly, we nailed down the sheets of corrugated iron and the roof was finished. It had taken many days of skidding around on the raw timbers that became slippery in the rain.

Meanwhile three large pits had been dug, the dirt in them loosened, and water added. In these the men walked round and round, tramping the mud all day. The brown clay had to be worked this way for three or four weeks. Before it was applied to the walls, the fine straw of a grass-like Abyssinian grain called teff was added as a binder.

With the iron roof overhead, the Soddu men could go ahead with the plastering. They threw handfuls of mud on the walls and rubbed it smooth. It oozed through the timbers and spread out on the other side where it caked and dried, giving the plaster strength. When the last finishing coat had been applied, with a little cow dung added for smoothness, we surveyed our labors. The walls were wavy, but it was the best we could do with the help we had. It would be a fine house.

Lewis was hearty and full of ideas. When some young men appeared on the station and started a simple dance to the tune of a native banjo, he invited them into the new house. "If they have to dance," he said, "they might as well tramp down the dirt floor."

At last Lewis returned to Soddu, leaving Nick and me to finish the building.

Four months had passed since I left Enid in Addis Ababa. We wrote to each other faithfully but mail traveled back and forth only twice a month. I had become a confirmed mailbag watcher. But not even the urgent necessity of opening the bag to get Enid's letters out in a hurry could interfere with the greetings to the postman:

"Are you in peace? Did you spend the night in peace? Are your people in peace? Are our people at Soddu in peace? How is the road? Did you arrive well?"

Having answered these questions for each other, we could open the bag without seeming to be rude. But the greetings continued, though less formally, as we dumped magazines and letters onto the floor. I recognized the writing on the letters I wanted to read first. Settling down in a chair next to the little window, the rest of the world stopped for a while as I read.

"Well, what's she doing now?" Nick asked one day, as I finally looked up from my reading.

"She's coming south soon," I replied.

It had been an exciting day for Enid when Dr. Lambie called her to his office to say that a party of missionaries would be traveling south early in August and that she could join it. On her arrival down country, Enid was to study Walamo. There was no room for her at Soddu so she was to go to Duromi in the Kambatta tribe. Duromi was twenty-five miles north of Soddu.

The rain poured down daily in August when Enid made the journey south. Her horse skidded in the mud a hundred times each mile. The rain beat through her American raincoat, "guaranteed waterproof." After that it did not matter so much when she crossed a swollen stream. She was already drenched. At Duromi she scribbled a note to me and sent it by the rest of her party which was going on to Soddu. When the letter finally dropped out of the bag, poor Nick had to listen while I told him the news.

"Enid is at Duromi!" I shouted.

It was good to have her that close. I was about sixty-five miles south of Soddu, Enid twenty-five miles north. Ninety miles did not seem far, though we did not reckon distances in miles but by days' travel. Uncle Nick must have been bored with my alternate bursts of enthusiasm and despair, depending on what kind of letters the mailbags produced, but he had to take it. People in love have to talk about it to somebody and Nick was stuck with me. But despair now vanished. Each day brought us closer to our wedding, though no date had been set.

First we would have to pass our language examinations. Then Dr. Lambie would inquire about our adaptability during our first year in the country. If our language work was acceptable and our general conduct and efficiency passable, we would be allowed to proceed with our wedding plans. Our engagement was in its fourth year, and I did not want to prolong it by failing in my language examinations. So I spent less time mixing bread and stirring chocolate pudding and finishing the house, and concentrated on my language notes and conversing with our neighbors.

I visited in the Gamo huts around us or sat with the children as they herded their cattle on the terraces that rose to the very tops of the mountains. There was plenty to do. Even so, time passed with excruciating slowness until at last the foggy days were gone and the roar of the wind and the falling rain diminished. September and October were done.

5

Some Trust in Horses

ON THE Tuesday afternoon before Thanksgiving, a boy came walking in from Soddu. He had a letter for me from Dr. Roberts, who had replaced Lewis as District Superintendent during the latter's furlough. I read the letter and started jumping. Enid was going to Soddu! The letter was my invitation to join her there for a few days' visit over Thanksgiving. It was a three-day trek to Soddu or two days' fast travel. I had just one day. Could I make it?

If I traveled in the usual way, I would hire a couple of pack mules to carry my tent and equipment. If I could find the mule men and work hard on preparations, I could reach Soddu for Christmas. But my invitation was for Thanksgiving—day after tomorrow.

With the first whoop after I opened the letter, Nick knew something was up. I told him about it.

"When are you going to go?" he asked.

"About three tomorrow morning," I replied.

It was already past five, and there was much to do to prepare for the arduous trip. As far as I knew, nobody had ever made it in one day. That was what I would have to do, traveling light. I would have no tent, no food except lunch, only enough drinking water for the day, and no facilities for boiling more.

Nick shook his head. "Haven't you got any sense?"

But Nick and I did not have the same point of view.

I had made only one hurried trip over the road. I remembered that in places it was a mere cow trail with many smaller trails that seemed as well traveled as the main road. There were stretches of uninhabited country where there were no guides. But I was in no mood to be pessimistic. I did not know much about the road but I knew what awaited me at the other end, and my dappled gray horse would take me there.

43

By three the following morning everything was ready and I had had a little sleep. Our local boy, Tola, who had just begun to work for me, had agreed to lead the way with a lantern until daylight. The boy who had brought the mail was to carry a small bundle of clothing to Soddu for me; it would probably arrive the evening of Thanksgiving Day. I jumped into the saddle. I had long since given up using a stirrup for mounting. As Nick and I said our farewells, my dappled gray started off briskly.

I followed Tola as he glided along in the darkness, the little lantern lighting the way. He took the sharp turns around tree trunks. He climbed over the broken-down terrace walls from one level to another. He hopped from stone to stone through the many babbling brooks, down the long bank to the river bottom, across the stream and then a hard pull up the other side. Up and down. Up and down. There was little level country to traverse.

At five o'clock the black sky began to turn gray. In the tropics it does not take long for day to dawn, once the first streaks of light appear. I called to Tola to stop, for now I could see my way. I would have to trot and canter over much of the road to Soddu far, far away. So I said my salaams to Tola and he said his to me, with a few extra for my lady whom he had never seen.

Tola was a sweet boy. It was doubtless difficult for him to understand my situation. Why all this sitting apart for so long? Why don't they get married without so much running around? Obviously a man of his wealth should be able to pay the bride price and go ahead with the wedding. Tola blew out the lantern and began the walk back. He had plenty to think about.

I pulled on the reins, touched my horse's flanks with my heels, and cantered off. The road, already high, followed a ridge that climbed to over ten thousand feet. The ridge was narrow and fell away sharply on both sides of the road. I could see mountains and valleys in endless succession to the right into the rising sun and to the left where it was still gloomy. There was a lacy fringe of clouds in the east, on which the sun began to shine before its rays reached me.

The air was thin and chill until I began to drop down to a more pleasant altitude. By ten o'clock I had done a long day's trek. I kept on trotting, cantering, and walking my horse, which showed no signs of fatigue. On steep uphill grades I used my own feet to rest him. Now I was down from the extreme height and a few thorny acacia trees with their flat tops began to appear along the road. I waved to the farmers as I passed. They were stacking grain for threshing.

Although the rains had stopped only a few weeks before, the pastures were still green. Cattle grazed restlessly as they drove off the flies. Tick birds slid over the backs of the cows in search of ticks. At two o'clock I stopped, watered my horse, and let him graze while I ate my sandwiches. A Gamo man squatted nearby to watch. I greeted him in his language.

"Are you going to sleep here?" he asked.

"No," I replied, "I'm going to Soddu."

The man looked puzzled. Not many foreigners passed this way. Practically all who did were missionaries and they were usually accompanied by a caravan of mules and head carriers laden with tents, boxes, and paraphernalia. I must have looked like a refugee instead of a Lochinvar.

The afternoon was wearing away and much of my road still lay ahead. I cantered across the lowlands, often called the Baroda Desert. Up out of the lowlands I rode, past Mt. Humbo. The rains of the recent wet season had dashed down its slopes, leaving new scars in the red clay. Last year's path had become a ditch two feet deep and already the feet of passing mule men and local farmers had traced a new one parallel to it. All over the country Ethiopia's topsoil was being washed away. To the north and west the soil was being carried by the Blue Nile all the way to Egypt where it became the wealth of that land. Mt. Humbo's soil was being deposited in the lakes we could see from Gamo Station.

I dropped at last to the Walamo plain, the last stretch of road I had to cover. It seemed endless. We cantered again and put chunks of the plain behind us. What an animal! By the time we were halfway across the plain, we had done nearly sixty miles. He was still going strong but I finally let him set his own pace. As daylight began to fade, I could pick out the location of the station. Roads crisscrossed everywhere in this populous area but there were few houses nearby. It was almost dark as I began to climb up out of the plain onto the ridge that ran to the station. I knew Enid was up there somewhere on the ridge but I did not know just how far away.

Before reaching the top of the rise, I heard soft noises behind me. My horse was suddenly restless. I jumped off to have a look around and in the dimness were the heads of three hyenas. I quickly picked up several good-sized rocks and threw them at the intruders. Or was I the intruder? I remembered the snapshot I had seen of the hindquarters of a mule owned by one of our missionaries. A hyena had torn a big hunk of flesh from the animal while it was being ridden. The mule had continued under its own power.

I began to wonder if I had been foolish to attempt such a journey in one day. Darkness, fatigue, and an uncertain road lower one's morale. It was now impossible to know which path to take and progress was slow.

Suddenly I saw a shadow against the sky. It was a hut. I called out and a Walamo tribesman emerged cautiously. We greeted each other at length, for I knew that not even in cases of extreme urgency could one omit the greetings. Then I told him my predicament and he was obviously relieved when he saw what I was. He knew missionaries did not cause trouble at night—nor in the daytime, for that matter. He accepted my offer of a week's wages to lead me to my destination, stating it would take an hour but that he wanted the dollar first. When I paid him, he handed the money to his wife and we started out. I was too tired to handle my horse so I gave the reins to my guide and slumped, relaxed, in the saddle.

It was eight o'clock when I saw lights. At the beginning of the Mission lane I met the night watchman. I jumped to the ground, said farewell to my guide, and told the watchman to put my horse in the barn.

"I'm not the horse boy," he protested. "I'm the night watchman."

He chose the wrong time to argue with me. I put the reins in his hands and was well on my way to the house. I had traveled about sixty-five miles to see my love and had been on the road seventeen hours.

I knocked on the door. Enid was still waiting, alone, in the living room; the others had given me up for that day. In those few moments at the open door I forgot the long way I had come, forgot my weariness, forgot the hyenas, forgot the puzzle of many paths leading nowhere.

The next morning Enid wondered if my horse were still alive. I suggested we had better go and see him. As we walked down the lane I grabbed her hand. I did not hold it long, much as I wanted to. People might not understand.

My faithful horse had been well taken care of by the night watchman. We found him standing in his stall, munching hay. As I pushed the door open, he nickered and I wondered what he thought of me. I told the boy who was bringing in the grain to give him all the barley he could eat.

"When did you stand up from Gamo?" he asked.

"Yesterday, early," I replied.

"Yesterday?" He stopped pouring the grain and his jaw dropped. "You left Gamo yesterday and arrived here yesterday? What kind of horse is this?" He shook his head. Some very important business must have called me, he quite evidently thought, for he asked, "And why did you come so quickly?"

"This is the girl I am going to marry," I said, pointing at Enid. "I came to see her."

The boy's face grew even more puzzled. White people did such strange things! This one tried to kill himself and his horse just to see a woman. He finished pouring the barley and went out the door. He needed to find one of his own kind to talk to. This was too good to keep to himself.

My horse finished his barley and I turned him loose in the paddock to see if he would walk. He was a bit stiff but he would recover.

Enid watched as he moved slowly across the field. "You shouldn't have done it," she said.

"I had to," I replied.

Years later, when I revisited Soddu after the reoccupation of Ethiopia under His Majesty Haile Selassie, I wondered how I would be remembered. I had not spent much time at Soddu in those early days. A whole new generation had grown up unacquainted with the missionaries who had been there in pre-Italian times. Would I be known as one of those, or because mine had been the first and only wedding held there? I knew I would not be known as the preacher or teacher or the one who knew the language well, for I had not been around long enough.

As I was greeting friends old and new in front of the village church, a friend of the old days was trying to explain who I was and how it happened that I knew Soddu so well.

"This is the man," he said, "who rode a horse from Gamo to Soddu in one day . . ."

6

Till Death Do Us Part

THANKSGIVING DAY passed and I said good-by to Enid again. I made the return trip to Gamo and Uncle Nick more leisurely.

"What's the news?" Nick asked, even before I had got down from my horse.

"Enid is to stay in Duromi until our wedding and I'm going to Gofa to be with the Andersons. Enid and I will be stationed there after our wedding."

Nick was surprised to learn that I was to leave Gamo. "But what about me?" he inquired.

"You've been appointed to Debra Markos. I guess you're supposed to go soon. I'll stay until the Streets arrive. I've got a letter here for you."

Debra Markos was as far north of Addis Ababa as Gamo was south. I did not think Nick would like being transferred so far away.

"Well, that's good," he said instead. "I've been studying Amharic all along and it will be more useful to me there than here."

Nick packed his goods. Then one day he climbed into his saddle and rode away. As I watched him disappear over the hill, little could I foresee all that would happen before we would meet again.

Soon the Streets arrived and it was my turn to leave. I took a last look at our skyscraper hut and the neat bungalow we had built for the Street family. Was this to be the pattern for the future—work on a station for a while, grow to love it and the people, then move on, to start all over again in a strange place with strange people?

It was early morning when I said good-by to the Streets and jumped into the saddle. I turned in a new direction, southwest this time. Ahead lay an unknown road. When I reached Gofa station one week later, I rejoined Merle and Lillian Anderson who had recently returned from Soddu where their baby was born. Kenny was two months old when I arrived.

My household duties were behind me and I now boarded with the Andersons. At last I was free to spend from six to ten hours a day on language study and visitation. Fortunately the Gofa language was the same as that spoken in Walamo and Gamo, with some variations. But marriage was not my sole objective. I wanted to start preaching.

I made such rapid progress with the long hours of study that by the end of my first month in Gofa I began preaching at the Sunday morning services. My talks were not sensational but it was satisfying to be able to speak to the people. And they understood!

When the mailbags arrived from Soddu, I received more sympathy and understanding from the Andersons than I had from Uncle Nick. When the long-awaited letter finally arrived, and I shouted, "We're going to get married!" the Andersons joined in the excitement. I was to get to Soddu as quickly as possible. Enid had already been there with the Robertses for nearly a month.

I made the eight-day trip to Soddu in five days. Enid was waiting to join me—in our first Walamo language examination. I had had the best opportunities for study and conversation, having been in the Walamo-speaking area the entire time. But the best marks went to Enid—a fine thing when in a few days I was to take over as the head of our new household!

March was near and we waited impatiently for final word from Dr. Lambie in Addis Ababa. His approval came at last in a letter to Dr. Roberts, which also suggested that another engaged couple be married at the same time as we. Harold Street would come up from Gamo to perform the ceremony. A lot of slow travel by muleback was necessary to get preacher, brides, grooms, and attendants together for missionary weddings in Ethiopia. It would be simpler to have a double wedding.

"When shall we be married?" we asked Dr. Roberts.

"As soon as everybody gets here. I'll send word off to Street and Couser"—the other bridegroom—"right away. You go over to town and see if you can get Sidamo on the phone. Tell them to get Flossie over here as soon as possible." Flossie, of course, was the other bride.

No lack of diligence on my part was going to delay our marriage. I ran down the road to the stable, saddled my horse, and galloped off toward town and the primitive telephone. If the phone isn't working, I thought, we'll have to send a runner to Sidamo and that will take time.

But the phone was working. I talked to one of our men and by much

repeating and shouting, as well as rattling the hook up and down, I got
the message across. "Flossie and Norman . . . double wedding with us
. . . get Flossie over here as soon as you can . . . we'd like to have the
wedding March 14." I hung up.

We had worked as quickly as possible but it was not until the second
day that Norman Couser arrived, grinning and disheveled. He had
ridden hard but the smile that seldom vanished was still on his face.
And that smile came right up out of his heart. Norman was short and
broad-shouldered and his hair sometimes resembled a mop. His work
with the Ethiopians was far too interesting to allow time for the care
of his clothes and hair.

On the third day Harold Street galloped in, and on the morning of
the fourth, Flossie rode in on her mule, escorted by Tom Devers. The
long trip across the lowlands had not upset her composure. She was just
a trifle shorter than Norman, and as careful about her personal appearance as he was unconcerned about his. It was easy to see that Norman
would continue his friendly visitation with his Ethiopian people and
that Flossie would follow along, keeping everything neat and in order.
She immediately set about to organize her part of the wedding.

Tom Devers had come to Ethiopia with Ray Davis, who was in charge
of building for the Mission. Tom had been assigned to Sidamo Province,
east of Walamo. He had been studying the Sidamo language hard for
he, too, had wedding plans. Tom was tall and handsome, a Canadian
who sometimes outdid the Americans in his good-natured banter. He
led our devotional gatherings with earnestness and evidence of a deep
spiritual hunger. Perhaps the Lord was preparing him for something
special.

"Isn't some member of the American Legation supposed to witness
the ceremonies or deputize one of us to do so?" Harold Street asked.

"Dr. Lambie wrote that the married couples could swear out affidavits
the next time they go to Addis Ababa," Dr. Roberts replied.

It seemed rather confusing to us but we were in no mood to delay
the proceedings by asking questions. Four years had been a long time;
but now the past did not matter. Soon we would forget the weariness of
waiting.

March 14 finally came. I had never shaved twice in one day but I
decided this was the occasion to do so. That was about the only extra
chore I had to take care of. The rest was much like getting ready for
church on Sunday. It was different for Enid. She had to fuss over the
white silk dress she had made, her flowers had to be arranged and she

had to have her going-away clothes ready though we were not going anywhere.

Mrs. Roberts had already done her part. She had gathered as many of the ingredients as she could for a wedding cake and had turned out a truly professional job. Her cakes were always like that, beautiful to the eye and pleasing to the palate. She had also prepared the sandwiches and cookies for the wedding tea, as well as the food for the supper that was to follow. All of us had worked together gathering palm fronds and calla lilies with which to decorate the Roberts's living room where the service was to take place.

Right on schedule I walked across the "street" toward the Roberts's house. The building was an oddity but a very useful one. Five thatched peaks poked their heads upward. They covered the five round rooms of the house. The three bedrooms and the dining room were set at the four "corners" of the round living room and opened on to it. The kitchen stood by itself, thirty feet from the dining room. The space between the two front bedrooms formed a veranda on the front of the living room. It was all so rustic, so African, that we really looked forward to having our wedding there.

I entered the house through the back door and handed the recording of the "Wedding March" from *Lohengrin* to Nurse Lois Briggs. We had had it sent out from England; the wheezy organ would not do for this special occasion. The fireplace formed the background for the ceremony, which would be in the living room. It was flanked by the palm fronds we had gathered. They still looked very much alive in their kerosene-can vases. Bouquets of lilies contrasted with the green of the palms. There were four missionary guests—Nurse Lois Briggs, Mrs. Roberts, Ray Davis, and Tom Devers; the rest were involved in the ceremony. Dr. Roberts would give the brides away. Down the sides and across the front of the living room sat the Walamo Christians and the men who worked on the station.

The phonograph was ready in the back of the living room. When the music began, Harold Street went over to the fireplace. Norman was about to follow, when suddenly I realized something was not right. I grabbed his arm and pulled him back.

"That's the wrong side of the record," I said. The phonograph had been playing Mendelssohn.

We could hear some scrambling in the living room. The music stopped, then began again. This time it was *Lohengrin*.

"You can go ahead now, Norman," I said with relief.

He walked out and took his place facing Street, and I followed. We left a space between us for our brides.

As Enid came down the aisle, I turned toward her. She was beautiful in her wedding gown. Her dark hair under the veil softly framed her flushed cheeks and her brown eyes shone. She was beaming. I was, too, but nobody noticed. The white calla lilies she carried contrasted with her lovely color. There had not been many flowers to choose from that day but as long as the choice was calla lilies, it did not matter. Christ had said, "Consider the lilies of the field . . . your Father careth for them." In the days to come we would have many occasions to remember that He cared for us as He did for the lilies.

I had nothing to carry and consciously kept my hands at my sides lest I betray my emotion. The little distance Enid had to walk from the bedroom door to where I was standing was the end of the road it had taken four years to travel. We need not have waited that long just to get married but our marriage plans had to fit into the Lord's plan for our lives. Now our marriage was a rededication to His work.

Enid was bringing her talents and deep devotion to the altar. For a woman to be willing to live and work in the isolated, primitive parts of tropical Africa, to raise a family there, and to keep her work with the Africans to the fore, required a special kind of dedication. At that moment I could not think of a thing I had to contribute. It was expected that men should roam the earth, play the pioneer, widen the frontiers of knowledge, and preach the gospel to all the world. Hers was the greatest gift.

As she stepped into the bower beside me I choked back tears of happiness.

At times Harold Street spoke to both couples but at the crucial points he addressed each couple separately.

"Do you, Malcolm, take Enid to be your wedded wife?"

I certainly did. Having been of one mind for four years I did not intend to change now. Norman and I produced our rings and Harold Street made his pronouncement over us:

"By the authority invested in me as a minister of the gospel, I pronounce you man and wife."

An uneasy thought crossed my mind. At home the ministers added "and by the authority of the state." No representative from the American Legation had come, and Dr. Lambie had written about swearing out affidavits the next time we were in Addis Ababa. The marriage ceremony was ended but it was not over. We were to find out about that later—much later.

The phonograph started playing again, Mendelssohn this time. We had no particular place to march to, so we wandered out onto the veranda. The Cousers had set up their camp about three hours' journey along the road to their station. They would ride away as soon as the wedding supper was over.

"Norman will learn not to be so optimistic," Dr. Roberts chuckled.

"Why, what did he do?" I asked.

"I offered to fill his lanterns for him but he said this was once when they wouldn't need any light along the road. So I filled the lanterns with water!"

I became aware that our Ethiopian guests were not only observant but critical of the unfamiliar ceremony they had witnessed. As I listened to Godana and Chaka, I realized that the worst was yet to come. The two men had worked on the station for several years. Godana was tall and handsome and carried himself well, and he naturally became spokesman for any group he had happened to be in. Chaka was short and stocky, genial and not the kind who looked for trouble. Both were promising Christians.

"What kind of wedding is this?" Godana was complaining. "There is no feast. Are they going to give us only bread and cookies and tea?"

"It is not good," Chaka agreed. "How can they be properly married without a feast?"

I took Enid by the arm and we stepped up to the two unhappy guests.

"We are getting married according to the custom of our country," I tried to explain. "There we don't have a feast after the marriage."

"Truly, truly," Godana replied, "it is the custom of your country but you are getting married in ours."

This was no small matter. Our Ethiopian guests were helping themselves to sandwiches and tea with a noticeable lack of enthusiasm. Was our happy wedding day going to end on a sour note?

"They really seem to be offended," Enid remarked disappointedly.

Just then we heard a scuffling sound out by the gate and hurried to the door.

"It looks like the chief," she said.

During her month at Soddu prior to our wedding, Enid had frequently visited the local chief and had made friends with his wife. She had eaten their food, given them the gospel with a mixture of Amharic and Walamo, and had, of course, told them about me. She had cheerily asked them to our wedding. It was the chief, all right, in his pointed burnoose, a heavy woolen, capelike garment which covered his *shama*, so that only the hem of the latter was visible. A *shama* is something like a shawl. A retinue of ten or fifteen servants followed him.

Two of the servants seemed to be struggling with an animal. They opened the gate and pushed and dragged a full-grown goat up the path and into the living room. Its bushy mane and long twisted horns indicated its age. It had eaten chlorophyll all its life but this fact had had no effect on its odor.

The chief stood before us, tall and erect. He had fine features, with a well-developed un-African nose and thin lips. A solid growth of black beard covered his face. His hair was fairly close cropped. He looked around the room, showing great interest and some amusement. He studied the Ethiopian guests, probably noting that they were farmers, tribespeople. Then he turned to Enid.

"You told me that in your country the bride gets gifts. Here, this is for you." He pushed the goat toward her.

Enid thanked him profusely, then had the boys take the animal out the back door. Her gift was passed on and the boys had their feast.

The chief had been attracted by the prospect of witnessing the first wedding of white people in his area. He had come a little late but he had come. He looked around at the palm fronds and the calla lilies, undoubtedly thinking that we still retained some nature worship. If he did not actually worship trees, he often rubbed butter on them and threw money at them to play safe.

We had greeted our guest on the veranda. In the house began a new series of greetings and blessings. "Ha! Ha!" he chuckled. "So you are married!"

It probably hurt his sense of modesty to see a bride boldly smiling and holding her husband's arm. She should have been huddled in a dark corner, a shawl completely covering her head. And the idea of two couples getting married together! What wasted opportunities for food and fun! But it did not really matter since there were only sandwiches and cookies and tea, anyway. Just as well to get it over with in a hurry.

We sat down together. Our friend munched gingerly at his sandwich. No telling what the mixture between the slices of bread might contain. It did not taste of red pepper, onions, or rancid butter. And the sandwich, once eaten, did not seem to occupy any space in the stomach.

"We have been waiting a long time to get married," I remarked. "Four years."

"Wouldn't her father listen to your talk?" he asked, pointing at Enid.

"It took me a long time to buy enough cows to satisfy him, and he raised the price twice."

The chief laughed. "You told me you don't marry with cows in your country." He scratched his head, which seems to help Africans solve problems. In his own way he was doing research. "When did your parents get together to arrange the marriage?"

I began to feel that we had not done anything right. There had been no feast for the guests, no cows for my father-in-law. Now still another confession remained.

"In our country young people meet, become acquainted, and fall in love. They tell their parents about it and then get married."

My words seemed almost immoral. At the very least, they would sound immodest to an Ethiopian. Our customs did not allow for very deep roots in family or clan, and parents received no reward for all they had done to provide wives for strange young men. Perhaps the African way was best for the African but I preferred ours. The most serious shock for the chief was yet to come.

"We promised to stay with each other and not to marry anybody else as long as we both live."

Our guest stopped smiling. He could excuse our other strange ways, but not this! He felt sorry for me. I was so young and no doubt I meant well, but to saddle myself with a woman without an escape clause! What if she turned out to be cantankerous as so many wives did? What if she were tiresome? And above all, what if she were childless? He said nothing about Enid's being saddled with me, for Africa is a man's continent.

The chief smiled again as we stood up. In spite of the confusion we had poured into his mind, he blessed us.

"May you have a man child," he said.

My wife—how well I liked the word!—and I stayed in Soddu for two weeks, managing the station while Dr. and Mrs. Roberts and Lois Briggs went to Addis Ababa. Instead of going on a honeymoon, we moved into the Roberts's house.

Ray Davis was slaving away on the new hospital buildings. He was still young but already had had experience in building. The lower walls of the hospital were being made of stone, the upper of mud bricks, and metal window frames had been brought from Addis Ababa. The hospital would not be made of sticks and mud. The lines Ray had laid out were straight and his walls true. When we took over the Roberts's house, Ray came with it as a boarder.

We had just settled down to the quiet of our post-wedding recuperation when two vacationing missionaries arrived, Daisy McMillan and

Frieda Horn of New Zealand. When the boys informed us that they had been seen leaving the main road and winding down the hill toward us, we dropped our bulky tropical hats on our heads and went out to greet them. There they were at the top of the road. Mosquito netting covered their helmets and hung down over their faces and necks to keep the flies out. Long coats covered their riding outfits.

"There are only two of them but they certainly look impressive," I said to Enid. "The mules seem to have absorbed some of the ladies' dignity. Don't they walk as though they were carrying the Queen to the Trooping of the Colors?"

The carriers, with beds, tents, food boxes, and suitcases on their heads, filed solemnly along behind. The Queen of Sheba could hardly have traveled with more pomp. Yet when the ladies had dismounted and stood before us, they were just Daisy and Frieda. They spoke a New Zealand English, but we had grown accustomed to that in our journeyings. Frieda hardly seemed built for mule travel in Ethiopia. Daisy was stronger and of a heavier build. Even so, it was only the call of God that brought these and other women to Africa to endure hardship for the gospel's sake.

Our boardinghouse honeymoon was pleasant enough until the evening of the fourth day.

"You'd better take my temperature," Enid said.

"Why?" I was alarmed. "Do you feel sick?"

"I don't feel very well."

She had a high temperature which continued for several days.

"Perhaps you should ask the girls to get the meals," Enid suggested.

"I'd rather do it," I replied. "They're on their vacation and I'm only on my honeymoon."

I tried to make a pie the first day. I should have stuck to chocolate pudding.

"This is good pie," Ray said.

"Excellent," pronounced Daisy.

"Indeed," Frieda added.

Christian people are often hard pressed to be kind and truthful at the same time. I knew the pie was awful.

I knew, too, that when the Robertses and Lois would return, we would gladly give their house back to them, complete with boarder and guests, and pack up for our real honeymoon journey to our new station.

7

African Honeymoon

THE ROAD to our first African home was a long one.

"Gofa isn't like Walamo," I told Enid as we talked over our travel plans. "I wonder how Hot Cross Buns will do in the mountains?"

Enid's horse was so named because of the scars crisscrossing his back. Ethiopian pack and riding saddles often rubbed sores into the backs of of the animals, and Enid's had had many such ulcers before she bought him. Ethiopian mule drivers had given him the "treatment" with their long branding irons.

I saddled Hot Cross Buns and went for a ride to see how sure-footed he was. Before long I began to wonder about this lumber wagon Enid had been riding around Ethiopia. His joints were stiff and there was no resilience in his stride. My teeth chattered with every step. How could a horse ride so hard? I returned to the yard and called Enid.

"How could you endure riding this robot all the way from Addis Ababa?" I demanded. "It felt to me just now as if he were walking on stilts!"

Her hours on the animal's back had worn Enid out but she had thought this was the inevitable result of horseback riding. She agreed with me that we had better sell him right away. We then bought a small mule. The first time I mounted her, she turned her head, bared her teeth, and tried to nip me. We called her Nippy.

Our rainy season supply of groceries had arrived. We had planned the order together and had sent it off to our business office in Addis Ababa. There were two boxes, each containing two five-gallon cans of kerosene, and together they made a well-balanced mule load. Cooking oil, pressed from Ethiopian seeds and refined in Addis Ababa, and sugar were packed in kerosene cans. The other boxes contained a few cans of fruit and vegetables, spices, and catsup and mustard.

57

At Gofa we would be able to grow a wide variety of vegetables, and buy limes, bananas, meat, and eggs from the local market. By American standards we would be living the simple life—but how we were to appreciate the abundance of Ethiopia later on in the Sudan!

The rains had begun and the mountainsides and valleys were splashed with many shades of green. There were green leaves, green grass, and green grain. We would travel over the mountains and through the valleys by day, and late every afternoon would pitch our tent in some faraway meadow. Even the anticipation was delightful and exhilarating. I had hurried over these roads before; now I would take it easy and enjoy it.

We said good-by to Soddu early one morning and with boys and mule men started out for Gofa. There would be only four missionaries there and we would have few visitors. We would be one of the most isolated missions in Ethiopia, perhaps in all Africa, but somehow, now, that did not seem to matter.

Our animals loosened the joints in their hind legs as they clambered down over the soft red rock toward the plain. The flat land ahead now did not appear so endless. Getting married had made me shortsighted. We wanted to ride side by side, but could not do so on the narrow mule trails. Ethiopians need only a one-animal track. The master-servant, master-slave, and husband-wife relationships do not require double-file traveling. That is one of the many ways the people have to show they know where they belong—in front or behind. Our American upbringing had led us to want to travel side by side.

I did not have to teach Enid much about trekking. She had learned the hard way, traveling from Addis Ababa to Duromi in August, the worst month of the rains. She took to her camp duties naturally. She had charge of the meals and I supervised the packing and the care of our riding animals.

Our alarm clock went off at four o'clock each morning. We had to awaken the boys because the local roosters had not yet given their second call. Enid helped her boy with the breakfast while I saw to the lowering of the tent. We often ate in the dark while the boys and mule men packed the tent and loaded the animals. The men and boys tried to squat by the fire as often as possible between efforts. We had to keep them moving in order to be on our way by six.

"Today we get to Gamo!" Enid almost shouted one morning. "I've tried to picture the place through your letters. It will be fun to see how accurate my imagination has been."

I began to feel very possessive. Gamo was my province; the mountains and the people were mine, too. I pointed out all the familiar landmarks to Enid.

"That's the road to the provincial capital. That's our mountain. We have to go all the way around it, the station is on the other side."

We were climbing higher and higher. The change in altitude affected our breathing.

"Here is the place Tola brought me to the day I rode to Soddu to see you," I said at last.

"I'm tired from doing it in three days!" Enid marveled. "I don't see how you ever did it in one." Neither could I.

We dipped down into the last stream bed. Finally, at the top of the bank, we could see the iron roof of the Streets' house and back of it our haystack, squatting on its haunches like a furry bear. We clattered down over the broken terraces and soon reined up by it and dismounted.

Enid looked at the tall structure. The grass on the roof seemed shaggier. I pushed the door open.

"Is this all the room you had?" she asked in surprise.

"Oh, no," I replied. "We had the upstairs, too." I pointed to the space above the bedroom. It looked dark and empty.

"It must have been very lonely at times," Enid said understandingly.

The Street family had gathered outside and were wondering why we had stopped.

"Enid had to see my bachelor quarters first," I told them, as we shook hands all around.

Suddenly I saw Tola. He was standing some distance away, by the corner of the house, eyeing us all and waiting for his turn to greet us. His face twisted into a half smile as he enjoyed our pleasure at seeing one another. He was trying to understand the "better life" we had talked about. His people greeted one another quietly, with almost religious dignity. We all laughed hilariously as somebody made a remark appropriate to newlyweds. Our greetings were soon ended and Tola thought he could advance safely. My heart warmed at the sight of him.

"Tola," I asked, "are you well? Are you at peace? Come and meet my wife."

He bowed slightly to Enid, holding out his right hand and supporting it with his left. The greetings were many and Enid returned greeting for greeting. Their hands parted and Tola straightened up and smiled.

"I am glad my master has a wife at last. May you bear a man child."

"We thought you'd enjoy sleeping in your old house, Mal," Harold Street said. "We've fixed up some camp cots there for you."

Our boys piled our goods and camping equipment on the ground outside our hut. We walked toward the Streets' house for the customary cup of tea.

"A few people are coming on Sundays now," Street informed us. "I'd like to have you speak to them tomorrow."

I agreed. In the five months since I had left Gamo I had studied hard and had done some preaching in Gofa. Still, I would have to do more work to be able to speak effectively. I chose a passage of Scripture and wrote out copious notes. Knowing the words of a language and putting them together correctly was one thing; getting a live message into the hearts of the hearers was something else. Could I bridge the gap?

Sunday morning I sat down on the front veranda with twelve older men. We had heard that these "elders" had agreed to listen to our talk first, then would later decide whether the women and young people could safely be exposed to it. Tirfay was there, a big fellow, broad-shouldered and seemingly muscular. He usually avoided hard work and was always quick to laugh and joke—a sort of African playboy. As far as he was concerned, everyone could come and listen.

The chief's father was also there. He was old and stooped. During his lifetime he had turned many a clod, had hoed many acres of grain, had harvested thousands of bushels, but he had never had an abundance of anything. His masters had exacted too heavy a tax on the fruit of his labors. Now this new thing had come in the form of people who were not interested in taxes or goods or domineering. They were interested only in God. The old man sighed, possibly reviewing the past. Perhaps he was recalling that life had brought him little but disappointment and sadness. Could mere talk change all that for the remaining days of his life?

For this first message in the Gamo language I chose John 3:16. I told the men that believers need not fear. "Perfect love casteth out fear. God so loved the world. . ." The greatest Spirit of all did not have to be appeased by men; God had provided the one perfect sacrifice sufficient for all men of all races and for all time. "He gave His only begotten Son. . ." Since this was God's work, there was nothing left for men to do but receive His gift of eternal life. ". . .That whosoever believeth in Him should not perish but have everlasting life."

I thought I understood their unspoken reaction, their nodding heads, their pensive faces. Probably they were thinking these were good words but was it safe to stop appeasing the spirits? It would take many messages and the fires of persecution itself to replace their fear by love. Fear was not easily removed; it had to be cast out.

I prayed and the men stood up. We said our farewells and they went down the path, single file, to their village. "He says God is good" were the last words I could hear from the eldest member of the group.

The next morning the mule men loaded their animals and resumed the journey for Gofa while we ate breakfast. We could easily catch up. After we had eaten, we gathered in the Streets' living room for a final word of prayer. As I looked around I noticed the fireplace. A few pieces of eucalyptus wood were smoldering, but the smoke was going up the chimney, not out into the room. Large glass windows admitted streams of light. The corners looked cozy with little tables crowded into them. What did one do for coziness in a round house? There was no piano but that did not prevent our singing. Harold Street read from *Daily Light*, a group of Bible verses for daily reading assembled by the Bagster family in England. Then we prayed. The "Amen" was like a good-by; it meant that fellowship was again being broken. How different the next meeting would be!

Saying good-by to our fellow workers did not take as long as the words of farewell with our Gamo friends and Tola. Finally we swung into our saddles and started up the path, the green hills unfolding before us. We followed the edge of the escarpment that fell away toward the lakes. The mountains reared their terraced heads to the right. The road was tucked into the ledge cut out of the cliffs like a modern American motor road. To the left the mountains dropped away to more terraces, cliffs, waterfalls, meadows, farms, and at last, far away, the lakes.

We looked at the terraces rising nearly two thousand feet above us to the very top of the peak. Only the sheerest cliffs had escaped the hoes of the cultivators. Many terraces were broken down and others were overgrown with brush. They had not been planted for years.

"The population must have been very heavy here at one time," Enid observed wistfully.

"It makes you feel sort of lonesome," I agreed, "to think of a large number of people just disappearing."

There were not enough people to cultivate the available land. Where had they gone? Much of the conversation around the village fires at night was of these missing people and the events leading to the depopulation of the province.

In the early lifetime of many of the old folk, there had been no central government. Throughout most of the nineteenth century intertribal warfare had destroyed many adult males, while the women and children were carried away. There had been little security. The Amharas themselves were divided into several kingdoms which often made war with one another. They were the first Ethiopians to get guns. The rest of the country was occupied by hundreds of tribes like the Gamos, Gofas, Gallas, and Walamos, who spent much of their time fighting one another or making raids for cattle and slaves.

Menelik II was the architect of modern Ethiopia. He subdued the rival Amharas and welded them into one nation, establishing himself as "king of kings of Ethiopia." Then he turned his attention to the tribes and because they had not been able to secure guns, conquered them and made it one country. Although Menelik II united Ethiopia, it was His Majesty Haile Selassie I who developed it and brought it to its present world position.

As I reflected on this subject, an oppressive silence seemed to hang over the mountainsides like the quiet after friends have gone. We rode on silently, only the clip-clop of the animals' hoofs breaking the stillness. That first day's journey brought us to the edge of an enormous valley that yawned like a chasm. We camped close to its edge at an elevation of eleven thousand feet.

In the morning we tried to get some breakfast while slopping around in the mud, for it had rained all night. The gorge by which we had camped lay before us, the road to be traveled skirting its edge. Soon we were making our way along the ever-narrowing pathway, the mountains rising sheer above us. Below was an empty void hemmed in by the cliff. Again and again the rain-swollen streams roared down from above us. They rushed across our narrow trail, and disappeared in a cloud of spray below.

Our animals were held back so the pack mules could go ahead. We followed along, keeping close to the rock on the upper side. A waterfall sprayed us as it splattered over the rough face of the cliff. We were in the center of the horseshoe formed by the immense valley gorge. There was time to look and plenty of room for looking. This vista dwarfed that of the Grand Canyon, but how many had ever looked upon this sight with appreciative eyes?

Down there in the forbidding valley people lived. Houses were perched on tiny terraces along the face of stone cliffs and others were scattered on broader shelves near the valley floor. The inhabitants had probably had trouble with relatives or chiefs and were trying to get away from it all, but not even there could they find complete isolation. Undoubtedly they rendered their weekly service to their masters and paid their taxes. Progress had not followed them but responsibility had.

We turned and led the animals along the ledge. It was at least three hours since we started and the mountains above began to lean away from us. Suddenly the shelf ended and the road turned abruptly up the steep mountainside. Our animals scrambled over the gravel and through the boulders. The incline was too steep for them to carry us so we dismounted, handing the reins to the boys. We held on to the animals' tails. In climbing a mountain at a high altitude a little thing like a tail can make the difference between success and failure.

The pack mules dug their tiny hoofs into the hard surface. Their shoulder muscles flexed and rolled. They had to go on; they could not be relieved of their loads. Toward four o'clock we swung away from the mountains and came out onto a little green plateau on the edge of the canyon. I called Enid and pointed across the wide expanse of emptiness.

"Straight across there is where we camped last night. I don't suppose it is more than three or four miles from here."

"How far have we actually come?"

"Oh, probably fifteen miles."

The next day we began our descent to the lowlands and travel and camping became more pleasant. The barley fields of the highlands gradually gave way to the corn of the lowlands. This area was monkey and baboon country, too. Villages dotted the countryside.

"It bothers me to travel through these hundreds of villages," I said to Enid, "knowing that another generation or two will die before the people can be adequately reached with the gospel."

"Our brief messages don't sink in. We'll have to come back sometime and sit with them so they can understand."

"We can't get enough foreign missionaries to come out here to reach all these people. We'll have to work for the building up of a strong church wherever we are. Then the Ethiopian Christians will have to come out to places like this to preach."

"That's this 'indigenous church' business I've heard so much about. Most of the older missionaries I've met talk about it all the time. They even got me to read part of that book by Roland Allen. I guess there are two of them. One is about St. Paul's missionary methods; the other something about the spontaneous expansion of the church. I suppose, Mal, you've gotten in on some discussions, too?"

"Plenty. But when you're traveling right past thousands of people who haven't heard about the Lord and who stand little chance of doing so in the near future, you don't depend merely on what books say. It's obvious that only converted Africans can do the job."

We started off again. For a short way the road was wide enough for us to travel side by side.

8

"And Rumors of Wars"

IT WAS our next to the last day of travel and we dropped down to a valley floor again and pushed our way through its elephant grass. Although I was high on my horse, the grass stretched another three or four feet above me. The early morning dew fell from the stalks as we touched them and soaked us. We spent the night in a native-style hut in the middle of our valley garden, the piece of land given us by the Governor so that we could raise fruits and vegetables we could not grow in the highlands. The next day would be the last and hardest of the journey. We would have to make the thirty-six-hundred-foot ascent to our station when the men and animals were worn out.

A downpour at four o'clock kept us in bed a while longer. At eight we were under way and soon climbing. We had not gone far when we saw a young boy coming toward us. I was surprised to recognize Samati, and learned later that the Andersons had spread word of our coming. Before I left Gofa to go to my wedding, Samati had asked me if he could be our "boy" when I returned with Enid. He had never really worked in a missionary house but he had learned from others who had done so a number of things about housework, washing and ironing, and the many other tasks that Africans did to earn money from foreigners. Later on, dozens of lads asked if they could work for us. The idea of hired servants in Africa was not initiated by Europeans; Africans themselves have had the master-servant relationship for centuries. Many Ethiopians consider it an honor to work for white men or "big" Ethiopians because they share their masters' glory.

Samati greeted us. "Did you arrive well? Did you arrive in peace?"

There was something heartwarming about the fact that he had come. To do so he had walked for nearly two hours over stony ground, just to greet us and to let us know he was ready to work. Now he had to walk back up the mountainside. More than anything else, this made Enid feel welcome. Among a strange people and in a strange place, she had met a lad who wanted to work for her. And he had walked all that way just to say so!

Samati turned around and went back with us. He walked by Enid's mule, his hand on the back of the saddle in customary Ethiopian master-servant fashion. The two carried on a lively conversation. Samati was a sweet lad, with an open happy face that radiated confidence. He and his parents lived on the edge of the Mission station. Even at fourteen he was leaving his boyhood behind and taking on adult responsibilities. During the entire time he was with us, we never thought of him as a servant. He seemed like a son in our house; we loved him and he loved us.

Often Samati tried to impress us with his appraisal of events in our Gofa world. His parents were confirmed Coptic Christians and could not understand how God could be worshiped without ritual, priest, and ancient language. There were some Copts who were evangelical at heart, including His Majesty Haile Selassie. But far away from Addis Ababa their religion had been influenced by the surrounding paganism.

As we traveled higher the grass, tall on the lower slopes of the mountains, grew shorter and there was only a scattering of trees. Occasionally the road was rocky and steep, but mostly a gradual grade had been maintained by routing the road into the ravines and then back out again. First we would be in brilliant sunshine, then in the ravine where the sun had not yet reached.

It was a long steep climb for the animals. Their flanks heaved and their muscles tightened as their tiny hoofs dug in. They would not quit. At last we came out on the top of the ridge. Now it was just an easy mile to our home. Gofa Peak still towered hundreds of feet above us but we had to climb no more.

Newsworthy events do not occur every day in African villages so our Gofa neighbors had been waiting for us. We had already provided them with nighttime conversation; now we would give them much more. We dropped down the little green slope to the Andersons' thatch-roofed house. They had been alone for three months and they welcomed us joyfully.

We could hear voices among the huts on the hillside. "They have arrived! They have arrived!"

Men and women, boys and girls, came scurrying down the paths to welcome us. They were profuse in their greetings but kept their eyes slanted toward Enid, appraising her. After shaking her hand they formed little groups, their heads together. I strained to hear their comments.

"She is quite short. . . . Is she not a child? . . . She doesn't stop smiling. . . . Where did she learn to speak like us?"

Her youth, her smile, and language ability would give Enid an open door to the people.

The Andersons and our neighbors escorted us across the meadow toward our new home. I discovered myself frantically making a hasty reappraisal of the building. Somehow, Enid's eyes now looked out of mine and my brain had to make the adjustment. The thatched roof poked its head up high. It had to be steep to shed the water but it made the house look twice as large as it was. I remembered that some of the walls had not been whitewashed nor had the palm-leaf mats on the floor been replaced.

Enid brought me back with a pressure of her hand. She was skipping along gaily, looking down over the grass and through the trees.

"It's so beautiful," she said.

The station was like a saucer with one broken side. Three buildings—two homes and a clinic—were set in the sides of the saucer, halfway up. Clumps of high, flowering thorn trees were scattered around and up the far side. The broken side represented the beginning of a ravine that circled around back of the station and below it, and finally ended up in the valley from which we had just come.

Strung along the edge of the saucer above our homes were the huts of our neighbors, half hidden by the broad leaves of the bananalike plantain stalks surrounding them. Some of them had been built down inside the saucer not far from the Andersons' home.

As we approached our house, the crowd began to thin out. We went through the gate and stepped into the shade of the overhanging roof. A few cobwebs, heavily powdered with borer dust, hung from the roof. I would have to get them down in a hurry. Enid looked around and up but she kept walking toward the door, a sheet of corrugated iron nailed to a wooden frame.

Together we pushed open the door and stepped inside. One could not help looking up first—it was that type of house. The center pole that supported the roof where it came together in a point poked out of the wall in front of us and disappeared in the darkness above. Braces went out from it to the rafters in all directions and other braces supported those braces. Between the rafters the straight bamboos lay row on row. They were tied with rope, the ends of which hung down. The thatch inside the house was not weathered and it, too, lay in rows. How many stalks of grass were up there? A million, perhaps? It would have been a wonderful place for monkeys but in their absence the spiders had taken over.

Enid looked up at the webs swinging everywhere. Again I told myself I would have to get rid of those spiders and their webs fast. We walked through the rooms. I knew Enid was mentally hanging her curtains and pictures, putting down her scatter rugs. We did not want our way of living to be a gulf between us and our Ethiopian people, but no matter what we did, our home would be a little bit of America.

Uncle Nick and I had helped build the house for the Streets at Gamo. Now Enid and I were moving into a house built by Walter Ohman and Laurie Davison. They had started the spiritual house, too, and we would build on their foundation. It would not even be necessary for us to struggle with an unwritten language, for Walter Ohman had done most of that work.

Our excursion through the four-room house did not take long. It was square, with the living room and bedroom occupying the front of the house, while the dining room and study were across the back with a pantry between. The kitchen, a few steps from the dining-room door, was set into the hill where an area just big enough to hold it had been excavated. The thatched roof had been extended to form a six-foot veranda all around the house. I wondered what Enid thought of it.

"Honey, it's wonderful!" she commented at last. "We're going to be awfully happy here."

And so we were—while it lasted. We forgot our fatigue in a new urge, the same urge that leads the weaver bird to tie knots, the woodpecker to drill holes, and the hammerheaded stork to plaster his nest. This was to be our first home. Instead of collapsing, we began to work on our nest. Our goods had arrived from Soddu. Much of Enid's stuff, containing many things for our home, had never been unpacked. We started to open boxes. How many dishes would be broken? Our Wheaton plate was smashed, and somebody in securing the banding iron on a box had driven a nail right through a mirror. But these things did not matter. We had to learn not to let our hearts grow too fond of material things.

"We'll have to tear those old mats out and put down new ones," I said to Enid, "and we should polish the dirt floors before we do it."

"When you say 'polish,' do you mean the same thing that they do in Soddu?"

"Of course! We'll get some men to make a mixture of cow dung and water, which will make a smooth finishing coat. It seals up the cracks and gives fleas fewer hiding places."

After the floors were polished, our workers brought split bamboo and wove them into a wall-to-wall carpet. We put down our newly purchased palm-leaf mats and had the boys stitch them together on top of the bamboo. When Enid produced our few scatter rugs, the bottom side of the house was ready.

There was so much to do that I neglected the thing that was causing Enid the most anxiety. I noticed her frequent glances upward at the jungle of spiderwebs, as she kept a watchful eye out for the spiders themselves. Her attitude was understandable for some of the spiders measured two inches in diameter and traveled so fast the eye could scarcely follow. And they appeared in the most awkward places. Between bed sheets, for instance.

One day a big woolly one, hanging between a table and the wall, caused Enid to let out a shriek. Samati came running. When he asked Enid the cause of her alarm, she pointed to the spider. Deflated, Samati looked at the harmless specimen and then at Enid.

"It is not a leopard," he said as he turned away.

Although we hired Ethiopians to do as much of the everyday work as possible, there were many things they could not do. None of them knew carpentry, so in my spare time I began to build a few essential pieces of furniture. Some Ethiopians, anxious to earn money, brought me planks they had hewn out of wild fig tree trunks.

A sideboard took shape, then a table. Now it was Enid's turn. She then dissolved potassium permanganate in water and applied the solution to the furniture with a rag wrapped around the end of a stick. The homemade stain ate up the rags but brought out the grain nicely. A coat of shellac finished the job.

With our floors polished, our goods unpacked, and our furniture under way, we turned to the neighborhood children and told them we were ready to begin reading classes. They had attended these under our former missionaries, Walter Ohman and Laurie Davison, and were clamoring for further instruction. The Andersons joined us and we divided the children into classes according to ability and progress already made.

The singsong of the recited alphabet arose from the four corners of our house. We had charts made containing the whole massive alphabet. Simberu, our first convert, carried his on a string around his neck, and struggled with it as he rested from plowing and hoeing.

Soon the ones who had studied under the previous missionaries began to read Gofa literature, which consisted of two small pieces—the Gospel of Mark, published by the British and Foreign Bible Society, and a compilation of Scripture verses called *God Hath Spoken*, published by the Scripture Gift Mission. The reading of the Scriptures and the messages we brought each day warmed the hearts of the children and young people. They came to Sunday school and the church services began to grow.

Each day we joined the Andersons in Station prayers. We exchanged information about people to whom we had spoken, mentioning those who seemed interested and those who were in trouble. Thus, whenever we would meet any of these people, we would know their problems and how to talk to them. The last Friday of each month was prayer day. Routine work was put aside and we met for Bible reading and for prayer. As we gathered together on this day, we realized how appropriate were the words "great is Thy faithfulness."

Much time was spent in language study. The Gofa language was changing. Its pure form was now spoken only by the backwoods people. One of the believers, Saka, had married a girl from a village beyond the mountain and her Gofa speech was unspoiled by contact with Amharas or foreigners. She was a jolly person and spoke in parables and idioms we had never before heard. It was like learning a new language. We frequently met with the Andersons and several of the believers to go over the language material for revision. The old language, such as Saka's wife spoke, would be useful but we would have to keep up with its growth and change.

On Sunday afternoons we rode out to villages four or more miles away and held services. Soon the people we spoke to began to come to the Sunday morning services and some visited us during the week.

Enid's linguistic talents gave promise of putting much Gofa literature into the hands of the people. We thought they would respond to the surpassingly beautiful yet grim truth of God's saving men through the death of His son on a cross. Everything looked rosy. We had set up our home and married life was all we had anticipated. At mealtime merry laughter rose from the little square table where we sat facing each other. Sometimes we moved the table into the living room and ate our breakfasts in front of the fireplace, for the mornings were cold.

Then suddenly Mussolini swept his hand across the land. The news came from Addis Ababa and in letters and clippings from home. Mussolini was conducting a civilizing mission to Ethiopia! We felt our personal involvement most when we received a letter from Dr. Lambie.

He wrote that the American Ambassador had ordered all American citizens to leave the country. This did not mean we missionaries had to leave but it did mean that we could not expect American protection. If at any time we felt that our lives were in danger, we were free to go to Addis Ababa. We did feel free and, together with all our missionaries in the country, chose to stay.

Finally we heard from Dejazmatch Abeba, whose feudal title is literally translated as "Governor." His "palace" was in the capital city of Bulki, two miles away, staffed by servants who were holdovers from the slaveholding days but were now free. He was a dignified and kindly appearing man in his black wool burnoose, his hair trimmed to stand straight above his light, fine-featured face. He administered Gofa and several surrounding areas, and guarded a piece of the Kenya border.

One day he called Merle Anderson and me to his sprawling bamboo stockade. His attendant ushered us into his "throne room." Abeba smiled but he did not look happy. We were sorry for him, for he always had the bright eyes of a child about to have a dream come true. Now his eyes were heavy. His discussions of world affairs had always been spirited. Now he had an inquiring attitude, as if he were asking, "Do you think we can possibly win this war?" He had just heard what was probably the worst news he would ever receive in his lifetime, yet he did not dispense with the customary greetings which included many inquiries as to our health and that of our families. He did not disclose the reason for his anxiety until coffee had been served.

"I am going to Addis Ababa," he said, as though he had been transferred to another province. "The Italians are getting ready to fight us and His Majesty has called me to go to war."

We felt unutterably sad. Dejazmatch Abeba was a kindly man and in our few meetings we had become very much attached to him. The tribespeople liked him and said he was a fair administrator, a rare tribute to Ethiopian rulers in those days. What could two young missionaries say in the face of such a pronouncement?

"We are very sorry. We hope you will quickly defeat the Italians and return to your province." We meant every word.

The Governor had one request. "We will pass through some desolate country on our way and it will be impossible to find meat there. Could you make me some sausages? I will furnish the meat, the spices, and the intestines."

Merle and I looked at each other helplessly. We wanted to do everything we could for our friend—but making sausages . . .

"We've never made sausages but we'll try," I promised the Governor.

We took our leave and upon returning home, laid the problem before our wives. A search through all their cookbooks turned up many recipes on how to cook sausage but none on how to make it. Finally we found what we wanted in an old book the Andersons had stored away, thinking they would never need it.

We conferred with the Governor and set a day for Operation Sausage. He sent a mountain of beef, what seemed like miles of intestines, and salt and red pepper. African sausages would not be much good without red pepper. Our two little family-sized grinders could hardly cope with the project. The boys turned the handles while we prepared the beef and stuffed it into the casings.

"How are we going to smoke them?" our wives asked.

"We'll have to hang them in your chimney," I told Lillian Anderson. "It's wider and lower than ours."

We scraped together all the wire we could find and hung the sausages over the Andersons' fire. For the next two weeks they had to keep it lighted whether they needed it or not. The fortnight passed, and the following day we climbed the ladder and pulled the sausages out of the chimney. They were wrinkled and black and had shrunk to half of their original size. We cut up one and tasted it.

"This isn't sausage!" Enid exclaimed. "It's dried beef!"

Whatever it was, it was cured and would keep while the Governor went to war. We presented the sausages with our apologies. The next day, he sent us a note asking us to order two cases of sardines for him from Addis Ababa. We thought we understood.

We were invited to visit Dejazmatch Abeba once more before his march to war. His servant came to us in the usual manner, head respectfully bowed, both hands outstretched and holding a note. It read: "Mr. and Mrs. Forsberg, Mr. and Mrs. Anderson, and Master Kenny are invited for dinner at six o'clock."

Six o'clock Ethiopian time was twelve noon by our watches. Kenny Anderson was not walking yet, so his father tied a pole to his cot and two boys carried it between them while we rode our mules the two miles to the Governor's residence.

Meanwhile, within the maze of the Governor's stockade, women servants were preparing for our coming. When their master entertained at the annual gathering for his men who were stationed throughout the province, he fed four or five thousand. We would be no problem, except

that we were considered very special guests and Abeba wanted to entertain correctly.

The masters of the servants, who were themselves servants, goaded
the cooks. "This isn't any ordinary day! Don't you know the foreigners
are coming? Hurry up with that chicken!"

Several chickens had already been killed and thoroughly cleaned, and
a clay pot had been placed on the fire. The dry plantain fiber wrapping
was removed from a ball of rancid butter, weighing about a pound,
which was put into the pot. Onions were sliced and sautéed in the hot
butter, and a quantity of ground red pepper was added, which soon
dominated the stew. Then pieces of chicken went into the mixture.
After it had cooked thoroughly, water was added to make a brown gravy,
thickened with pea flour, along with two kinds of locally grown seeds
which were ground up and used to season the stew.

Nearby was a special hut for making *injera*. These resembled large
pancakes, described later by an American war correspondent as "turkish
towels." The women prepared a batter made of the Abyssinian grain,
teff. A pottery griddle sat on three stones over the fire and was greased
with a piece of cloth soaked in beeswax. Then the batter was poured
round and round several times, and spread over the entire griddle with
the hand. The *injera* cooked quickly, forming bubbles just like pancakes.
Then they were piled on a little basketlike stand.

Even the Ethiopians need some kind of liquid with their meals to
cut the pepper. They favor two alcoholic drinks, one made with fer-
mented honey, the other from barley. The Governor served us unfer-
mented honey water, which the Ethiopians rarely drank.

Dejazmatch Abeba knew exactly how far we were from his home
at any given moment. When we rode into his enclosure, he came toward
us, arms outstretched in welcome. He was gracious and charming as
always, his face serene, although a new anxiety, war born, occasionally
revealed itself in a look or expression. He shook hands with all of us,
a stream of familiar Amharic greetings flowing from his lips. He had
special words for little Kenny who was still too young to understand.

"You are white, but you were born in our country, weren't you?" He
bent over the crib and kissed Kenny's pudgy hand. Turning to the boys
who had carried Kenny, he told them to bring the child in. Ordering
people around came quite naturally; he had been born to his position.

We entered a mud-walled room, the floor of which was strewn with
fresh grass. The Governor's wife and two daughters greeted us timidly.
We felt sorry for them, for we knew it was an ordeal. Servants brought
low tables and placed them before us. The chicken stew, now known

as *wat*, was poured on top of a large round *injera*. The Governor took the first mouthful and then, selecting a morsel for Enid, placed it in her mouth. After that he urged us all to eat. We broke off pieces of the *injera* and dipped them in the gravy. It was delicious.

As we relaxed after the first course, the Governor ordered the lions brought in. They came, two of them, half-grown. They rubbed their heads against us like overstuffed kittens and Kenny jumped with delight. The lionkeeper had only an ineffectual-looking piece of split bamboo to restrain them. The Governor noticed our uneasiness.

"They won't hurt you," he assured us. "They have just been fed."

The lions circled around us, as though they craved action. Kenny kept squealing happily but Abeba saw our discomfort and ordered the lions driven back to their cages. As soon as they were gone, Kenny began to cry.

"He wants the lions. Bring them back," Abeba ordered again.

So the lions returned and continued their smelling and investigating. We enjoyed this private showing—more or less—but presently another course of *wat* was brought and the lions were led out. We drew a relieved breath.

Abeba sat between us and his conversation was stimulating. He urged us to eat. We had been doing just that for an hour, much longer than we spent at a meal in our own homes. When we stopped, from sheer inability to eat another morsel, he picked up a choice piece of chicken, wrapped it in *injera*, and put it into the mouth of the nearest guest.

"Do eat," he said. "There isn't much pepper in this *wat*."

Perhaps he was right, but we had to drink a stream of honey water to keep flames from breaking out in our mouths. We loved the food but our capacity was not as great as the Governor's kindness.

At last he yielded to our protestations that we could eat no more. But we were not through. He wanted to impress us with his knowledge of modern dishes, too, and calling to his servants, produced what was intended to be a custard. It was actually scrambled eggs.

"We must go," Merle said finally. "Kenny is getting tired."

"That is just the way we talk." The Governor smiled understandingly. "When we want to leave a friend's home we say, 'The baby is tired.'"

We exchanged bows and greetings with the Governor and his family. We had feasted with them and had had a pleasant time. Tomorrow some peasant or former slave would invite us to a meal. The local people kept to their social strata but all welcomed us. They seemed to know instinctively that those who preached the Word should not be bound by caste.

9

Taboo

THE SPIRITUAL work on Gofa Station was still in a primitive state when we arrived, but a foundation had been laid, for the Ohmans and the Davisons and others had preached and taught. Simberu and, shortly afterward, Saka, a serf, had believed though they had not yet been baptized. It was our job to give them instruction and to prepare them for membership in the church of which they would be the charter members.

And then there was Dafarsha, who represented another problem. He called on us one day, standing at the gate until one of our boys informed us of his arrival. People from his tribe did not often get much farther than the gates of houses in the provinces. A Gofa might go in but Dafarsha was not that high in the local caste system. We called to him but he hesitated at the door. He had been in our house many times before, yet he was so accustomed to being one of the people farthest back that he could not bring himself to enter without a personal invitation.

Dafarsha was soft spoken, almost bashful, and his face was gentle. He wore only a loincloth, but his lack of clothing did not seem to bother him. He had urgent business to discuss.

"When are you going to visit us?" he asked after the customary greetings.

His village was two hours away. He belonged to a people whom the Amharas designated as Shankala. They were the remnants of tribes once enslaved by their stronger neighbors, and lived along the edges of the more civilized Amharas and tribespeople. In the early days they had borne the heaviest brunt of slave raiding and were a subdued people. They called themselves Ara, and although they had their own language, those living close to the Gofa people were bilingual, so we could speak to most of them. We promised to visit them.

One day Enid and I packed our trek goods and made the trip to Ara country. It was a big day for Dafarsha and his brother, Dabalki, when they welcomed us to their people. We looked around at those who had come to greet us. The men wore loincloths for the occasion; they did not always have that much on when we met them in their fields. The women wore only bunches of leaves. Even for Africa they were a backward people.

They told us to pitch our tent in the meadow and that they would gather the people that evening to listen to the talk.

On the hillside above us was a platform supported by four poles about seven feet high. What was on the platform did not look like grain or firewood and I asked Dafarsha what it was for.

He hesitated. "Our people don't bury their dead quickly the way the Gofas and the Amharas do. They keep them on a platform like that for a year."

I wondered if Dafarsha were dissociating himself from the practice by his choice of pronouns. Dafarsha and Dabalki were believers. They had first heard the Word from the Ohmans and had walked to the mission station many times since for instruction and fellowship. Now they wanted their neighbors to hear the gospel.

Dafarsha's conversion had presented him with a whole new set of problems. He timidly indicated that he hoped our few days in his village would help him to solve some of them.

Taboos, especially those which degraded women, were basic to Ara culture. Enid found this out on our first visit to one of their huts. Then there were two small stools in the center of the room. I was offered one of them. Enid thought the other was for her and started to sit down.

"Don't sit there!" the lady of the house cried. She reached for the stool and pulled it out from under Enid, who landed on the dirt floor. "Stools are for men!" she added, amazed at Enid's ignorance. "It is taboo for women to sit on stools."

A plantain leaf was brought for Enid. Accepting her position as a woman, she sat on it. I was exalted on the stool.

This custom was not the only means the Ara people had devised to keep their women in subjection. Dafarsha wanted to tell us about his present situation. As we walked toward his house, which was set among the bananalike plantain stalks on the hillside, he tried to prepare us.

"My wife is still out in the little hut," he said. "She's had a baby."

She had been there for twenty days and Dafarsha wanted to bring her back to his house, though the usual forty days had not yet passed. We dodged the dew-laden plaintain leaves as we made our way to the hut.

Suddenly in front of us, in a tiny clearing, was the hut. It was obviously a temporary structure. The walls were woven of bamboo over thin poles and the thatch was carelessly laid. It looked like a shelter for sheep or goats, but as we approached we saw the fuzzy head of a woman just inside the low doorway. Her body stretched the full diameter of the house.

Dafarsha explained that if his wife were brought back to the main house, everything in the house, including the cattle that occupied half of it, would be considered polluted by his neighbors. His cattle would not be allowed to graze with the village herd. That would work a hardship on Dafarsha as it was customary for the men to take turns herding. Dafarsha would have to herd his own cattle daily. In other ways too he would be isolated from all his friends.

How Levitical it sounded! The light of the gospel, shining out from his inner being, had shaken his faith in the rightness of this treatment of Ara women.

We greeted Dafarsha's wife and she held up her new son for us to see. He was fat and black and roly-poly, evidently thriving on his mother's milk. He gurgled happily, unaware that his birth had precipitated a crisis. The mother did not seem to feel any resentment. Custom had taught her that it was correct for her to lie in the dirt of her hut. She probably had no desire to organize the women of her village to demand a change in their condition. The victims of paganism ask no questions, seek no remedy. But conforming had not solved the Aras' problems. They still had to offer sacrifices to offended spirits and walk carefully down the narrow pathway of taboo.

Enid sat on the ground and began to talk to the mother. The woman's look of surprise turned to one of wonder. Her thoughts were reflected on her face. She quite evidently wondered why a woman would risk pollution to talk to her.

"There is nothing wrong with giving birth in the house," Enid said.

Dafarsha's wife looked troubled. The seed had been sown; she began to question in her mind the customs of her tribe. We prayed that she might continue to question. Dafarsha still had the problem of boycott. Could he break taboo and survive? We left Enid at the hut and walked back to the main house. After the little hut it looked like a palace, though cattle occupied half of it. We sat down inside in the semigloom.

"No price is too great to pay for the grace of the Lord," I said. "You yourself are sorry because your wife is out there. You have come to believe this practice is wrong."

Some anthropologists would have suggested that for people like the Ara, the gospel should be interpreted within the context of the local culture. But Dafarsha was the interpreter of his own tribal culture and as far as he was concerned much of it would have to go. For him the gospel would be the dominating force.

Here was the Ara church in embryo. Someday, we hoped, it would be strong enough to ignore the sanctions of the tribe. But all that was for the future. What was best now? A blatant defiance of the old? A quiet conformity until there were more believers to make the break together?

We discussed the matter. We prayed together, asking God to give Dafarsha and Dabalki wisdom in facing their situation, strength to do His bidding, and faith to believe that He would lead them and many others into the freedom and light of Christ.

Our visit to the Ara people ended and we returned to our station to resume our own affairs. Saka and Simberu had to be baptized. We wanted Walter Ohman to examine our two candidates and to take part in their baptism.

Walter Ohman had come to Ethiopia with the first party of missionaries of our Mission. His wife, then Marcella Sholl, had followed and they had been married in Addis Ababa. Marcella was tiny and attractive and always busy. She was a demure little person, who was careful to do everything correctly so as not to offend anyone.

Walter was less concerned with protocol. He was a hard worker and efficient but he did not believe in letting his work become drudgery. He might have been a left-handed shortstop on a professional baseball team had not the Lord called him into the vastly more important work he took up in Ethiopia. In fact, an apocryphal story persisted that he had once played baseball for the Cleveland Indians. The Ethiopians knew nothing about baseball but they did call him "Lefty." Part of the time Walter made his missionary work a game that he delighted in playing. Metaphorically, he would dash up and down the third-base line, worrying the opposing team. His Ethiopian friends loved it.

"Pull up your socks!" he would call out in Walamo to one of his workmen. The phrase had no meaning in that language but it sounded very funny to his fellow missionaries who knew both languages. Walter explained the expression to his workmen. It was all clear then, and there was nothing humorous about it. "Do you know your onions?" he would ask some other unsuspecting Walamo. The man would look at Walter in utter confusion. He knew all the words but how could one know an onion?

Walter was the District Superintendent for Walamo, Gamo, and Gofa. He and Marcella had been on furlough and had but recently returned. They agreed to make the long trip from Soddu and Ray Davis came with them.

We found there were now three candidates for baptism. Saka's brother, Sonkura, had been attending the classes but was worried about the consequences of baptism. He finally asked to be included with Saka and Simberu. We were glad to have Walter Ohman's help in questioning the candidates. The baptism of these three men would be our first step toward establishing a native church.

On mountaintops streams are not big. They start out as brooks and do not become rivers until they have run for a while in the valleys. On our mountaintop there was no stream big enough for our kind of baptism. Although the Andersons and we were Presbyterians, "our kind" of baptism was immersion. In the very early days of the Mission, before the turn of the century, Dr. Bingham's Baptist friends had insisted that he establish immersion as the mode of baptism in the Mission. Dr. Bingham preferred not to set any precedent but his dilemma was solved from an unexpected quarter. The Church of England Mission in Nigeria had a group of Christians ready for baptism before the Sudan Interior Mission did. For some reason, never fully understood by Dr. Bingham and his associates, they performed the rite by immersion. At that time our senior missionary in Nigeria was a Presbyterian, and he decided to follow the example set by the Anglicans. So now we had to find a place to baptize by immersion.

"The only thing we can do," Walter Ohman suggested, "is to dam up the little creek down in the meadow."

Together with the three candidates for baptism, we carried stones and dug dirt and built a little dam. The next Sunday, after the morning service, the congregation walked across the meadow to our pond. Walter stood by the edge of the water and looked up at the crowd gathered in a bower of green shrubs. He began the ceremony.

"These men have become believers in Jesus. They are going to be baptized but this will not save them. Christ went into death and rose again for them. These three believe that and have already been crucified with Christ and raised with Him. They will go under the water and be lifted up again to show you that they have been raised to live new lives. May many of you believe and be baptized."

I helped him as we immersed the three young men. Some of the bystanders screamed, for they had seen only sprinkling by Coptic priests. When the service was over, one of our young neighbors said, "That was truly baptism!"

That night we had our first communion service with the three new members of the Gofa church. But the gates of hell would almost prevail against it before we were to see any substantial growth in it.

A few days after the baptismal service, one of our boys came running. "The Dejazmatch is coming!" he called excitedly.

We looked toward town and saw that the road was full of people. Merle Anderson and I quickly saddled our horses. We must ride out a short distance with our friend. He was mounted on a beautiful mule, more horse than donkey. Merle fell in on one side of him, I on the other.

"We are off to fight the Italians," the Governor said. He seemed determined but not very confident. His manner was friendly but preoccupied. "I have left one of my men in charge. You will be all right."

We talked as we went. We had gone about two miles when, in polite Ethiopian fashion, he said:

"Return, you have come far enough. We will soon drive the Italians out and come back to you."

We dropped out of the procession and returned to the comfort of our homes. Thirteen years were to pass before we would see him again, and under vastly different circumstances. The war would affect us all.

10

Some Were Healed

THE GOVERNOR had gone and so had the Ohmans and Ray Davis. Enid and I settled down to our work again for there was still language material to classify. We had gone over much of it with Walter Ohman and he had given us many new leads.

Since our neighbors often invited us to eat *wat* and *injera* with them, we decided to reciprocate in some way. Our purpose was to be friendly as well as to evangelize, so we began a round of entertaining. Enid felt we should not serve our kind of food. Besides, our supplies and vegetables would not go far and the guests would leave hungry. Therefore, we asked a new neighbor to bake the big pancakes and make the stew. Her name was Shashotie.

Simberu had first told us about this slave girl, whom he had brought to his tiny hut to rot when she could no longer work. Only a hole remained where her nose had been and another had eaten through her skull. Her joints were "frozen" and she could do almost nothing, for she was dying of syphilis. Simberu thought our medicine might save her; he had done what he could but his efforts proved useless.

Many years before, Shashotie and her mother had been abducted from Kaffa Province, to the west, and sold separately in Gofa Province. They had not seen each other since. Shashotie's mistress had been a "big woman" but was now a derelict and had abandoned her.

As a slave, Simberu had no income. He worked hard but there was scarcely enough food for him and his master's family. But Simberu shared his meager supplies with the dying Shashotie and taught her to give thanks before eating. There was nothing impressive about Simberu's appearance. His body, broad at the shoulders from millions of strokes with the pick, tapered down to spindly legs that seemed hardly strong enough to support him. His cheekbones protruded and he had a long pointed chin. But when he spoke, with mellow voice and earnest words, a glow from within completely obscured any physical lack. The gospel, coming to Shashotie from such a source, had been irresistible.

When we had first visited her, we said that Merle Anderson would give her a series of treatments with "needles." She jumped at the magic word. Needles were only for those who could afford them. She had seen landowners, soldiers, and government officials ride off to some distant mission station to get relief from the disease she knew so well. They had come back with ulcers healed and strength restored. But that was not for slaves. Or was it?

The needles did wonders for her general condition. The ulcers healed and the hole in her scalp closed over. Enid went to Shashotie's hut several times a week and exercised her legs in the hope they could be made less rigid, but the damage had already been done. She crawled about the house and sat with her things around her doing her work, but she never walked again.

Simberu was doing his work, too, and soon Shashotie became a Christian. It did not seem right to them or to us that they occupy the same hut though it made no difference to their master and mistress. We built a bamboo hut near our house for Shashotie and one day carried her to it. Shashotie's mistress was furious; she wanted no one else to help the slave she had abandoned. Sometimes compassion makes it necessary for missionaries to go against local custom. When we saw human suffering, we could not be silent.

After her disease was arrested, we asked Shashotie to cook *wat* and *injera* for us. Now that she was a Christian, she wanted to give expression to her new faith. To have some way of serving gave her much joy and satisfaction. Later, when we said we would come to her house to eat her food, Shashotie was overwhelmed. For the first time in her life she had been shown respect. The gospel had found her; she learned to read and write; she gained dignity. She could entertain Americans in her own home! How could this come about except through the gospel?

With the Governor gone, public security rapidly deteriorated. Old feuds were revived and there were frequent shootings. Merle Anderson was kept busy treating knife and gun wounds. Then an epidemic of unknown origin suddenly swept the community.

"What is it, Merle?" I asked. "Typhus?"

"It doesn't fit the description of any tropical disease in the books I have," he replied.

The disease had no outstanding symptoms apart from high fever, though we could predict its duration. The crisis came exactly seven days after the onset. On the morning of that day the patient either sank into a coma, without warning, and died in three or four hours, or just as suddenly began a slow recovery.

When Simberu became infected, we were alarmed. Merle went to see him. His master gave us permission to move Simberu to Shashotie's hut where he would receive the care he needed. We nursed him, fed him light foods, did everything we could—and waited for the seventh day. Never had we been so close to a disease so predictable—yet so unpredictable.

Early on the seventh day we were with Simberu, for we knew the crisis would come shortly after daylight. We could only pray. By nine o'clock it was evident he would not recover. Sonkura and I were with him when he died at one o'clock. It seemed that a foundation stone of the Gofa church had disappeared into the bowels of the earth, leaving a corner of the structure sagging.

"We can't bury him," his master said when we told him. "He can't be buried as a Copt, for he is one of you. You must bury him."

Here was a circumstance we had not foreseen and whatever we would do that afternoon would probably set burial precedents for future Christians. With no time to plan, we had to go ahead immediately with funeral arrangements. There was an unmarked plot of ground over the hill where other non-Coptic persons were buried. We would lay Simberu to rest in it. Those who were not averse to digging a Protestant grave gathered at the spot. While they dug, we made a coffin, and by five o'clock we were ready to carry the body to the grave. As the coffin was lowered to its final position in the ground, we held the service.

I had never before conducted a funeral service in Africa and only once at home. We sang some of the hymns and I read from the Scriptures or paraphrased what was not yet translated into the Gofa language. "I am the resurrection, and the life: he that believeth in me, though he were dead, yet shall he live: And whosoever liveth and believeth in me shall never die. Believest thou this?" I told them that because of Simberu's faith, he was now with Christ.

They were quiet until we began closing the grave. Then women and men alike began to wail in the Gofa style because they knew no other way to express what they felt. They believed in a future life but they were not sure their religious practices would guarantee it to them. In the presence of death they felt sorry not only for the dead and for the bereaved, but for themselves. They saw themselves in the gaping earth; they could not see clearly beyond the grave.

I looked around at the crowd. This was one of the biggest funerals we had witnessed in the whole area. The Amhara aristocracy was there, as was the pagan Gofa aristocracy from many surrounding villages. Slaves and peasants had come too, to honor a slave at death! Suddenly I realized the significance of this scene. When Simberu had become a Christian, and particularly after his baptism, his master and his superiors in the village thought of him in a different way. Conversion had raised him to a higher level.

The people could not understand or explain what had happened to Simberu that they should adopt such an unorthodox attitude toward him, a slave. The last scene in Simberu's life, there at the graveside, was evidence to us of what had happened. A slave had been born again and the freemen around him were unconsciously and unwittingly acknowledging his spiritual superiority. Christ had made him a free man! Simberu was a symbol of what was happening in Africa wherever the church was rising. Social, racial, and color distinctions were going into the church melting pot. There would come out of it no slaves, no bond, no free; all would be one in Christ.

In the days that followed, life seemed difficult without Simberu. He had preached regularly in the villages and always witnessed to his neighbors. He was a living epistle in the community and we missed him terribly. Also, the war news was disturbing and we needed all the stabilizing influences we could find. Rumors were flying:

"The British are coming in from the Sudan. . . The Germans have bombed Rome. . . The French have taken Addis Ababa. . . The Italians are only three or four days' march from us."

At first we thought there must be some truth in them but eventually learned to discount them all. Sometimes we were told the roads were unsafe for travel, at other times that travel was quite normal. We had become increasingly interested in travel conditions ever since Enid woke me one night to say, "I've got a sharp pain right where I think my appendix ought to be."

Those were the last words we wanted to hear, for the nearest doctor was a week's journey away. A person with a diseased appendix should not bounce on a mule for that length of time, and what if the appendix burst?

Merle and I gave our joint, strictly nonprofessional diagnosis and treatment. We recommended that the patient stay in bed until the attack passed. It did pass but others recurred at intervals, so Enid and I finally decided to go to Soddu. Our boys accompanied us. She survived the trip and Dr. Roberts removed her appendix successfully. We lingered at Soddu while she recuperated, and the doctor and Walter Ohman brought us up to date on events.

The Emperor of Ethiopia had fled and the news had reached most of the country. Many Ethiopian soldiers, knowing their time was short, returned to their villages to await the coming of the Italians. But other soldiers were trying to gather as much wealth as possible by any means before the arrival of the Italian forces. They were a menace to the countryside.

One day Samati ran in with news. "God be praised! The Gofa children have returned from the war and are camped near the town. All of our boys are safe."

There was good reason for joy; some Gofa villages would soon learn that they had no men to welcome back. Our boys had been prayed for daily—and now we were happy that all had returned. But it was time for us to decide our next move; we discussed our future many times with Walter.

"Conditions are likely to get worse before the Italians break through," he reasoned, "and we don't know when they'll get here."

"Either we should return to Gofa or the Andersons should come here to Soddu," I insisted. "Perhaps we could join a caravan taking salt to Gofa. The men would be well armed and it would be safe to travel with them."

We remembered that two of our missionaries had already been killed. Cliff Mitchell, Tom Devers, Allen Smith, and Alan Webb had been stationed east of Soddu, in Sidamo Province. When government and public security collapsed, old warfare between the tribespeople and the Amharas, and between tribe and tribe, resumed. Mitchell's wife and child, and Devers' fiancée were already in Addis Ababa. When a large group of Amharas decided to make their way to the capital city, Mitchell and Devers went with them. They were never heard from again.

Mitchell and Devers were not the only missionaries to lose their lives. Dr. Robert Hockman, of the American United Presbyterian Mission, had joined the Red Cross. In trying to remove the detonator from a bomb, he had lost his life.

The Governor of Walamo was still in Soddu and his presence there helped to keep the peace. Should we leave the comparative safety of his province to return to the insecurity of Gofa? We prayed. The more we prayed the more we felt led to return. Reckless though it seemed, we thought our decision to go back was right. We heard that some muleteers of our acquaintance were organizing a large caravan to transport forty or fifty mule loads of salt to Gofa, and arranged to go with them. Once again we opened our hearts to the sky and the road, as our mules and horses clip-clopped toward home.

It was a happy reunion with the Andersons. They had been under severe strain during the return of the soldiers. The uneasiness caused by heavy drinking in the town and the uncertainty of our return had given them considerable anxiety.

The future itself was uncertain. We thought we should spend most of our time giving the gospel to the villages on the outskirts of our area and teaching the believers. But although we settled back into a routine of work, life was never the same again.

11

"The Orange and the Blue"

THE ENTRY of the Italians into Addis Ababa had cut us off from our office there. For months we had received no funds and were close to economic disaster. Fortunately, the rains continued intermittently all through what should have been the dry season. Our gardens flourished and we had an abundance of fresh peas, lettuce, root crops, and cape gooseberries. Never before had we had so much rain and such good gardens. Still, we had to buy meat, milk, and eggs. Chickens, bananas, limes, and potatoes were plentiful but they also cost money. In addition to buying produce, we had to have cash to pay our boys.

"Let's sell some of the clothes we never wear," Enid suggested one day.

There were a few we could easily spare. Our missionaries had warned us of the cold Ethiopian highlands, and recommended we have winter underwear. Although we had survived without such apparel in the sub-zero weather of America's Midwest, we dutifully carried several sets to Ethiopia. These we had never worn, so now we gave our boys the first chance to buy what they wanted.

"I would like this pair," said one, and Alamo disappeared with the warm underdrawers.

The next time we saw them, they had become a sweater without any alteration.

Ethiopians were fond of jackets, vests, and coats. We were sentimental over our senior jackets from college days but did not really need them either. Our old ones would do. So we asked each other if we should sell them. We stalled until our money gave out again. There they were—blue with orange piping, our Wheaton College colors which we used to sing about in the Alma Mater, "We will e'er uphold thy colors, the orange and the blue." The college seal was there too, in Latin, "*Christo*

86

et Regno Ejus, For Christ and His Kingdom." The boys took the jackets and their wages were thus paid for about two months.

Our supply of flour dwindled and our sugar was all but gone. We had plenty of fresh food; nevertheless it was difficult to relax and the Ethiopians, as well as ourselves, were feeling the tension. Rival officials were still maneuvering for the top spot. Our boys frequently brought us reports of killings in town. We heard enough shots fired during every twenty-four hours to cut the population in half. Night usually brought ominous little sounds . . . imaginary movements in the shadows around the house . . . the measured footsteps of men who never came.

Our friend Geeza was worried about us. He was the Emperor's special representative in Gofa Province whose job it was to secure his King his share of the revenue from the area. Before being appointed to this post, Geeza had been a soldier of fortune, roaming about the lowlands toward the Sudan, shooting elephant and selling the ivory, and trading in iron from the mines at Dimmie. He knew his own language well and could also read Geez, the ancient dead forerunner of modern Amharic. A big man, of middle age, like Abeba he was friendly and forward-looking. He believed as we did that salvation came to the individual through faith in Christ, not through works. Still, he followed the practices of his church, for they were an inherent part of his life.

In the absence of the Governor, Geeza had shown more concern for our safety than any other man in or out of the government. We held him in high regard and trusted him. He thought we should have some armed men to stand guard, but after a few hours we found this arrangement tiresome and sent the men back.

There was also the growing possibility that we might have to leave Gofa hurriedly, without warning, so we packed the few essential supplies for the road. We did not bother with tent or beds; a few blankets and a duffel bag would do. We would take the remaining cans of food, along with the remnants of sugar and tea, and a saucepan and a teapot. Some needles and thread and our medicine, and we would be ready. In an emergency, there would be no carriers available. We would have to use our own donkeys and hope that at least one boy would go with us to handle them.

One morning Merle Anderson came over with the distressing report that Lillian had pains in the region of her appendix. The Andersons loaded their pack animals, mounted their mules, and soon disappeared over the notch in the hill. They reached Soddu safely, never to see Gofa again.

We turned away from the problems of the outside world to face a new one of our own. After months of waiting and disappointment, our first baby was expected. Without this added complication we might have been able to stay in Gofa indefinitely and hope for conditions to improve. Now it was necessary to plan to be near a doctor before it was too late.

"What do we do for baby clothes?" I asked Enid.

"I'll have to make some things out of Ethiopian homespun," she replied. "We won't need much."

Some soft locally woven cloth, after it was washed well, proved to be ideal for diapers and nighties.

Visits to our neighbors continued but we did not go very far afield. Then one day we had a pleasant surprise. Tucked away on a little shelf on the mountainside below us was the village where "Sleepy" Hailu lived. Whenever we visited there, he was always more hospitable than the others, and one morning he sent word he wanted to see us. In Hailu's dark hut we watched as he prepared coffee for us. He crushed the leaves and put them in the pot to boil while we visited, then, as the time to drink his brew approached, he added salt and red pepper. Finally, he poured the contents of the pot into the cups that had been lined up on a low table in front of us. Before we were served, a piece of rancid butter was dropped into each cup. It was hard to believe that the people really enjoyed this mixture but we wanted to be sociable and friendly, so we sipped the drink.

Conversion is not always dramatic. We had had no indication that Hailu had become a believer. Yet, as we sat in his hut and talked with him, we suddenly realized we were addressing him as a believer and he was responding. When we returned to our home, we reviewed the progress we, together with the Andersons, had made in our work.

Our church was slowly growing. The people in Kencho and Baga, behind the mountain to the west, were coming for visits regularly and holding prayers in their villages. And there was Samati, and also Saka's young wife, who had heard the good word for the first time after her arrival in Saka's village. She had understood and had believed eagerly. Shashotie, too, came often. She was dependent on us and on the Christians. They carried her to our house for meetings and then home again. Shashotie had grown up in sordid surroundings and had spent much of her adult life in a compound where she was exposed to lust and lewdness, but her faith in Christ had obliterated all the outward marks the old life had left on her.

"It's good to take stock once in a while," Enid said. "The results we look for don't always come from the open windows of heaven. Sometimes it is 'first the blade, then the ear, after that the full corn in the ear.' "

We had had no mail from home for six months, but Walter Ohman sent the mail carrier from Soddu fairly regularly to keep in touch with us. One evening he came again.

"The Italians have entered Soddu!" he announced.

It was almost ten months since the Italians had proclaimed their final conquest of Ethiopia and we had not seen them yet. Enid and I were the only missionaries left in the uncertain areas of the land. The others had all been taken into the Pax Romana for better or for worse. We wondered when our time would come to leave.

12

"They That Wait upon the Lord . . ."

ONE MORNING the Ethiopian wife of one of the two Greek merchants in Gofa appeared at our gate to warn us that her husband and the other Greek were leaving immediately for Soddu because it was rumored the town was to be looted that night. The Ethiopian wives were to be left behind. If the town were looted, our homes would not be overlooked.

This seemed to us the final signal. If the Greeks were thus led to go, might it not be best for us to go also and seek whatever kind of peace the Italians had brought?

"If we're going," Enid said, "we'd better travel with them."

We would have to hurry to go with the Greeks. They were already passing us on the road below.

"Come on into the bedroom," I said. "Let's pray about this before we do anything."

There was not much time left for prayer; the answer seemed plain if disappointing. We called Alamo and Saro, who had agreed to go with us. They saddled the donkeys while I attended to the mules. Our emergency outfit had been kept intact and the boys now loaded it onto the donkeys.

As we said our last farewells to the Christians—Shashotie, Saka, and Sonkura—we somehow sensed we would not be returning from this trip. But they would not be alone. The villages behind the mountain had been stirred, and the church was coming into being there with a nucleus of about twelve men. We had told our neighbors many times to trust in the Lord and not be afraid. It hurt us to be fleeing, but there seemed no other way.

We pulled our mules through the gate and down the hill to the narrow mountain trail, where we mounted. Saka followed us down the mountainside. Only a few short months before, we had baptized him. After Simberu's death, Saka had become the leader of the church. Through our preaching he had isolated himself from his family and they had turned their backs on him. He had joined the small group we had sponsored and now we were leaving. But his Lord was with him. Jesus had said, "I am the good shepherd . . . My sheep hear my voice, and I know them, and they follow me: And I give unto them eternal life; and they shall never perish, neither shall any man pluck them out of my hand."

Our last picture of Gofa was Saka standing in the path, weeping. Our hearts were weeping, too, as we followed the path around the mountain that cut him off from our view. It was five o'clock and soon would be dark. We traveled down the steep mountain trail as fast as we could go. The Greeks seemed to have left us well behind; their riding animals were better than ours. Two hours elapsed before we reached the bottom, and there found the two Greeks sitting. Actually, they were not waiting for us but for some Ethiopian traders who also were leaving.

"It's a good thing you caught up to us," one of the Greeks said. "You'd never get through to Soddu without our help."

He proved to be a poor prophet.

We knew there were certain danger spots along the road, some of which we would have to pass at night. It was dark and foreboding. There was much thinking but little talking. Under normal conditions a group such as ours would have been lively, and engaged in spirited conversation, even a little quarreling, perhaps. But on this journey there was only the occasional low murmur of voices, now speaking in Amharic, now in Greek, now in English, now in Gofa. We were all thinking the same thing: What would it be like ahead?

Mule hoofs plodded through the sand, kicking up the loose gravel. *Up, down, scrape. Up, down, scrape.* How many complete cycles of this motion would there be before real rest was found? People usually do not count footsteps, only hours or miles. In my breast pocket was a small old alarm clock, which I pulled out periodically as our mules trudged along. Our lovely watches, gifts from relatives, had given up long ago and had been safely packed in our boxes at Gofa to be taken someday to Addis Ababa for repair.

We had been on the road a long time but it was only nine o'clock. Danger spot number one was still an hour ahead; we would have to pass it and travel another two hours before resting. At ten o'clock we could see the dark outline of huts and conversation stopped entirely. There was only the *clip, clip, clip* of mule hoofs and the *grit, grit, grit* of walking feet. In a few minutes the village was left behind. Conversation began again, softly at first, then, when nothing unpleasant happened, somebody laughed.

"We fooled them," a voice in the dark said. "The people they think to be the wealthiest in the province just passed their village and they didn't know it. They'll have to steal a lot of chickens to make up for the loot they missed tonight."

Everybody laughed but there was some restraint, for most of the road still lay ahead. I had decided not to use Enid as an excuse for stopping to rest. I knew she would tire easily in her condition, but I also knew she was plucky and would not want us to camp unless she had come to the end of her strength. Just after midnight by the little alarm clock we turned off into an open glen separated from the main path by several clumps of trees. Our parties camped a few feet from each other. Enid and I pulled our blankets from the duffel bag, spread them on the ground, and lay down gratefully. But it was hard to find a comfortable spot among the little stones, and our minds would not stop whirling. At last we fell asleep—but we would soon be up again and on the road.

We did not expect trouble on the second day. We plodded on, and although we skirted farm lands and passed close to Gofa villages, we received only the usual attention. The mourning doves raised their doleful songs from the branches of the trees and sounded even more discouraged than we felt. We stopped to stock up on food in the few villages where *wat* and *injera* were sold.

By noon we left the valley and began to drop down even lower to the Mazi River crossing. There, in the shade of the trees, we rested while the mules and donkeys thrust their muzzles upstream in search of the clearest water. Ahead of us lay the road back up to the highlands, three hours of almost vertical climbing. We hung on as the mules began the scramble. On an ordinary trek we would have camped and reserved the climb for the cool hours of the morning when the animals were fresh. Now they had been carrying us since dawn and the big climb faced them in the midday heat.

Finally we reached our camp site at the top. There was no village nearby so we unloaded the donkeys, unsaddled the mules, and staked them out to graze. It was easy to camp; there was no tent to set up, nothing to cook, no camp beds to assemble. We nibbled at the remains of the Ethiopian food bought along the way, and then sat down for the inevitable fireside conversation.

Piety was not lacking even in the most profane. Our words of warning and comfort from the Scriptures were greeted with "Amens" from all quarters. It has always been that way. Men live carelessly and give God no place in their lives until trouble comes, or death stares them in the face, then suddenly they want God's help. Though the day had been long and exhausting, we talked on. Some of the group would never forget the words they heard that night because of the circumstances that brought them forth. All of us knew that the following day would bring the final decision. We would meet people at the next village who could tell us whether it would be possible to get through to Soddu.

Daylight saw us on our way again. It was cooler than in the valley and we were happy to have our old warm jackets. Before long we arrived at the village where we settled down in a hut to rest and then began the lengthy process of gathering accurate information. It would not be available at once; information was now a commodity. We would have to bargain for it and show our willingness to part with a little silver. What we could finally piece together from the village headmen was that it was impossible to get through to Soddu. Many of the returning soldiers had refused to surrender to the Italians when the latter came into Soddu and were preying on the road we would have to travel.

Although this news was expected—and probably exaggerated—it was depressing. Then Enid and I found someone in the village we knew. On a previous trip we had drunk coffee in his home, and this simple sharing of his hospitality had made him our friend.

"You can get through," he told us, "if you travel at night. There is heavy drinking at Bola every day. If you go through the town about four in the morning the drunks will be asleep and others won't be up yet. You can go beyond the town for a couple of hours and spend the day in the woods away from the road. Then you'll be able to get into Italian territory the next night."

This advice was what we were waiting to hear. We walked back to where the Greeks were sitting, but they told us they were not going on, that it was not possible to get through. Their decision was somewhat of a relief to us, for we could plan the rest of the trip ourselves.

The local headmen were paid twelve dollars for whatever services they had performed for us, and at four o'clock we started out. Who was doing the right thing? The Greeks by stopping? Or we, by going ahead in the face of warnings? We heard the Spirit's soft voice, "This is the way," and pressed on.

At six o'clock we left the road and spread our blankets under the trees.

If we started out again at ten that night, we would pass the danger point at just the right hour. We ate our supper, such as it was, and rested again. The moon was setting and the road would be dark. We prayed fervently with our boys. By ten we were on our way.

Of course I felt some anxiety for Enid. This was no treatment for an expectant mother—and her first offspring at that. "Are you all right?" I would ask over and over again, and invariably she would say, "I'm all right." But I could detect the measure of "all-rightness" by the tone of her voice. Sometimes it was tired, sometimes anxious. I was thinking mostly of her welfare; Enid was concerned only about the welfare of the little unborn one who had been on the way five months.

We had traveled only about an hour when I looked back and saw lights on the road.

"Here they come!" I shouted. "Get off the road!"

I grabbed my mule's reins and began to pull. We were on top of the mountain ridge and the ground dropped away on both sides of us. I disappeared from view.

"Mal, where are you?" Enid called.

"I'm down here," I replied. There was a crashing of underbrush and the cry of a hyena as it disappeared down the slope. I had skidded down a ten-foot embankment.

"It's a good thing we didn't fall any farther," Enid gasped as she soon came beside me. "At some points along here we could have dropped a hundred feet."

The boys were standing on top of the bank watching the torches. Lights at night can be deceptive.

"They aren't coming," Alamo finally said in an unnecessary whisper. "They are probably farmers out looking for cattle."

We had been afraid they were bandits, come to rob us where there would be no witnesses. Presently we returned to the road and plodded on. There was not a trace of light, so that when we walked, we stumbled, and when we rode the mules, they stumbled. The boys kicked their bare feet against stones until they were raw. I thought of Moses and "the darkness which may be felt." I could understand now, for the moon had long since set and even the stars refused to give their feeble light. Trees leaned over the road and added to the blackness. The gloom began to enter our minds and we did not know how much longer we could steel ourselves. Then we prayed and were conscious of God's loving care; the light inside brightened.

All at once the road dropped down through a boulder-strewn gulley.

The mules could no longer carry us so we walked. Enid fell and I fell trying to help her. When she lost the heel from one of her shoes we got down on our hands and knees and crawled.

"This isn't the road," Enid cried at last in desperation. "It's a rocky stream bed going down the side of the mountain!"

We stopped and sat down among the boulders. We could see each other only in outline. Suddenly a verse that would carry us through came to Enid like a flash of light through our darkness: "They that wait upon the Lord shall renew their strength; they shall mount up with wings as eagles; they shall run, and not be weary; and they shall walk, and not faint."

"Let's go!" she said, and limped off minus a heel.

It was past midnight by the old alarm clock. Fortunately, we could see its luminous dial without having to strike a match. Soon we were back on the road. At three o'clock we sat down to rest and to have a sip of water. By now we were sharing our canteens with the boys. We moved on again, quite sure we would not get through Bola before daylight.

It was four-thirty when we saw the first huts dimly outlined against the dark sky. There is something ghastly about squat thatched roofs at night, especially so when one has to pass through a village of hostile people. It was deathly still. Then a rooster crowed. We prayed the dogs would stay quiet. Now we had passed the upper section of the town and, driving the mules mercilessly, clattered through the stones. When we reached the lower section of the town, it was light enough to see. As we came to the first hut, an Ethiopian was standing in the doorway.

"Foreigners!" he exclaimed, as he turned back to inform the people in the house.

I was riding hard and Enid's mule was dropping behind, but I did not slow down. She would have to keep up. We could hear women at their grindstones; the day began early for them. At the last hut a man stood by the door, rifle in hand. Perhaps we took him by surprise for he did not move.

The road began its descent toward the Demi River, still several hours away. Three hundred yards from the last hut a waterfall splattered over the stones right beside the road. We stopped in plain sight of the man with the rifle, for we had to have water and might not find any more the rest of the day. We drank thirstily. The water had not been boiled but that was of no concern to us now. While we filled our canteens the mules drank deeply. Then, without waiting to catch our breath, we mounted the mules and drove them down the mountainside. Several men with guns were now standing on the edge of the embankment above us and we could feel their eyes boring through our backs.

"They probably think our mule caravan will follow," I said. "They no doubt plan to let us go on and concentrate on that."

We had been on the way an hour before we decided it would be relatively safe to leave the road for the day. Anybody wanting to molest us could easily follow our mule tracks, anyway, so we went off some distance into the thornbrush and spread our belongings on the ground. There were no leaves on the trees and the sun at this lower altitude was hot. We welcomed the thin shade provided by one lone acacia. Our bread had turned to crumbs in the pillowcase in which we had been carrying it, but we were glad to eat the crumbs.

"We might as well open a can of cheese, too," Enid said. "It will never taste any better." So we nibbled cheese with our crumbs.

We were tired but found it difficult to relax. One more dangerous stretch of road lay ahead of us and again we would have to travel by night. After removing our shoes and stockings, we stretched out on our blankets and finally fell asleep. When we awoke two hours later, we were no longer in the shade, and the morning sun had left our legs unnaturally warm and red.

The crumbs and cheese lasted throughout the day. We resumed our journey as soon as darkness fell. Any bandits preying on the road would hardly expect travelers to pass at night. I had to lift Enid onto her mule, and it would now have to carry her continuously. Her legs were swollen from the sunburn and from her condition, so she could do no more walking. Also, the soles of her shoes had been torn off. We finally reached the Demi River beyond which lay the last stretch of dangerous wilderness. We filled our canteens again while the mules drank for the first time in many hours. As we crossed the river, conversation stopped. Only the hollow sound of animal hoofs on clay soil broke the stillness.

Midnight came and we began the gentle climb out of the lowlands to the Walamo plain. We did not know whether Italian authority extended to this outer edge of Walamo territory. An open area suddenly appeared beside the road.

"This is the Sunday market!" Alamo said out loud. Our hearts leaped with joy, for now our dangers were all behind us and we were safe.

We found a grassy spot near the market place where people came from villages on both sides of the wilderness to do their Sunday trading. The rest of the week it was just a flat piece of earth. Our blankets were spread out again—for the last time, we hoped. How safe and comfortable the hard ground seemed! Before we slept we staked the animals out but they were too tired to eat the luscious grass. When we awoke it was light and the sun was rising.

"It's going to be a long flat ride today across the plain," I said to Enid unenthusiastically.

"I don't care," she replied. "It's so wonderful to be here and to know the trouble is all behind us."

The slow pace of the mules was agonizing. We tried to drive them, to pull them, but they would not be hurried. At best we were making only about a mile and a half an hour, but at nine o'clock we reached the first Walamo village and stopped under a huge, spreading wild fig tree. The boys went to the nearest hut and asked to buy food. The woman brought out two gourds and set them before us. It was a time to give thanks so we bowed our heads. Then we ate greedily.

"This is the most delicious meal I have eaten in all my life," Enid said excitedly.

Sour, clabbered milk, and cold, boiled sweet potatoes . . .

With anxiety at least partially gone, we settled down to the ordinary weariness of the road. On the ridge ahead we could see the iron roofs on the mission buildings but they were in another world. We needed help. We stopped while I scratched a note announcing our impending arrival and asking for fresh animals. Then one of the boys disappeared with it down the road.

About three-thirty we saw puffs of dust rising from the road ahead and shortly afterward a group from the Mission dashed up on fresh horses. Peg Phillips slipped off her animal and she and Enid were soon in tears. I turned aside and choked back mine. They had a horse for me and a fresh mule for Enid. I prayed silently as the journey neared its end.

Dr. and Mrs. Roberts and Lois Briggs had fixed up the only room available on the station. As soon as I explained to Dr. Roberts that Enid could not walk, he reached out and grabbed her mule's bridle, led her down the path to the hospital, and through the door of the operating room that was to be our quarters. We slid her out of the saddle and onto the table. Then the mule was led out, and Enid transferred to a bed that was waiting for her. After everybody had gone, Enid and I looked at each other as we thought of the past ten months and the five days we had just lived through. We were grateful.

As far as money and clothing were concerned, the Soddu missionaries were no better off than we. They, too, had sold most of their clothes for needed cash; nevertheless, in a few moments clothing began to arrive for us. There were willing hands to help Enid get cleaned up and comfortable. It was good to eat . . . it was good to rest . . . it was good to be clean . . . it was good to *be*.

Italian military planes had been shuttling men and supplies weekly between Addis Ababa and Soddu. They had also brought mail for the missionaries and we eagerly opened the first letters we had received from our parents in many months. They all said the same thing. The Mission had told them we were all right, but they had had no word from us and hoped they would soon hear we were safe. Happily word would go to Addis Ababa on the next plane, and from there a cable would be sent to our loved ones through the New York office of our Mission. We would rejoice together, though at opposite ends of the earth.

Our Mission officers in Addis Ababa were now having to deal with Italians instead of Ethiopians. The news was not good. Italian military authorities informed them that all Mission property in Ethiopia would be confiscated for "political and sanitary reasons." We were not told we had to leave the country; the Italians merely made it impossible for us to stay. Some of our number, crowded onto Soddu Station, were due for furlough and almost all of us needed one. It would be a long walk to the capital but nobody need walk. The Italians would be only too happy to take us by air. Enid and I decided to arrange for an early departure.

At Soddu we met the Cousers, who, with their fellow workers, had been in hiding eight months with the Gudeila tribe. A small group of Christians had come into being through their preaching and two of them had reached Soddu with the Cousers. Every day they sat with Norman under a tree in the Roberts's yard, translating the Gospel of Mark.

There were difficulties to overcome other than mere words, for though Norman tried to concentrate his thoughts wandered. Would the Italians allow the book to be printed in Ethiopia? Or if it were printed abroad, would the Italians let it into the country? If the military authorities were arranging for our expulsion, what might they not do to the Ethiopian Christians? One day Norman closed his manuscript for which there seemed to be no future. Tomorrow the plane would come for him. What last word was there to say to his Gudeila helpers?

"Sometimes the Lord removes our fathers from us so that we ourselves may become strong," he began. "We are leaving you but the Lord will be here. Preach the message of salvation to your people. We will never forget you and we will pray for you."

Ethiopians seldom lack for words but Norman's friends found that theirs had flown.

"If God wills, we will return to our homes and preach to the people," they said feelingly. "We will not forget. If God wills, you will come back to us again."

There was little to say at the air field; the real farewells were going on under white and black skins. The missionaries were *going* home but here they seemed to be *leaving* home forever.

When it was our turn to go, we said our farewells to our faithful boys and took our places on the bombracks of the Italian Air Force plane. As it rose in flight, we looked down at the airstrip until everyone was swallowed up in the distance.

From our fellow missionaries in Addis Ababa we learned more about events of the past horrible year. At first, those who had been in the capital at the time of its fall had been in great danger, but the interval between governments had been short and order was restored. Enid and I asked about the prospects of work in the Sudan. The directors of our Mission, we were told, had visited Khartoum and had made a trip up the Blue Nile to a group of unevangelized tribes along the Ethiopian border. We had a vague feeling that it might be the place for us in the future, but we were not quite ready to think about it seriously. Not now, at least, for our furlough had begun.

At the railroad station we had another funereal farewell and when the Addis Ababa-Djibouti express train of the Franco-Ethiopian Railway chugged out, our feelings were confused. We were happy at the prospect of going home to America in time to welcome our firstborn but this was more than tempered by the almost certain knowledge that we would never see our Ethiopian "babies" again. We stared out of the window at the landscape that was slipping away from us.

"It's like winding up and unwinding again," I said.

My remark puzzled Enid.

"When we came into this country," I explained, "we wound everything up on a string—the smell of eucalyptus trees and fires, frying onions, red pepper and spices, the sight of typical Ethiopian houses and dress. Now we are leaving it, sort of unwinding the reel. When we get to Djibouti we will have lost it all."

In almost every town an Italian-style concentration camp had been set up near the railway station. Unco-operative Ethiopians or patriots were herded behind the high barbed-wire fences where Italian soldiers, in their ill-fitting uniforms and oversized shoes, stood guard. Eventually the Italians would reach Gamo and Gofa. How many of our friends would end up in stockades like these?

Our thoughts jumped ahead and jumped back again as the train carried us steadily down toward Djibouti. This was the end—or was it? We had decided that nothing could ever dislodge the Italians from Ethiopia, but suddenly we realized how foolish all our pessimism was. Of course we had left our Ethiopians behind. But we knew God was there too!

PART II

The Anglo-Egyptian Sudan

. . . then the ear . . .

13

We Get Married Again

AS WE sailed up The Narrows in the warm May sunshine the entrancing Manhattan skyline gradually came into focus. A little group of Americans on the foredeck began to clap and we hustled toward them to see what was happening. There, just off portside, was the Statue of Liberty, holding her torch high.

Two of Enid's college friends were waiting on the pier. The emotional reunion was reminiscent of college days. Then Jean and Peg stepped back and gave Enid a long look, taking in her borrowed hat and ill-fitting coat.

"I'm going with the girls," Enid said hurriedly, as they disappeared in the direction of the taxis.

Two hours later at the Mission home, a new, smiling Enid appeared. Jean and Peg had outfitted her completely from head to foot.

In Addis Ababa I had seen some beautiful men's suits in the shops recently opened by Italian merchants. Since they were on sale for only sixteen dollars—I figured the same suit would cost me forty dollars in New York—I had decided to buy one. But I had not been in New York long before my self-consciousness grew and I realized that my Addis Ababa suit was not worth forty dollars and that I was not as well dressed as I had anticipated. I was beginning to adjust.

Our hostess in New York, knowing something of our ordeal, fed us bountifully on roast beef, potatoes, a never-ending variety of vegetables, and easy-to-eat desserts. But when she was not looking we slipped out to the corner grocery store to buy celery and saltines. The next day we smuggled some apples into our room. It was unnecessary to hide them there; they did not last that long. We did not want our hostess to think us unappreciative but we had missed some things more than roast beef.

Much as we liked New York—on a short-term basis—there were good reasons for us to move on. Soon there would be three of us, and Enid's family in Milwaukee, who had spent ten anxious months waiting for word of our safety, was becoming impatient. My own family, in Tacoma, would have to wait a little longer.

"Won't it be wonderful to go to church!" Enid sighed blissfully that first Sunday in Milwaukee. "I've been looking forward to it so much."

At this remark, her mother seemed troubled. Enid should know better than to appear in public in her condition. During our stay in Africa we had come to accept the fact that an expectant mother went about as usual until labor pains began. We went to church anyway.

The service began the way we had hoped, with the singing of the doxology. How we would enjoy this! As the first notes sounded from the organ we rose with the congregation and began to sing with them: *"Praise God from whom all . . ."* I stopped and reached for my handkerchief. I had not been prepared for this, and hoped the people around me would think I had a cold. Enid had stopped singing, too, and was wiping her eyes. Several months later I was to hear and fully understand the sage words of Harry Stam, who spent many years in the Congo:

"When I have been home on furlough and wonder about my fitness to return to the field, I always know I am emotionally ready if I can hear the doxology sung in the morning service and join in myself without crying."

We had to make arrangements for Enid's care during her confinement. Prospective parents do not usually wait until the baby is eight months along before consulting a doctor or making a hospital reservation, but that is what we had had to do. The doctor was willing to help us but the Milwaukee Hospital was booked for the month of June. However, the director kindly offered to admit Enid as a "house case" and made arrangements for one of their finest doctors to take care of her.

Our baby was born early on the morning of June 5, 1937. Enid had a girl's name—Dorothy June—all picked out, so certain were we, but things seldom work out as planned. We searched for another name. Leigh Hunt had written a favorite poem of mine, "Abou ben Adhem." I was not interested in calling my firstborn Abou but the name Leigh intrigued me. Besides, it would be easy for Africans to pronounce. So Leigh it was.

With the arrival of our son, the need to make a trip to the courthouse for an opinion on the validity of our marriage became most urgent. We had a beautiful rose-covered certificate signed by the minister, the Reverend Harold B. Street, and witnessed by Dr. and Mrs. Percy Roberts, but there was nothing to indicate that any branch of local government had issued a license. Two years had elapsed after our wedding before we reached Addis Ababa, and by then the Ethiopian government had yielded to the Italians. The American Legation had closed; in fact, the staff had traveled to Djibouti on the same train that carried us. There had been no opportunity to discuss the matter with anyone.

One day I finally made my way to the Milwaukee County Courthouse and approached the desk marked "Marriage Licenses." Behind it stood a well-proportioned man, puffing on a cigar. I felt ill at ease as I began my long involved story—

"Ethiopia . . . wedding . . . expulsion . . ."

As I spoke, I slowly pulled the preacher's certificate out of my pocket and pushed it toward the clerk. It told him the story.

"Thunder and lightning, man!" he exploded. "You ain't married!"

We were quite certain we were, but we realized it would be better to have our marriage recognized by some branch of government.

Most of our furlough was spent in Dallas, Texas, where I studied at the Dallas Theological Seminary. As the spring of 1938 drew near, we went to see Dr. Lewis Sperry Chafer, president of the Seminary.

"We would like you to marry us," we said.

He had rightly understood that I was one of the married students. In fact, with our son, we had had dinner with Dr. and Mrs. Chafer in their home. When we explained our difficulties, he chuckled.

"Of course I'll marry you," he agreed.

Another courthouse trip was necessary. I wrote out our names as though we had never been married, and I paid the fee—for the first time—and took the license home. On March 14, 1938, the third anniversary of our marriage, we went to Dr. Chafer's office. Our friends John and Dorothy Kopp stood up with us and so did Leigh, now nine months old. The Kopps also were from Washington State and had one child. We had been doing things together during our months in the seminary.

Dr. Chafer did not ask us to love, honor, and obey. He merely had us reaffirm the vows we had previously taken in Ethiopia.

At last we were married!

14

Return to Africa

IN SEPTEMBER, 1938, Hitler began his first serious fist-shaking. Europe's statesmen ran back and forth seeking a formula to satisfy *der Führer* and prevent war. If Enid and I had any doubts about returning to Africa, the realization that war would prevent our going proved that Africa was where we most wanted to be. We listened apprehensively to the radio many times a day.

Neville Chamberlain finally instituted direct negotiations with Hitler in Munich. Enid and I crowded against the radio as though by doing so we were assuring Chamberlain of success. We prayed by the radio that we might return to Africa. Then the announcement blared out, breaking the tension: *"Peace in our time."*

Uneasy peace though it was, we sailed again for Africa, this time to the Anglo-Egyptian Sudan. It was December, 1938. We crossed the Atlantic, sailed the full length of the Mediterranean, then entered the Suez Canal, where we spent most of the day leaning against the rail and watching the sand go by. Lonely Arabs rocked along on their camels as they crossed the desert into oblivion. The passage through the Canal with its exotic background, its people, towns, and passing convoys was much more interesting than the weary expanse of ocean. The sun set in a scattering of lacy pink clouds and that night our ship slipped out of the Canal to begin its run down the Red Sea, setting its course for Port Sudan.

There we docked one morning three days later. Some of Kipling's "first-class fighting men," the Fuzzy Wuzzies, squatted docilely on the pier to await the signal that would have them scrambling on board to unload freight and baggage. Everything seemed to be under control. We were led by our agent through an orderly process of disembarkation, customs inspection, and boarding of the boat train for Khartoum, capital of the Anglo-Egyptian Sudan. The activity had made us hot but we kept telling ourselves that it just couldn't be hot. Christmas was only a few days away! The train, like all Sudan trains, was quite comfortable.

It moved slowly out of the station and across the coastal plain toward the Red Sea hills. As dusk approached we could feel the train forcing its way up the grade, and through the window we could see rocky peaks looming darkly against the sky. When morning came we looked out again across the endless expanse of desert stretching westward to Atbara where we would meet the Nile.

After thirty-six dusty hours, our once-clean train crossed the Blue Nile Bridge and pulled into the open-air station in Khartoum. We were glad to spot familiar faces in the crowd. Glen Cain, our immediate superior, had come over from Ethiopia to direct the opening of the Sudan work. He had been in the first party that entered Ethiopia and had also entered the Sudan with the first party to represent our Mission. Like many Australians, he was tall and lithe. There was a slight stoop to his shoulders, and he spoke with an accent that was more British than Australian. Norman and Flossie Couser were there, too, awaiting their appointment.

It was Christmas morning and the station was alive with porters, railway officials, taxi drivers, and townspeople who had come to meet the train. Railway and government officials, Sudanese and British alike, were dressed in khaki bush coats and shorts, their pith helmets bearing the insignia of the department and province they represented. The Sudanese townspeople wore an assortment of Western suits and felt hats or the long gowns and turbans of the Arab world.

"Merry Christmas!" we called from the train window.

"Merry Christmas!" came back to us from the station platform.

We were driven through the streets of Khartoum to the rented house that was called Mission Headquarters. Victoria Avenue, which ran from the station to the Palace, residence of the Governor General, was wide to accommodate the crowds that flowed down it by car and on foot after every train arrival and departure. The streets leading off from it were paved down the middle with a strip of black-top, but the rest was dirt. Europeans and well-to-do Sudanese occupied most of the stuccoed houses in the main part of Khartoum. The people with lower incomes lived in the mud-walled houses in the suburbs.

An open-air trolley crossed the avenue several blocks in front of us. Near the streetcar line was a sign with a familiar name—FORD. Fords and Chevrolets mingled with donkeys and bicycles. We arrived at the comfortable six-room Mission house. Its four bedrooms were no longer adequate for the new but growing work of our Mission in the Sudan, but room was made for us.

Christmas Day passed and we set about getting acquainted with a new world. There was vague talk of the Sudanese being granted their independence someday and the British were training nationals in administration, although there seemed to be little sense of urgency on either side. We had not heard of anything like it in the colonies of other European countries. However, the British were performing an admirable job of establishing the framework for education, adequate medical services, and justice. The time would come when the pressure of world-wide nationalism would fire a drive for independence in the Sudan. There would even be talk of "throwing off the yoke of the oppressor." The British would have to put up with such ingratitude, but in 1939 nobody, Sudanese included, called British rule in the Sudan oppressive.

We were told that Protestant and Roman Catholic missions in the Sudan were operating in their respective restricted areas defined by the government. There was some overlapping, of course. The Catholics, for the most part, kept to the west of the Nile. South of them, in Equatorial Province, the Church Missionary Society of the Church of England was working. On the Nile and to the east of it, the United Presbyterians were well established. Almost all the educational work in the south was carried on by these missions. Farther north and to the west, the Sudan United Mission, an organization like our own, was working in Kordofan Province among tribespeople.

Christian missionary work in the north was confined principally to the large cities where there were schools, hospitals, and some visitation in homes. In several centers the Egyptian Evangelical Church had congregations serving mainly Egyptian nationals. The British had their Anglican Cathedral and the Greek and Coptic Orthodox their places of worship almost exclusively for nationals of Greece and Egypt respectively. The northern Sudanese themselves were almost entirely Moslems.

Like all missionaries, Enid and I were anxious to know what lay ahead of us. Finally Glen Cain called us into his office.

"We would like you to go to Chali," he said, as we seated ourselves opposite him. "Uncle Nick and Alan Webb are working with the Uduks there. Alan is being transferred to the Dinka work at Melut but Uncle Nick will remain at Chali with you."

Nick and I had not seen each other since we parted in Gamo. He had felt a call to the Sudan work and preceded us there. Getting together again would be exciting. Chali had been just a name to Enid and

me and the Uduk people an unknown tribe. Now we began to feel possessive, for once again we had a station and a work. Chali was five hundred
miles south of Khartoum but only fifteen miles from the Ethiopian
border. Perhaps it would not be as unlike Ethiopia as we had been led
to believe.

"In the Sudan you'll have a garden for only two or three months of
the year," Glen warned us. "You'll have to buy a large supply of canned
goods here in Khartoum. The roads will close in May, so you'll need to
have enough food to last until they open again in December." He said
further that we would be leaving for Chali early in January.

We were soon to learn there were practically no roads in that part
of the Sudan nor were any roads planned. That the Ethiopians lacked
any concern over so vital a matter was understandable, but the British
attitude was less comprehensible. There were immense areas to be
administered which the British could reach only six months during
the year because of the heavy rains.

The lack of a proper sewage system in so large a city as Khartoum
was also puzzling. Every residence in the metropolis had its little house
backed up on the street and equipped with a heavy bucket and a trap
door. Nightly, our sleep was disturbed by the slamming of trap doors
and the sliding of buckets in and out. The bucket men spoke softly
enough and the well-padded feet of the camels that pulled the wagons
made no noise, but nothing was ever done to control the odors.

We were anxious to go south. In Ethiopia we had always traveled
"down country" out of Addis Ababa, presumably because we headed
"down south." In Khartoum our missionaries spoke of "up country." We
learned that the "ups and downs" in most of the Sudan were determined by the northward flow of the Nile. We were to travel for three
hundred and fifty miles through ruts and poor roads along the Blue Nile.
At Roseires we would leave the Nile and travel southward another
hundred and fifty miles to the land beyond the Nile.

Enid had to make up her menus for the next eleven months in order
to estimate the amount of canned goods to buy, and when our supplies
were all assembled we could have opened a grocery store in the bush.

Our plans for the trip south involved no saddles, no pack animals, no
horses. We were to do all our traveling in Dorcas, a Ford, so named
because she was "full of good works."

In Ethiopia our problem had been how to keep warm; now we would
have to find ways of keeping cool. Glen suggested that since most
Europeans in the area wore khaki shorts, that I might better have some

made. The tailor down the street measured me and soon the shorts were finished. I dreaded my first public appearance with bare knees, and although shorts could be seen everywhere, I felt more self-conscious than when I appeared in my first long trousers. I soon realized that nobody took notice; the struggle was all inside me.

We had learned something of the history of Ethiopia during our time there, and now we began to read up on the Sudan. In 1882 the Dervishes, under their religious leader, the Mahdi, had revolted against the Egyptians and defeated them. General Charles Gordon was loaned to the Egyptians by the British to launch a counterattack from Khartoum and to re-establish Egyptian rule in the Sudan. In 1885, when Gordon reached Khartoum, he discovered that he would need reinforcements. The Dervishes were closing in on the city and he had to prepare for a long siege. The reinforcements did not arrive in time and Gordon's Khartoum fort was overrun and the general killed on the steps of his palace. Sixty hours later reinforcements appeared and were routed by the Dervishes.

It took thirteen years for the Anglo-Egyptian forces to regain control of the Sudan under the leadership of General Kitchener. A young soldier named Winston Churchill was with the army that met the main body of the Sudanese near Omdurman. The Mahdi had died and his Dervishes were being led by the Khalifa. They could not stand up to the Anglo-Egyptian attack and were defeated, the government of the Sudan being returned to the hands of the British and the Egyptians. Their joint rule was called a condominium and the land was renamed the Anglo-Egyptian Sudan. The year was 1898.

To us newcomers, Egyptians seemed to have little place in this condominium rule. The British were administering the country and they were bringing the Sudanese, not the Egyptians, into the government with them.

Khartoum was really three towns. The capital itself squatted on the tongue of land formed by the juncture of the Blue and White Niles. This tongue was the shape of an elephant's trunk, hence the name Khartoum. Across the Blue Nile was a residential and industrial town, Khartoum North, and on the other side of the White Nile was the large native city of Omdurman. All three were connected by tramways.

Donkeys, taxis, bicycles, and pedestrians moved down the left side of the street toward their many destinations—stores, government or private offices, workshops. Most of the residents, European and Sudanese, lived behind high walls. The Moslem's religion required privacy for his women, and the rest of the people needed it because they slept outside most of the time. Along the Blue Nile the large houses of the senior government officials hid behind tamarisk hedges. Broad lawns surrounded the houses and in the winter season there were masses of flowers along the edges. Tea parties, "drinks" parties, and dinner parties were in progress each afternoon and evening somewhere along Khartoum's Blue Nile waterfront.

We visited the palace where the British Governor General was in residence, and near it the statue of General Gordon riding on his camel. Gordon's name appeared everywhere—Gordon College, Gordon Avenue, and also a Gordon Bar and a Gordon Cabaret. We wondered what the General would think about some of these ways of honoring his memory. The name and personality of Gordon were beginning to chisel themselves into our consciousness. He must have been a great man.

In developing the Sudan, the British made a distinction between the Arab north and the tribal south. In the past there had been long years of exploitation of the southerners by the more sophisticated Egyptians and Arabs. This exploitation was ended when the British declared the south a closed area. It would remain closed until its people, through education, could meet with the northerners on a more equal footing. Our travels would be shaped by the closed-area regulations. Before we could go south, Glen Cain would have to secure a permit for us. Once we entered Upper Nile Province, we could not leave it without the permission of the Governor. The Sudan had a government and in the days ahead we were to be conscious of it.

15

Up the Blue Nile

WE WERE ready by seven on the morning of our departure for Chali, and shortly afterward Glen Cain pointed Dorcas' nose toward the south. Dorcas had been bought as a chassis with windshield; then Glen had designed and local artisans had built on an open-air plywood body. The driver's compartment and a long seat just behind it held a total of seven people and in the back there was nearly enough room for the passengers' baggage. Missionary vehicles seldom had enough room for all of it.

The road was good black-top for about three miles, beyond which lay four hundred and ninety-seven miles of dust and dirt. Beside Glen and ourselves, Phyllis Hawkins and Zillah Walsh were traveling south. Phyllis was a new missionary who had come out with us from England. After the customary year of language study and adjustment, she would be married to Alan Webb. Phyllis had red hair and some of the lively disposition that goes with it. Zillah had come to the Sudan from Ethiopia; Enid had lived with her for a short time at Duromi.

Leigh also was with us. He was nineteen months old and his blond hair still lay in waves, though his long curls had been left behind in a New York barbershop. He was very fair, with blue eyes, and was the sharpest possible contrast to the Africans around him. He had started to walk on the day following his first birthday, and was sturdy and healthy. We hoped that he would stay that way in his new surroundings.

"Green trees and grass don't last long once we leave the riverbank, do they?" I remarked to Glen.

"No," he agreed, "there's desert wherever the water doesn't reach."

We were now well into the desert and could choose any one of a hundred tracks, switching from one to the other without waiting for a cross-road. The desert was our road and an hour after we left Khartoum we came to the endless fields of the Gezira, a vast tract of one million irrigated acres lying between the Blue and White Niles. Once an unproductive wilderness, it was now a maze of canals, roads, railroad control points, and towns.

The whole area was laid out in squares. It was no haphazard affair but had been thoroughly engineered. In addition to providing a good living for the tenants, the Gezira Scheme was the government's largest source of income. We had to do our own engineering to find our way through the checkerboard. We crossed main canals, subcanals, and railroad tracks, and then crossed them again, asking the way of local camel drivers or cotton pickers waist deep among the plants.

"That's the Sennar Dam over there," Glen was saying several hours later. "It holds back the waters of the Blue Nile. This is the end of the irrigated area. We should be in Singa in less than two hours."

As we traveled through the Gezira with its network of canals and growing cotton, we realized the truth of a statement once made to us by a Sudanese: "Water is our greatest natural resource."

The Sennar Dam controls the water for irrigation in the Sudan. Farther north, on the White Nile near Khartoum, the Egyptians had built the Jebel Aulia Dam to hold the water back until needed in Egypt. Before many years were to pass, we would hear of proposals by the Sudan government to build a dam on the Blue Nile above Roseires to increase the amount of irrigated land. We would hear, too, of Egyptian objections to this plan. Also, upon seeing the Sudan's increasing population and expanding economy, we would think the Sudan entitled to more than the 5 per cent of water allowed her under the Nile Waters Agreement. She could at least be given the water that ran into the Mediterranean each year.

Still later we would hear of Egypt's proposal to build a high dam at Aswan. The dam would be needed to irrigate more land for Egypt's rapidly increasing population, for the green strip along Egypt's Nile was already the most heavily populated area in Africa. But the proposal would bring many difficulties. For example, the inundation of several hundred square miles of Sudan soil together with the town of Wadi Halfa, one of the more important points in the north, was a matter to be arbitrated. Egypt would ask the United States for a loan with which to build the dam. The increased production of cotton made possible by the dam would be thought to add to the difficulties of the Southern farmers in America. Dams solve many local problems but create many international ones.

The Nile was carefully watched by the Egyptian Irrigation Department. Engineers measured the flow at various points. In fact, the payroll of the Ministry in Malakal alone exceeded that of the entire Sudan government administration for the whole Upper Nile Province in which Malakal was located.

It was winter in the Sudan and it stayed a cool 90° all day. Still, we were glad when we drove up in front of the rest house at Singa. The building, which at one time had housed a government family, had brick walls two feet thick, a living-dining room, two bedrooms, and a bath, complete with tub, although there was running water only when the barrels outside were filled. There was a porter in charge and he knew what travelers in the Sudan would want first—a cup of tea, then a bath.

"You never had anything like this in Ethiopia, did you?" Glen asked.

"No," I replied, remembering the tent we always carried, "and we didn't need it. On the other hand, I wouldn't want to do much camping in tents in this country."

During the morning we had passed through the city of Wad Medani, capital of Blue Nile Province, and there Glen had paid his respects to the Governor. Again at Singa he reported to the District Commissioner, through whose territory we would be passing the next day. We were learning to go out of our way to keep up good relations with the government.

"We won't have very good roads from now on," Glen warned us. "We should get up early and try to leave by six." Then he added: "No matter at what time of the day you meet British or Sudanese officials, they will always be clean-shaven. I think it would be wise for us to shave before we start out."

For me, this practice was quite a contrast to living among bearded Ethiopians, but I agreed that we ought to keep up appearances. Next morning I shaved in the faint light of dawn. In the years that followed I came to appreciate Glen's gently given advice. Too often people were careless about shaving and embarrassed me in front of officials. I shaved by the light of a tiny lantern, or in the dark by feeling my way. I shaved out in the bush when there was not the slightest chance of meeting a government official.

The next day the road was inferior but not bad, although our progress was much slower. But it was not the fault of the road that the gear shift ceased to function at noon. When we removed the cover from the transmission and experimented with the parts inside, we did not really know what to do but hoped we would discover the trouble accidentally. We were getting nowhere when an Arab came along in his truck. Apparently he knew what to do, for in a short time the gears were working and we were on our way again.

"It was good of him to stop and help us like that," I said.

"They always stop," Glen replied. "They're very helpful out here in the bush. Sometimes we're able to help them."

The desert had given way to scrub growth and palm trees now that we were entering the equatorial rain belt. The day we left Khartoum we covered two hundred and twenty miles; the second day we were on the road longer but did only one hundred and twenty miles. That was the difference.

We were still in the northern Sudan. The towns and villages we frequently passed through were inhabited by northern Arabs, or by Nigerians who were the remnants from the pilgrimage to Mecca. During the previous decades so many Nigerian Hausa pilgrims to and from Mecca had been stranded in the Sudan, that they now formed large communities along the banks of the Blue Nile. We were interested to see that the Moslem women were free to leave the enclosures around their homes. We saw them, blue shawls draped around their shoulders, gathered around the wells or coming up, single file, from the watering places in the river bed.

The rest house at Roseires sat high on the bank of the Blue Nile. It was in the process of being rebuilt of ironwood and mahogany planks, so we set up our camp cots under the spreading trees. The river looked inviting. The water had come down from Ethiopia, all the way from Lake Tana. What was going on in Ethiopia? How were the Christians faring? We were not far away, but we might as well have been in America, so tightly had the Italians sealed all sources of information. That was our last point on the river; our road would take us away from and beyond the Nile.

The third day we reached Kurmuk. Halfway there we stopped in the area occupied by the Ingessana tribe, the first tribespeople we met. They were attractive in their cloth or skin garments draped from the waist. When we stopped, the men moved slowly away and the women ran. They were lagging far behind the people farther north and would need sympathetic help in moving from the tenth to the twentieth century.

"We asked the government to let us open work among this tribe," Glen said, "but we've been turned down. Officials seem to think that because these people border on Moslem tribes, bringing in a Christian testimony might cause religious rivalry."

"From the government's standpoint, who is going to educate them?" I asked. "They're giving education to the people in the south through the missions. How will they bring education to the Ingessana?"

"Government officials seem to want to bring this tribe into the northern pattern," he explained. "If that is their purpose, they'll establish government schools here."

Whatever they did about education, I thought they ought to let these people hear of Christ. He could deliver them from their very real fear of evil spirits and witch doctors. There ought to be enough religious freedom to allow them to hear the gospel.

We roller-coasted the hills and there it was, the business section of Kurmuk, crowded against the foot of the mountain. Only thirty-two miles separated us from Chali. Kurmuk would be one of our trading centers, although on a very limited scale. During the dry season the government brought the mail to this point weekly by truck, and, during the rains, fortnightly by mule from Er Roseires.

We were soon passing the huts of the Kurmuk people. The rainfall made it impossible for the compounds to be shut in with mud walls. Instead, grass, tied to a frame of poles and bamboo, provided the necessary seclusion. In this part of the Sudan the townspeople were mostly northern Arabs, many of whose ancestors had intermarried with the local tribespeople. Now Sudanese of mixed blood were numerous. When we passed the customhouse and enclosure Ethiopia was only half a mile away.

We drove into the middle of the business section of Kurmuk and parked Dorcas in the shade of a banyan tree. The one-room shops were lined up on four sides of a square. Most of the shops were operated by Greeks who made their money not so much from local trade as from the coffee they bought from Ethiopian mulemen and from the goods they sold them in return.

Glen Cain led us to the store of a Greek who spoke English and who acted as agent for the missionaries at Doro and Chali by forwarding their mail to them and supplying some of the few items missionaries could use. Kerosene lanterns and enamel bowls hung on and over both sides of the door. Inside were bins of coffee, rock salt, and rice, and boxes of tea and sugar. The shelves which reached to the roof were piled high with yard goods and blankets, and there were smaller shelves for flashlight batteries, canvas shoes, and laundry soap.

Behind a desk a Greek was weighing a tiny quantity of gold flakes. A Sudanese man was watching the weighing closely to see how much it would bring. He had dug quantities of dirt from his shallow shaft in the poor gold-bearing area south of Kurmuk, then carried the dirt for half a mile, often two miles, to some stream or water hole where he had washed it in a wooden "pan." Each panful had yielded five or six flakes of gold and now he would know the reward for his hard labor—the equivalent of two dollars!

We spent the night in the comfortable stone-and-brick rest house in Kurmuk. The next morning we were on the road, passing through the well-populated country of the Berta tribe. We were traveling through bush and scrub and the once-tall grass was brown and crumpled. Smoke columns from grass fires were visible in almost every direction. In a few hours we would be in Chali.

16

The Uduk People

"WHEN WE cross this dry stream bed we'll be in Uduk country," Glen announced at last.

We began to observe our surroundings more closely, since we would be living here. For how long? Until another war came? Until illness sent us home? Until retirement, perhaps forty years hence? The countryside looked desolate. All around were low rocky hills and we were to learn that the Uduks believed the spirits of their dead lived in the air above one of them. Between the hills the ground was seared and flat, not at all like Ethiopia. But then we had not come in search of a pleasant place to live; we had come because of the people.

"Here are your first Uduks!" Glen called out.

We leaned forward, eager to get a good look. There they were, a man and a woman, husband and wife, presumably. Their color made them seem more like American Indians than Africans but the red was an oily substance they had smeared on themselves. Only a little black around the eyes betrayed their true color. The man walked ahead, bow, arrows, and spear held tightly in one hand; a basketful of corn was balanced atop the woman's head. They were dressed in typical Uduk fashion. Not a thread appeared on the man anywhere except, perhaps, for the cotton strands holding his many beads together. The woman wore a small, low-slung apron in front and back; once white, it was now a dirty red. That was about all we could see as we drove past. Indeed, the people were as desolate looking as the country in which they lived.

"It appears as if there will be plenty of work to do here," Enid commented.

The road twisted and turned until finally we came out into an open space. Glen pointed.

"Do you see that big baobab tree up there? It's on the Chali Station."

One more turn and we left the main road to start up the rise to our new home. We could hardly wait to get there—especially Phyllis, who had not seen Alan Webb for quite a while. Uncle Nick and Alan welcomed us warmly in front of the fieldstone bungalow they had completed just before the rains. We would soon be well acquainted with its corrugated iron roof, low ceilings, and dirt floors.

"Here's your nephew, Uncle Nick," I said, holding Leigh out to him. Nick took him in his arms and began a one-sided conversation. Although Leigh was more than a year and a half he had not bothered to talk yet.

"You've lost a lot of weight, Nick," I observed.

"Forty pounds." At my inquiring look, he went on. "We came here from Ethiopia. You know how it was there. We were able to grow most of our food and could buy meat, eggs, and milk from the people. We thought we would do the same here, but when we arrived we discovered that there were no markets in this part of the country and that the people wouldn't sell us even one egg. We soon learned that compared to the people we had known in Ethiopia, they were poor." Nick shook his head mournfully.

"When the rains came in May," he continued, "we planted a garden about a mile from here where the Uduks raise their corn. The plants came up and then the rains stopped. We planted again in June and finally we got a few tomato, bean, and pumpkin plants to grow. They were about to produce when the river overflowed its banks. A few plants survived the flood and Alan swam some pumpkins across the stream. That's about all we got. So we didn't have enough to eat."

Nick Simponis and Alan Webb had had a rough year at Chali. They had spent long hours supervising an Arab contractor as he built the house, but had had to do most of the finishing themselves. There had been the shortage of food so that much of the time they just managed to stay alive. Here was not the Africa of the efficient servant, luscious tropical fruit, and markets bulging with meat and eggs. It was an inhospitable, difficult Africa. The missionaries' struggle for survival that first year was hardly less grim than that of the people; locusts had destroyed three-quarters of their crops.

Glen Cain, who had seen Alan and Nick once before that season and who knew of their hardships, had decided earlier that they needed a change. He discussed his plans with me.

"We'll spend the night here and I'll take Nick and Alan with me tomorrow. Nick's going to Khartoum for a vacation and Alan will be staying at Melut for a while. I'll leave Phyllis here with you. Zillah will be going on to Doro."

Upon Uncle Nick's return, Phyllis could go on to Melut Station to begin her study of the Dinka language and to await her marriage to Alan.

We could see difficulties looming ahead. Phyllis, Enid, and I had been in the country less than a month. We knew no language that was spoken in the Sudan and could not even converse with the boy we had brought with us from Khartoum.

Our one contact with the world around us was a small booklet of Arabic phrases designed to help people carry out a minimum of their responsibilities. The phrases were of much more use in metropolitan Cairo or Khartoum than in the bush. We could think of many more important things to say than "Bring us our tea at 6:00 a.m." or "We'll be having our drinks on the lawn this evening." And now we were to be left in this place about which we knew nothing. It would be essential to obtain as much information as possible from Nick and Alan.

While we stood and thought about these things, a few Uduk stragglers wandered slowly up to us. They held out their hands and we extended ours, expecting the usual handshake. However, they held out only two fingers, and when they saw that we did not know what to do, they showed us, with a few grunts and gestures, how to snap fingers. We pressed each other's middle finger between thumb and middle finger. We withdrew our fingers with a loud snap.

"We want to see the baby," they said. Uncle Nick interpreted.

We introduced Leigh to them and they immediately lost interest in us. Nick said they were asking whether he was a boy or a girl, what we fed him, and why, since he was so big, there was not another baby. We were glad to have Nick answer their questions in his own way.

Later that day we had our own questions to ask him. "What do we do for water?" was one of the more important queries.

"We have a couple of boys here who will help you," Nick said. "One of them brings water from the stream. We have a wooden frame that serves as a saddle. It holds four kerosene cans. He brings three donkey loads a day."

It sounded rather precarious to us as we wondered what we would do if the boy quit.

The next morning Glen left with Alan and Nick. The latter gave us their few notes of the Uduk language. We appreciated their efforts in gathering these words and phrases, but nearly all of the language work still remained to be done.

Chali Station had but one solid structure, our stone house with floors of pounded earth. The lack of other buildings and cement floors was directly traceable to the depression in America. Our immediate need was for a house to live in and Nick and Alan had provided one. When the Uduks were willing to gather for church, school, and clinic, we could think of putting up additional buildings.

Phyllis occupied one of the bedrooms, Enid, Leigh, and I the other. That left the center room for living and dining. The screened-in veranda was piled high with boxes of groceries and supplies; evidently Nick was not planning to starve again. Leigh had several hundred square miles of front yard to play in but we were hard put to find a quiet place for study because the bedroom was small and we all lived in the living-dining room. There were not enough rooms in the house. We unpacked our goods hurriedly, put shelves in a big box that would serve as a china closet, set up our new beds, put our camp cots away, and went to work.

"We'll have to get acquainted with the people around here before we can do much," I said to Enid. "Each morning I'll visit with the men wherever I can find them. You can probably find some women in the villages during the afternoon."

So we sallied forth daily, notebooks in hand. The notes Alan and Nick had given us included the phrases "What is this?" and "What are you doing?" With the former we were able to compile a good list of nouns and with the latter a useful supply of verbs, but we spent most of our time writing down sentences we overheard. Back in our house we analyzed them and thus gradually built up our grammar.

"When we know them better, we'll probably be able to get some of them to come here to the house to help us with the language," Enid suggested. "That way we can make more rapid progress."

Since the Uduks were very friendly, we wondered why none of them would sit with us. With or without such help, we would have to dig out their language, for the future of the work depended on our success in this area. When even one Uduk understood and believed, the next part of our program would be undertaken. Primers would be prepared, reading and writing taught, and portions of the New Testament translated. The children would be invited to attend school; perhaps a boarding school might be opened. One day we would hope to have a nurse with us to treat the many sick Uduks, teach them to guard their health, and train some of the young men to do simple medical work. And if any of the children could go on to become preachers, doctors, teachers, or administrators, the Lord would lead in that. We would preach the whole counsel of God and seek to bring salvation to the whole man.

We soon learned the reason for the Uduks' refusal to sit with us.

First of all, it was considered unmanly to stay in the village during the day. An Uduk man either worked in his field or, in the dry season, spent his time hunting or lolling in the shade of a tree with his friends. Only a beer drink would keep him near a village. Then, too, the loss of their crops during the previous rainy season forced the hungry Uduk men, women, and children to spend much time searching for edible and semi-edible roots, digging rats out of their runways, and carrying on their mass hunts for waterbuck, hartebeeste, and other game animals.

Our names presented another problem. "Mr. Forsberg? Mrs. Forsberg?" the Uduks said. "Why do you both have the same name?"

Then we noticed that our surname was suddenly dropped and I became "Jo Li" and Enid "Ko Li"—Leigh's father and mother. They were following their custom of calling us by the oldest child's name and we liked it.

We had been at Chali for several weeks when we recalled a visit to one of our cousins. He had been attending college, and was interested in our missionary experiences in Ethiopia.

"We were talking about missionaries in our psychology class the other day," he had said. "Our professor stated that civilized people often go out as missionaries to primitive tribes to satisfy their egos. They are too inferior to dominate people in their own country."

"I wish the professor could see us now," Enid remarked. "He'd have to overhaul his theories."

For although we had been at Chali for some time, not one Uduk had worked for us, and members of the nearby Berta tribe stayed just long enough to earn money to pay the small head taxes. The two boys Nick had mentioned had quit. The morning following each monthly payday was one of concern to see if we had any boys left to help us. They never gave advance notice.

On one such morning after our boys had gone, I announced to Enid that I was going to take the donkey down for a load of water. It was five-thirty and I could make the round trip before breakfast. The meal would be late anyway, as Enid would have to chop some wood, make a fire, and then wait for the porridge to cook. I placed the wooden frame and the four kerosene cans on the donkey and started in the direction of the stream bed. The water had long since stopped running and stood in pools fouled by the village animals. I removed my shoes and waded out into the water to fill the cans, then loaded them on the donkey and started for home.

"This doesn't smell good," Enid said, as she poured out water for the laundry after breakfast.

I agreed, and drove the donkey off to the stream again. It would take a lot of water to keep the house going that day, and three donkey loads were a minimum requirement.

This time I noticed a number of women going off in another direction to fill their gourds, so I followed them. They looked my way and laughed—laughed, I presumed, at a hapless foreigner who had to haul his own water and did not know how to do it. I observed, however, that the women did not dip water from the pools. Instead, they dug in the sand close to the water's edge and poured clear water into their gourds. So I borrowed one of their dippers and slowly filled my cans.

"Where did you get this water?" Enid asked, as she sniffed at the cans I had just brought back. "It's much better than that other stuff."

I told her how I had learned my lesson.

When I returned with the third load of water and Leigh perched atop the cans, it was 113° by the back-door thermometer. Then I stared in amazement.

"What in the world are you doing?" I asked Enid, as I lifted the heavy tins from the donkey.

"We thought this would be the easiest way to do the laundry," she replied cheerfully.

She and Phyllis had put the clothes in the washpans, had added soap and water, and both women were now standing in the pans and treading the dirt out. At the same time they were soaking other articles in pans on the table. How quickly they had lost their dependence on washing machines! This procedure, fortunately, did not have to be repeated, for Berta boys turned up again and released us for our language and visitation work. Eventually we partially solved our water difficulties by digging a well on the far side of the stream, for the hill we lived on was solid granite. We still had to haul the water a mile, but it was the best we could do.

The Chali trading center consisted of one native-style hut in which several brothers carried on their business. One of them, Abdalla, knew the Uduk language quite well, although he spoke it with a foreign accent. The brothers belonged to the Berta tribe, were friendly, and we visited their store often. From Abdalla we acquired a considerable Uduk vocabulary, but we could not depend on him for pronunciation or accurate definitions.

"I feel sorry for the Uduk children," I told Enid one day after I had returned from the trading center, "but I don't feel sorry for the adults."

"Why, what's wrong now?"

"Every time I go to the store, Uduk people bring in their bundles of corn to trade for beads and bracelets, while their children starve."

We knew the little grain the Uduks had been able to salvage from the locusts would not keep the people alive until the next harvest. In spite of this, they kept up their purchases of beads and trinkets. Also, grain enough to last a family for several weeks was consumed in one day at a beer party. It was all not only disgusting but discouraging.

We decided to have our Mission truck, which brought goods and building materials from our station at Melut one hundred and fifty miles away on the White Nile, bring grain from there, for the locusts had not harmed the crops of the Dinka people. With this surplus grain we would try to help some of the hungry children who appeared daily at our back door. The babies were strapped by a saddle to the backs of their older brothers or sisters or cousins and carried around all day. Some of these older children were not much bigger than those they were carrying.

"We'll give them the grain," we agreed, "and the older girls can grind it and cook it here the way they do in their own homes."

The only music we could use with the children was a simple chorus we had written to the tune of "Oh, Happy Day." They enjoyed singing it and rocked back and forth to the rhythm, the babies on their backs moving with them and sleeping better because of it. We could not determine how much of the message of salvation got through to the children. A few basic phrases were checked for accuracy, and then, as the children ground their daily ration of grain, we told them the simple story of God's love. They memorized our first bit of translation, "In the beginning God created the heaven and the earth."

Superstition and fear often plagued the children. Kwaat, one of the older girls, was raised by parents who were more superstitious and fearful than their neighbors. There were several witch doctors in her family. The only female witch doctor we knew was a relative of hers. Kwaat was bright and friendly. She brought eight or ten children each day for a week, then suddenly, about the middle of the second week, stopped visiting us.

"Aren't you coming any more?" Enid asked one day when she met her on the path.

"We like the food and we like to sing," Kwaat replied, "but our parents say you are going to run away with us, so we can't come any more."

We were sorry to lose the close contact with Kwaat and the other children, although they continued to appear irregularly. Someday we were to learn that the brief teaching of those days had not been in vain.

Bringing up our own baby in Africa was more difficult than it would have been at home. One day just before lunch there was a loud scream from Phyllis.

"What's the matter?" we chorused anxiously as we converged on the scene.

"Leigh just handed me a scorpion!" she sobbed, quite evidently in pain.

Leigh was standing by us, alarmed and bewildered by the commotion. We helped Phyllis to bed. We had heard frightening tales about scorpion stings but nobody had bothered to tell us what to do about them. Enid stayed with Phyllis while I went out to hear Leigh's side of the story.

"Where is the scorpion, Leigh?" I asked.

He pointed to the corpse lying where Phyllis had ground it into the dust with her heel. Leigh looked at me fearfully. He knew something had gone wrong but was still ignorant of the part he had played. I picked up the scorpion by its tail and pointed to the stinger.

"That is very bad," I explained. The demonstration went on for some time as I tried to show the connection between him, the scorpion, and Auntie Phyllis' crying. Perhaps Leigh was wiser than I had thought, for he had picked up the scorpion by its stinger and it had not hurt him. It had not injected much poison into Phyllis and in two hours she was free of pain.

Several weeks after we had been at Chali, we heard that the British District Commissioner was to visit the area. He and his assistant were stationed on the White Nile two hundred miles to the northwest of us. The two, with their minor Sudanese assistants, administered an area twice the size of the State of Connecticut. The district commissioners were the agents in their areas of all the branches of government. They were responsible for local projects of the departments of agriculture, education, and public works, and kept an eye on the veterinary and medical work. They administered justice, maintained public security, and collected the taxes.

When the District Commissioner arrived at the rest house down the hill, we sent him an invitation to lunch, which he accepted. He was the only government official close to us, so we looked forward to a friendly visit. At the lunch table we discussed everything from Hitler

to anthropology. When it was time for him to go, I walked down the
hill with our guest.

"I hope you don't intend to put clothes on these people," he said.

"Well, not exactly," I stammered, quite unprepared for the remark.
"When they become Christians they will have to decide that for themselves." But I could not stop there. "We want to help these people all
we can," I continued, "and we think the best way we can do that is
to give them Christ. We don't intend to convert them to our Mission
or to some foreign church. We want to get them established in their
own churches so they will run their own affairs."

"I'm very glad to hear that," he said, relaxing visibly. It was obvious
that this missionary objective was all new to him.

I did not share my hope that before long many of the people would be
believers and wearing clothes.

17

The Polygamy Problem

IT WAS just getting light and from the direction of the village female voices were pouring out wild sounds.

"Somebody is being killed!" Enid exclaimed, jumping out of bed.

I rushed to the kitchen to ask the boys what the trouble was, but they were quite undisturbed.

"The silly Uduk women are probably fighting," they said. "Women are so foolish. They get upset when their husbands take second wives."

We wanted to find out all we could about the Uduk people, so we went to the village. As we neared the scene, the shouting grew louder and angrier. One of the men had taken a second wife the day before and his first wife was giving vent to her wrath.

We found the two women standing ready for battle in a clearing between the huts. They glared at each other across a distance of about fifteen feet. Both were stripped of beads and other decorations and each held an eight-foot bamboo stave. They were furious; as they shrieked insults, a second woman stood dutifully behind each dueler to shout further curses and insults at the opposing fighter. The fiery talk of the seconds exceeded that of the injured women. Male onlookers were absent and we learned that the men were disgusted because wives would not live together, so they never watched these fights. It was time for the duel to begin.

"You'll take my husband away from me, will you?" shouted Wife Number One.

She lunged forward and took two quick cracks at her adversary, one with either end of her stave. Wife Number Two deftly swung her stave into action and defended herself, then the first woman stepped back. Apparently there were rules for this kind of fighting. The second wife poised her mouth and her stick.

"You with the face of a hyena, you aren't going to drive me away from the man who wants me," she screamed.

Then she let loose the two blows allowed her as Wife Number One warded off the attack. The sticks cracked like rifle shots as they met. There seemed to be no rules to govern the war of words, as the seconds kept up a machine-gun stream of vituperation. They were profane, with no evil deed of either contestant left unmentioned. The insults added fury to the already fiery emotions of the fighters.

"Nobody will have you," shrieked the first wife, "so you try to steal my husband!"

Her stick came down—one, two!—as the defender warded off the blows with her stave. We wondered what the ultimate object of the game was. How many innings would there be? How would the winner be determined? The battle went on, back and forth. Each contestant got in her two blows; then it was the other's turn.

Wife Number One, who had the most to fight for, was tense and efficient. When her turn came again she poised, swung her stave and the first blow fell with animal-like dexterity. The second came with the speed of lightning. Wife Number Two did not move fast enough and her opponent's stave got inside hers, skidded down the length of it, and tore the skin from her wrist. She looked dismayed at the blood on her arm. The fight with staves was over but not the war of words. We wondered if anything had been decided. It was later that we learned the two wives had settled down in separate houses and avoided each other. Eventually, when Wife Number Two could endure it no longer, she picked up her few belongings and returned to her mother.

"But the African can't grow enough grain to keep himself and his family alive unless he has several wives to work with him," our District Commissioner had said when we complained about polygamy.

"If there are fifty people in the village, they can only do the work of fifty," I had protested. "If several of the women are married to one man, that doesn't add to the number of people doing the work."

The District Commissioner, who had not worked it out by simple arithmetic, agreed.

Some years later, when a chief in the western part of the country was alarmed at the number of young unmarried girls in his tribe, he ordered them brought to the market. There the men who were seeking second, third, or even fourth wives were allowed to bid for the girls. Some of the Khartoum newspapers commented favorably on the chief's method of providing husbands for the excess women. A few days later

Double wedding at Soddu:
(*center*) Malcolm and Enid Forsberg, Norman and Flossie Couser

Our African bush home. Uncle Nick (*r*) boarded with us at Chali

Alan Webb

The old Uduk witch doctor

(*Below*) Four Uduks sipping beer through straws cut from a special grass

Mona before he became a
Christian

Mona (r)
and son Kona

Mary Beam

The Chali church

The church elders and Betty Cridland at Chali

Nurse Bea Noffsinger and helpers at Chali

Mary Beam

Mary Beam

National Guidance Office, Khartoum

Election official briefs a voter

Ethiopians with their alphabets

Sudan Interior Mission

Mary Beam

Triumph over superstition: Rasha and Susgay, the first Uduks to raise their own twins

Mary Beam

Susgay, the mother of twins, is baptized

Mary Beam

Borgay and Thoiya—Praise and Prayer—the first Uduk twins to live

Our children in 1952: Leigh, Dorothy June, Jayme, and Kim

Karakashian, Khartoum

(*Above*) Railway station, Khartoum

(*Left*) Sayed Meccawi Suleiman Akrat, Permanent Undersecretary, Ministry of the Interior, Khartoum

(*Below*) Extraordinary Session of the Sudan Parliament on motion for evacuation of foreign troops from the Sudan, August 16, 1955

National Guidance Office, Khartoum

one of the newspapers printed a letter to the editor. It was not from a missionary but from the head of the Department of Statistics in Khartoum. He was not concerned about morals or religion, but gave a statistician's view and we were grateful for his support. He commented as follows:

World statistics show that the number of men and women in the world at any given time is almost equal. There are sometimes slight imbalances. But these merely mean that the persons belonging to the sex having the larger number at any given time will have to wait a year or two longer before being married. Statistics do not uphold the theory that without polygamy many females are destined to remain unmarried.

But polygamy was not the only family problem of the Uduks.

"Bargay is sick," Enid said one day when she returned from one of the villages. "Perhaps you could take some medicine to her while I prepare supper."

We discussed the symptoms and decided some atabrine would help.

"But don't go to Janna's village," she said. "Bargay has left him and is living with Puna."

"How are we going to keep up with these people?" I asked. "Every time we go to a village the wives and husbands are scrambled again."

This constant exchange of mates resulted in the widespread transmission of the major contagious disease in the community—syphilis. We assumed everybody had it. Babies only a few days old had the telltale ulcers and older children were brought to us with ugly sores where their noses should have been. The people obviously needed more than medicine. Drugs could mask the symptoms but syphilis would continue to spread unless marriage was stabilized. We had the cure for the underlying trouble but the people were not yet ready for it.

With mothers circling from one husband to another, it was also difficult to know which father belonged to which child. Even when we thought we knew, we would find children living, not with father or mother, but with a third party. We wondered how the people kept their family affairs straight, and decided at length to question one of the village boys.

"Where do you live, Dugu?"

"With my mother's brother."

"But why don't you live with your mother?"

"Uduk children don't live with their mothers after they are able to chase the goats." Dugu sputtered his disgust.

It was not until later in our work, when old Elephant Chief died

—that was his name; he had nothing to do with elephants—that the pieces fitted together. Elephant Chief left a few cows and goats. One day his nephews came up to his hut and drove them all away. Elephant Chief's son was sitting on a log nearby but did not protest. What his cousins did was perfectly all right. We discovered that in the Uduk tribe a boy did not inherit from his father but from his mother's brother.

"There is a word for that," I recalled.

We went to our anthropological books and found a description of the situation obtaining at Chali. The Uduk people were "avuncular"; that is, the maternal uncle was the most important person in the family, the children often going to live with him and always inheriting from him. Thus the Uduks offset the instability of the home.

"What will this mean when we have Christians?" Enid asked.

"The Scriptures make the parents responsible for their children," I replied. "It would be sad to see a Christian couple send their child to live in the non-Christian home of the child's uncle."

Many such difficulties were to face us in the days ahead.

18

The Night the Wind Blew

WHEN UNCLE NICK returned from Khartoum, Phyllis went on to Melut Station for Dinka language study and to await her marriage to Alan Webb. It had been decided that a second house at Chali should be built for Nick, so he brought back lumber for doors and windows, corrugated iron roofing, and hardware. It was too late to start building that year; the work would have to await the end of the rains. This meant Nick boarded with us that first year, so our food problem was a joint one.

Nick had earlier bought three small milk goats and they supplied our minimum needs. Each dry season nomad Arabs brought their large herds of fat-tailed sheep and goats into the area for pasturage along the Yabus River to the south of us, and we bought more stock from them. Since we had nobody to watch our little flock, we frequently spent the last half hour of daylight, and sometimes the first hour of darkness, hunting our goats. Getting food took about as much of our time as learning the language. We had cans of vegetables and fruits, and other supplies, with macaroni and rice substituting for potatoes, but without meat, milk, and eggs, meal planning was difficult.

"We're going to have to do something about meat," Nick said one afternoon. "I've got my rifle and you've got a can sealer and pressure cooker. How about canning some meat—that is, if I can shoot something?"

We did not like to break into the week's work with personal projects any more than we had to, but Nick could not guarantee to shoot his animal on Friday so that we could do our canning on Saturday.

"I'm going to try for one of the big ones," Nick said determinedly.

A "big one" was a hartebeeste. There were herds of them running in the forest but they had to be found, stalked, and killed. Other fairly plentiful game included roan antelope, kudu, tiang, reedbuck, and oribi, as well as lions, leopards, and warthogs.

"If you shoot a hartebeeste three or four miles from here," I asked Nick, "what will you do with it?"

"Well," he replied, "I'll take a couple of boys and a couple of donkeys with me. If we get a big one, we'll carry it home in pieces."

Donkeys would certainly be needed, for a full-grown hartebeeste was as big as a cow. Nick left about four o'clock on Wednesday with his little train of two boys and two donkeys. About eight o'clock we heard a clattering at the back gate.

"I got one!" Nick bellowed.

We went out to see and sure enough, there was the pile of potential steaks, roasts, and hamburger. The animal had been skinned and cleaned in the woods.

"We'd better get everything set up for tomorrow," Enid warned. "It will be an all-day job."

First the meat was hung from the rafters on the back veranda and then the home-sealing cans removed from the cartons. Next we studied the sealer, instruction book in hand, after which we pulled the nineteen-quart pressure cooker out of its box.

The next morning, after an early breakfast of porridge and coffee, our assembly line went into action. The little kitchen was crowded. Nick cut the loin into steaks and the hindquarters into roasts; Enid seared the meat in the frying pans and put it into the cans; and I sealed them and put them into the pressure cooker. The boys washed cans, passed meat and cans along the line, and kept the fire stoked. Things were really happening; there was never a dull moment.

Leigh was busy running from one point to the other. There was fun for him, too, when the boys threw scraps of meat into the air to be snatched in full flight by the kites, a native bird of the falcon family.

The cutting, searing, canning, sealing, and cooking went on all morning and well into the afternoon. The stove and the sun co-operated, and soon we were dripping sweat and blood. There was no ceiling in the kitchen and the iron roof conducted a maximum of the sun's rays onto our heads. Finally there were only scraps left, which we ground up and made into hamburgers, then fried and canned. We looked at one another, satisfied with our day's work.

"What have we got?" I asked.

"Twenty cans of steaks, twenty of stew meat, thirty-two of roasts, and ten hamburger," Enid replied.

In addition, we had given away a lot of meat and had left some un-cooked for our immediate use. The main work was done but I still had to stay with the pressure cooker. I finished processing the last batch that night at eleven-thirty.

So with the little herd of goats we had milk, and with the rifle and canning outfit we had meat. We built up a flock of scrawny chickens and they kept us supplied with a few eggs. Breakfast usually consisted of dried fruit, porridge made of local sorghum ground in our own little grist mill, and toast and coffee. Seldom were we able to vary this menu. We ate our main meal at noon, which was more varied but usually consisted of meat, rice or macaroni, a can of vegetables, and dessert.

Enid frequently had to ask the question, "What shall we have for supper?" Soup was always good but we did not need it to keep warm. Extra eggs were available only when the hens co-operated and that was not often. During the rains we ate large quantities of wild mushrooms which the children brought us in exchange for empty cans. We also noted the weeds the Uduks ate so we used some in salads and cooked others. But the evening meal was always a problem.

On Friday afternoon of that week Nick decided to go to Kurmuk.

"There's a truck at the trading post. I want to see about a contract with a trader to handle our mail during the rains, and I want to line up some Arab masons for next season's building, too." He took his canteen, rifle, toilet articles, and pajamas, and disappeared down the road.

At midnight we were awakened by a sudden blast of wind which roared and tore at the house. The corrugated iron sheets were rattling on the roof and the shutters were banging against the wall. Suddenly there was a splintering of wood, a massive creaking and crash of sheet metal. I went into the living room and found half the roof gone. I looked into Nick's room. The rain was pouring in and the wind was still shrieking. I rushed back to the bedroom.

"Wrap Leigh up and stand in this doorway," I yelled over the roar of the wind and the beating of rain on what was left of the roof. "If the rest goes, you'll be safe here from falling stones."

I went back to Nick's room. He had stacked the bags of cement for his house in a corner and rain was drenching the pile. I grabbed his raincoat and spread it over the bags. Stones from the top of the wall began to fall when the mud mortar holding them together softened and crumbled from the rain. A small stone hit a picture, which crashed to the floor. I carried books, papers, and clothing out into the still-dry half of the living room. Although I was wearing my raincoat over my pajamas, I was already soaked, but I was too busy to feel wet. There was not much more I could do but watch the destruction and think about the morrow.

"It's a good thing part of the roof stayed on or we'd be in a bad way," Enid commented as she came into the living room to survey the scene.

"And it's a good thing Uncle Nick brought the building material for his house. We'll need the roofing iron and lumber tomorrow."

We looked over the damage before returning to bed. Back of Nick's room was the pantry and behind that the kitchen. The wind had caught the kitchen roof and pulled it off with the rafters, at the same time tearing big holes in the stone wall. It was unusually dark outside and soon we saw why. The roof had folded over like an enormous door, on hinges, one end over the other, and was now dug into the ground in the front yard.

At daylight the damage looked even more dismal. The kitchen was a shambles. Large stones had fallen into it and some had landed on top of the stove and broken the lids. The boys set to work carrying out stones and dirt. Then we inspected the pantry. We could push the door open only a few inches but just enough to let us see what had happened. The uprights holding the pantry shelves had been fastened to the roof. When the roof had blown off, the shelves broke loose and collapsed to the floor with all their contents.

I reached inside and pushed away the debris so that we could get in. The sight was so ridiculous that we burst out laughing. Bulk coconut, dried beans and peas, lentils, macaroni, rice, cinnamon, sugar, salt, cloves, and broken glass were in a jumbled heap, sprayed with mud and smashed by stones from the walls. We were still laughing when the boys came in to see what had happened. They said that if the spirits had treated them as we had been treated, they would not be laughing. We were glad we knew the Lord. Without Him we, too, would have been wondering what spirits we had offended. The Lord let us laugh and the tension left us.

While Enid began to reorganize the inside of the house, I went out to see what could be done there. The meat grinder had flown over the house from the back veranda and landed on a stone, and was smashed to pieces. A serving dish had sailed over the house, too, but it had not even a crack to show for it.

"I'd better get some kind of temporary cover on the house today," I told Enid. "When Nick gets back, we'll have to rebuild the tops of the walls and re-lay the roof."

The timbers were so broken up that it did not take long to pry the twisted roofing from them with a crowbar. I was standing on a ladder pulling off the iron sheets when Gari, our nearest neighbor, went by.

"Look!" I called to him. "The wind took our roof off last night."

"Uh-huh," he said, but kept right on going.

I looked after him as he disappeared into the grass. I was shocked and disappointed. He was my neighbor and, I thought, a good friend. Why this complete lack of neighborliness in my distress?

Enid called to tell me the porridge was finally cooked. I climbed down the ladder, still pondering Gari's attitude. As I told Enid about it, I realized what the trouble was. The spirits had been angry with us and Gari did not want to get involved.

"He didn't dare stop," she agreed. Then she laughed. "If their spirits suddenly left this country, nothing would ever happen. It would be very dull."

By the time we had finished breakfast, I had the reroofing figured out. But roof or no roof, there was much to be thankful for, so as usual we took time to read from *Daily Light* and gave thanks.

The sun was streaming through where the roof had so recently been.

It was Saturday morning and I did not want to spend Sunday roofing the house, so I tore the old wreckage apart and then dipped into Nick's building supplies for lumber and roofing sheets to construct a temporary cover. Darkness had already fallen before the last sheet was laid. Since there were no timbers to which to nail the rafters, I placed large stones on top of the iron to hold it down. Tornadoes do not usually strike on successive nights and we would be protected from the rain.

Sunday morning I heard a truck grinding up the hill and I ran out to tell Nick the news.

"I heard about it in Kurmuk," he said. "A truck driver who came through here yesterday told me. He said the house had been completely destroyed."

"It's not that bad," I assured him. "More than half the roof went but we have it temporarily covered. A lot of your stuff got wet or smashed."

The next day I mixed mud mortar and carried it and the stones up the ladder to Nick. When the walls were repaired we re-laid the roof. We put new shelves in the pantry but did not fasten the uprights to the roof. By the end of the week the job was finished.

19

"For of Such Is the Kingdom . . ."

"I WAS up quite a lot with the baby last night," Enid said one morning shortly after the roof had been repaired. "He has a high fever and is very restless. I don't know what's wrong with him. Malaria, I suppose."

Our anxiety, never very deeply buried, rose to the surface. We suddenly realized the roads had become impassable with the rain. If Leigh became seriously ill, we would be unable to have a doctor, nor was there even a nurse to advise us. Theoretically, we had faced this situation, and had decided we would trust the Lord. We did not realize how much trust we would need.

We were ready to treat Leigh for malaria when suddenly the dreaded symptoms of dysentery appeared. More than once in Ethiopia we had been stricken by this filthy disease and had seen Africans die from it. We were alarmed, yet we hoped we could treat Leigh's case successfully, for we too had often received injections of emetine, the specific remedy for amoebic dysentery. We pored over some of our medical books.

I hated to stick the needle into my own baby but there was one thing worse than giving him an injection; that was not giving it. I followed instructions carefully and administered the correct dose that morning, in the afternoon, again in the evening, and once more the next day. With four injections there should have been some improvement; instead, his condition worsened. His diapers, soiled every half hour, were red with blood. Milk we tried to give him turned sour in the glass; he lay pale and still. We tried not to think what he looked like. Unless we could stop the dysentery, we knew he would not last much longer.

"Let's look through some of our other medical books and see if we've missed something," I said, feeling we did not have much time left. "I'm going to send a telegram to Earl Lewis. He might somehow be able to get through the mud with Phyllis."

I wrote out the message and found a boy who was willing to take it the thirty-two miles to the Kurmuk telegraph office. The trip would require nearly two days so it seemed almost useless.

Meanwhile, Enid had found an old medical volume among Nick's books and was reading the chapter on dysentery.

"Listen to this: 'If diarrhea and vomiting persist, call a doctor'!"

"That's the trouble with most of these books," I replied. "Just when you want to know what to do, they tell you to call a doctor!"

Enid put the book back on the shelf. The one next to it had lost its spine. She pulled it out.

"Here's Chesterman!" she exclaimed. It was an old copy of Chesterman's *Handbook of Tropical Diseases*, written in a simple style. That was what we needed—something simple enough for us to understand. Enid went over the chapter on dysentery line by line.

"Here's a chart that shows the difference between the symptoms of bacillary and amoebic dysentery," she said. Light dawned. "Look here! Leigh must have bacillary dysentery and we've been treating him for amoebic."

"What is the treatment for bacillary, then?" I asked eagerly, scanning the book over her shoulder.

"The book recommends the German drug Yatren. Isn't that what we have in our medicine cabinet?"

I hurried to the bathroom to see and found the bottle of pills on the top shelf. We had had no occasion to use it before. I crushed and mixed half a pill with a spoonful of jam. We had to force it down. The little hope that had revived with our discovery in the medical book died, for Leigh brought up the pill. We tried giving him another in sirup, but again he brought it up. We tried it whole with water. Still the pill would not stay down and the vomiting weakened him all the more.

All during Leigh's illness our Uduk neighbors would press their noses against the window screens and ask, "How is the child?" We could not hide our anxiety from them and they were becoming concerned.

Whenever we had inquired about a very sick baby of theirs, they usually replied, "He is." That was about all we could say of our baby, but we did not want the people to misunderstand our anxiety.

"We tell them to trust the Lord in their sorrows," Enid said. "Now we'll have to show them that we trust Him in ours."

Although we had prayed constantly for Leigh, we were distressed to the breaking point and now felt the need for special prayer. Uncle Nick was summoned.

"We thought we should ask the Lord to keep the pill down," we told him.

Together we knelt in the living room. The "Amen" still echoed when Enid spoke as though by revelation.

"Let's throw the pill down his throat!"

Would it work? It was our last resort. Enid held Leigh on her lap as I knelt beside her and tipped his head back. She held his mouth open and threw the pill as far down his throat as she could. He gulped and it stayed down. At noon we repeated this performance. Our tense faces began to relax a little. That evening he had another half tablet.

The next morning we were awakened by a thin wail: "Mommie . . ."

"He must be feeling better!" Enid cried.

He was. He did not lie so listlessly that day and a smile occasionally appeared on his wan little face. The pressure relaxed somewhat and the Uduks could tell by looking at us that things had changed.

"It was God," we said.

The boy with the telegram had left on Tuesday morning, and on Thursday afternoon we heard a familiar grinding of gears. Lewis and Phyllis had made it! They were relieved to see Enid standing on the veranda with our still very sick baby in her arms.

"Praise the Lord!" Earl said, as he walked up to the house.

Leigh had been getting his medicine, now it was our turn. Our friends' visit hastened the healing process in us. Phyllis made out diet sheets for Leigh and told us how to take care of him during his convalescence. Their presence had refreshed us but the rains were threatening, so the next day we waved farewell to Phyllis and Earl as their truck disappeared down the road for the last time that season. We returned to our house, to our work, and to our baby.

Not long after this, when I was out making the early morning rounds, I saw a small crowd gathered near one of the houses. Early morning crowds could mean only one thing—witchcraft. When I returned home I told Enid about it. We decided to go over before breakfast.

We found Gari's wife, Kwatgay, sitting on the ground, her baby in her lap. Both Gari and Kwatgay were steeped in the superstitious traditions of their people. Five witch doctors were seated in a ring around the mother and baby. No one paid the slightest attention to us except Kwatgay, who looked up and smiled. The witch doctors were dressed in their ceremonial skin "diapers," their magic roots strung around their necks. Each had his fox-skin bag which contained more roots and charms that would cure almost anything.

"Quite a contrast to an M.D. or a surgeon," Enid commented. I agreed.

"They're going to treat Kwatgay's baby, by the looks of things."

Without a word the five stood up and leisurely began their work.

"It's strange that the most villainous-looking men usually treat these sick people," Enid said.

"Maybe their bondage to the devil makes them look that way," I suggested.

The first witch doctor walked up to the baby, leaned over, and sucked its stomach. Then he stepped back into the grass, pulled a slimy-looking object from his mouth, and threw it onto the ground. Presumably he had sucked this object from the child's stomach. It looked like a piece of raw wet cotton. I could see that Enid was getting worked up and I hoped she would not do anything rash.

When the next witch doctor performed, the baby began to cry, and by the time the fourth one leaned over him, he was screaming. After several rounds of this sucking, each witch doctor picked up his spear and a handful of grass. The first one pressed his spear against the child's stomach, then pretended to catch something between the head of the spear and the bunch of grass. He pressed the two together and walked some distance away to get rid of whatever he had caught. There was nothing visible.

I felt Enid's growing impatience. Two cultures were meeting on a rather low plane and something had to crack. Either we would have to go home and forget about it or—

"I can't stand this!" Enid exploded. She jumped up. "Give me that baby!" she cried, as she snatched him from the arms of his surprised mother. She started for home and Kwatgay followed her.

The witch doctors stared after them in blank amazement. Then one of them burst out laughing.

"Ko Li didn't like what we were doing," he said.

I had been ready for trouble but at this display of hilarity I relaxed. For all their pernicious ways, the Uduk people could be gentle, and after all the witch doctors would be paid anyway. They could afford to laugh! They sat down to eat a meal which Gari's mother served them. They would not collect their fees in kind for several months, during which time the baby's hair could not be cut. This custom had provided the Uduks with a word for being in debt, which translated literally was "to be with hair." When payment was made—a goat or two —the parents would brew beer, prepare another feast, and the witch doctors would gather again. Then the baby's head would be shaved, the long, tangled hair falling off.

I arrived at the house in time to hear Enid's health lecture to Kwatgay. "The baby is sick from a mosquito bite," she was saying, and went on to explain as simply as she could the cycle of malaria in the mosquito and in a human being—parasites, the host mosquito, infection of the body when the mosquito draws blood.

Kwatgay laughed. "Mosquitoes don't make people sick. A baby gets fever from its mother's milk." And she took her baby home.

"I suppose I shouldn't have done it," Enid sighed later at breakfast, "but what are you going to do when five wretched old men are pummeling a tiny screaming baby? I just couldn't help it."

The story of the mosquito bite and fever, often repeated by us, had become a stock joke among the Uduk people. But one day we were rewarded when a mother brought her baby for treatment.

"My baby is sick from the mosquitoes," she said.

Perhaps the only way to expose the cult of the witch doctor was by the lesson of mother love and a lecture on the mosquito.

20

We Accentuate the Negative

DURING LEIGH's illness the rains had diminished. As he improved, our minds were freed to take up a new concern—our neighbors' fears over the lack of rainfall. The Uduks had not tried to help us with the foreign spirits that had caused Leigh's illness but they were ready to do something about their own, who were preventing the rain. We were never to discover all the ways in which they appeased their spirits but we did learn some of them.

One morning Enid looked out of the window and noticed half a dozen men and women parading around our baobab tree. Apparently they had danced at other trees, for their oily bodies were streaked with sweat and they had tied bunches of grass to their heads and other clusters hung around their waists. They waved green branches, evidently hoping this demonstration would show the spirits that the foliage needed rain, and they chanted their appeal to the spirit in the tree.

"What are you doing this for?" we went out to ask them.

They paused, and, as they seemed to wonder themselves, sat down on the rocks.

"Can't you see it isn't raining?" they asked finally. "The spirit in the tree stops the rain and we have to chase him away."

Then, perhaps impressed by their own words, they arose and began throwing rocks at the topmost branches. But gradually their enthusiasm waned when the rain did not start immediately. They complained to us that things were not as they used to be. Once they had plenty of rain and good crops but now the rains were poor and the locusts ate what little they could grow. They blamed the English, who, by not permitting them to kill the people with the evil eye, exposed them to all kinds of trouble with the spirits.

And there was trouble for one of their chief rainmakers, too. During the long dry spell, the grain that had been planted earlier had dried up. For days Uduk men and women sat around sullenly; there must be a reason for their plight, and they discussed several possibilities.

"If Babu can make rain and doesn't," they concluded, "then it's his fault."

Babu was the most highly respected of the local practitioners.

The Uduks finally decided the local police should step in and sent a delegation to the police station. They told the corporal that Babu was not using his power to bring the rain. Consequently, they would all die of hunger. They asked the corporal to lock up the guilty Babu until he did something about the rain.

The police had been ordered to keep the peace. They wore uniforms and carried guns but their instructions omitted anything about witchcraft. They did not know what to do, so they came to see us. They really feared the people. The Uduks were a docile tribe but when they were stirred up about something they could become surly and menacing. It was not for us to meddle in the affairs of the government but we told the police they were right about their orders.

"The rain comes from God," I told them. "No man can make it rain or stop the rain."

The police went away, relieved to have their orders confirmed.

"Whose side are you on, anyway?" Enid asked after they had gone. "You're trying to teach the people to give up witchcraft and now you use your influence to keep the worst one out of jail!"

When the police overlooked his witchcraft, Babu began to worry, for if the rain did not come, the people might take things into their own hands. So he announced that it was time for a rain sacrifice.

"They don't have a sacrifice like this very often," I said to Enid and Nick when I heard about it. "Let's go down in the morning and see what happens."

At Babu's village a bull had already been slaughtered and the blood caught in a gourd and mixed with water. Babu washed his ten smooth white rain stones in the mixture and sprinkled the blood on the roofs and around the doorways of the houses, in a ceremony reminiscent of the Passover in Egypt. The rainmaking was finished and we went home.

The next afternoon it poured. Babu's witchcraft had worked and it had saved his life. It would be useless for us to tell the superstitious Uduks that the rainmakers could not make rain. When they had a sacrifice one day and it rained the next—well, that was that.

The people thought we had a very careless attitude toward rain, at times suspecting that we wanted to stop the downfall so the trucks could run and bring us supplies and medical help. Yet they should have known that we wanted rain as badly as they did, for whenever a shower came, we watched the barrel that sat under the eaves of the house. During a hard rain a down spout emptied water into it, filling the barrel quickly. But we needed even more water than it could hold, so Nick and I would don raincoats and go out with thirty or forty five-gallon kerosene cans which we filled one by one as the water poured down the trough. When they were full, we stacked them in the back veranda away from the thirsty goats.

Rainmaking, witchcraft, and beer drinking made us suddenly aware that we could easily find ourselves preaching only of morality.

"We've got to be careful not to make the gospel a mere matter of do's and don't's," Nick declared.

"That seems particularly true among the Uduk people," I said. "Their sins are so open—lewdness and debauchery. We set up the don't's simply by being unwilling to join with them in their affairs."

"When we have Christians here," Enid said, "there is really going to be a difference."

One afternoon I strolled down to the village to call on Babu.

"Come have a drink," he said. I told him I had not come to drink beer but to talk. "You can talk better if you drink some beer," he urged.

The beer was inside the hut, in enormous earthenware pots. The hut was full of people; perspiration poured from their bodies as they squatted on the ground and sipped the beer, to my surprise, through straws cut from a special grass.

I sat down outside and, as usual, had a list of words in my notebook to check.

"What is this?" I asked, pointing to my Adam's apple.

"Wait for beer," the men replied, laughing.

"I mean the name of this bump on my throat," I said, wondering if they were joking.

"What else would you call it?" Babu asked. "We call it 'wait for beer' because that's what it does."

In my word list, opposite "Adam's apple" I wrote "wait for beer." I had unwittingly started the conversation along the very line I wanted to avoid.

"When are you going to take another wife?" I was asked.

"People who believe in Jesus," I replied, "marry only one woman and stay with her until one of them dies."

The group around me laughed unroariously. What a joke that was!

"New marriages are very tasty," Gari said.

The conversation was offensive to me, although my friends were thoroughly enjoying themselves.

"I'm going to my village," I announced, and, getting up from the log where I had been sitting, left the people to their beer.

"O Lord, how long?" I groaned as I turned toward home. The negative aspect of the gospel was growing in the minds of the Uduks. Christians were people who did not drink beer, who did not talk about sex, and who married only one wife. To counter this negative approach, we preached Christ as much as our limited knowledge of the language would allow. Were they fearful? Christ came to deliver from fear. Were they sad because of a home broken by polygamy? Christ came to bring peace and love and stability to the home.

When misfortune did not demand their concentration on appeasing the spirits, the Uduks danced. There was nothing formal about this. Any Uduk could pick up a dance block, put it between his legs, pound out a few hot licks, and draw a crowd. The people were often too tired to work or talk to us, but they were seldom too tired to dance. The first time the drums beat I went to the village to see what was happening. I told Enid about it later.

"It's pretty primitive," I reported. "They have six men in a tight circle, each with a crude flute in his left hand. The flutes are of different sizes and different pitches and each man also has a block of wood between his legs, which he pounds with the stick he holds in his right hand. The people go round and round the band in a circle, men with men or women with women. It looks rather monotonous and harmless."

Eventually we learned that the dances were not always so harmless. A dance which followed a beer drink lasted until dawn, or sometimes for forty-eight hours, and was lewd and sensuous. Men and women, boys and girls, danced opposite one another, motioning erotically. Old men, nearly blind, shuffled around the outside of the circle as they kept time by tapping their sandals on the hard ground. Middle-aged people danced for a while, then went to sleep, and even women with babies saddled to their backs danced, the baby rocking to the harsh drumbeat. Young married people felt the impelling beat of the drums and danced feverishly.

Often a dance was the beginning of illicit courtship, broken marriages, and polygamy. Men and women would disappear into the night and the next day in the village the first and second wives would prepare for battle over possession of the man. The dance was especially suited to the restless impulses of the young people, who danced wildly as the drums waxed hotter at midnight and beyond. The older people would go home and the younger ones would pair off and disappear in the bush.

The day after I had watched my first night dance, some young men came up to see me. "How did you like the dance last night?" they asked, squirming and giggling, as they nudged each other knowingly.

We did not want our gospel to be negative but we were dealing with matters beyond our control. So I merely answered, "God doesn't want us to behave like animals."

Then one afternoon we discovered that the part of Uduk life we objected to most had entered our own home.

"Come here a minute, Enid," I called from the bedroom.

She opened the door.

"Look at your heathen son," I said.

Leigh was lying on his back, sound asleep, his left hand clenched around an imaginary flute, and his right hand beating out a rhythmic tattoo on his knee. We were suddenly brought face to face with the results of our living in Africa. The dance, like the snakes around us, had turned up inside our house.

"Oh, my goodness!" Enid burst out. "What are we going to do? What's going to happen to Leigh growing up in a place like this?" Her voice was full of concern.

"We'll have to find a boarding school for him eventually. He shouldn't spend much time here after he is seven."

Leigh's fondness for the rhythms of the dance continued. Frequently the drums called at nightfall in the village, less than a hundred yards from our back door, and often the dance was still going several hours after sunrise. Sometimes the small children in the village, Leigh's playmates, gave a good imitation of their elders. Leigh would put one of our shoes between his legs for a drum and use the other shoe as a drumstick. Any stick served as a flute. When the locusts came in hordes during the rains, the witch doctors called a halt to the dancing, and Leigh turned to other forms of amusement.

We kept closer supervision over our son. And we prayed more earnestly for the change that would help us in this difficult situation and for the coming into being of a strong Christian community at Chali.

21

A Name for God

ENID WAS bent over the scraps of paper and lists of words and reference books that made up her language study material. Presently she straightened up and tapped the desk with her pencil.

"If we could get a few more necessary words into our vocabulary, we would probably get further with our preaching. What we need most is a word for 'believe.'"

She realized she was not saying anything new. We could tell people to "*take* the Lord" or to "*put* God's word in your livers," but we could not say "*Believe* in the Lord Jesus Christ and thou shalt be saved." So far we had not discovered the Uduk word for "believe," but were quite sure that when we did so, the word would have some relation to the action of the liver or the stomach. To the Uduks, the heart was just the part that had a lot of blood in it, at least in an animal, the liver was the seat of the affections, the stomach the seat of the will.

One day Enid was telling a group of men about the power of Jesus to raise the dead and heal the blind, and they countered with their own hero.

"That sounds just like Leina," they said.

"And who is Leina?" Enid asked.

"He's the biggest Maban witch doctor," Gari replied.

Enid was disturbed at the comparison but Gari went on to tell her about Leina.

"The District Commissioner didn't like what Leina was doing, so he took him to Kurmuk and chained him. That night Leina slipped the chains off by his own power and escaped. When the District Commissioner tried to catch him, Leina sat under the water in a stream for three days and they couldn't find him. After they went away, Leina got out of the water and went home."

Gari saw the look of disbelief on Enid's face. "You don't join my word to your body," he said.

Enid knew all the words in the sentence but she had never heard them put together in that order before. "Why, of course!" she said to herself, excited over the discovery. "Join word to body means 'believe.'"

She could scarcely wait to tell Nick and me the good news, and we could hardly wait to use the new idiom on the people. Join Jesus' word to your bodies!

We seldom obtained the words we needed directly. They came out when we were doing something other than language work. I discovered the word for "reconciliation" quite by chance and all because one of the men, Hadeen, attempted to elope with his neighbor's wife.

There was a native court to try Hadeen, but the woman's husband preferred the methods of the good old days and challenged Hadeen to a duel with bows and arrows. The bows were about six feet long, made from solid bamboo with strings of carefully braided hartebeeste or antelope sinews. The arrows were made of elephant grass, the heads carefully carved from ebony. These heads were about six inches long and notched so they would break off, leaving most of the barb embedded.

Hadeen had to accept the challenge and the two men met in a clearing in the brush that bordered their cornfields. They took their positions and began shooting. Most of the arrows wobbled and flew wide of their marks. Then Hadeen turned to pick up an arrow and as he did so his neighbor let fly and caught Hadeen in the neck. The ebony arrowhead burrowed four inches into the flesh and broke off. Early the next morning we arose to find Hadeen waiting at the door for medicine.

The back of the neck was the last place I wanted to do any amateur surgery. I treated the wound as best I could and told Hadeen he would have to endure it until the rains ended and we could get him to a hospital. As I worked on him, I asked if a duel with bows and arrows was the way the Uduks settled their quarrels. Hadeen said it was the way they settled their private ones but when there were arguments between villages, they had big fights.

He went on to say they used bows and arrows in more serious disagreements, too, the men of one village lining up on one side of the field opposite the men from the other village. The men then took turns shooting at one another. Quite a few were killed, of course. I was curious to learn how they knew which side won and was told the fight went on until somebody from another village came along and tried to stop them.

"Would the men listen to him?" I asked.

"Yes," Hadeen said, "but to stop the fighting for good they had to bring a lamb. It was killed and then all the men dipped their fingers in the blood and snapped them with their enemies. That made peace."

I jumped up excitedly from where I had been squatting beside Hadeen.

"Honey!" I yelled. "Come here a minute!"

"What's the matter?" asked Enid, who came and stood just inside the screen.

"Say that last sentence again," I said, turning to Hadeen.

"They snap fingers in the blood of the lamb and are friends again."

Before Enid could fully understand my excitement, I had to explain about the arrow in Hadeen's neck and the story of the village fights.

"That is what we have been telling you about God, Hadeen. He wants to snap your fingers in the blood of His Lamb, the Lord Jesus." I did not want to miss making the first application.

Enid quickly went for her notebook. "*Gwam*," she wrote, "to reconcile."

Now we could translate Colossians 1:20: "And, having made peace through the blood of his cross, by him to reconcile all things unto himself."

Enid, Nick, and I brought our language findings together daily. We were not always unanimous about our discoveries and many of them had to await further research, but on one thing we were agreed. Every tribe on earth had a name for God, we thought, yet we had found no such name in the Uduk language.

"In your notes you have *arum* as meaning 'God,' " I said to Nick one day. "The way the Uduks use it, it seems to mean 'spirit,' especially the spirits of the dead."

"God is a spirit, isn't He?" Nick rejoined.

"Yes, but His name isn't *spirit*. According to Uduk ideas, when we call God *arum* we are saying that He is the spirit of a person who once died, a ghost. I don't think that they believe in any one spirit who has only had spirit existence from the beginning."

Many breakfast, dinner, and supper conversations later, we decided that it was misleading to call God *arum*.

"I studied phonetics in Bible school," Nick said one day, "and we were told that if there is no adequate name for God in a language, we should just use the English name. After all, no matter what word we use, we'll have to describe Him to the people and tell them who He is."

We did not feel qualified to argue, so we started to tell the people about God. Our first attempt at a hymn, set to the music of "We Praise

Thee, O God, for the Son of Thy Love" (but not a translation of the hymn), looked like this:

> *God diid imis*
> *God diid imis*
> *Akim bidi yuka Yesus.*

We taught the people to sing it but it did not sound quite right.

"That English word 'God' sounds terribly out of place in the Uduk hymn," Enid observed one day.

"I don't like it either," I admitted.

"Nick is right in saying that we'll have to tell the people what God is like regardless of the name we use for Him," she continued, "and since that is so, I'd rather adapt a word of theirs that fits into the language and then tell them who He is."

Nick, too, had begun to feel that the word "God" fitted rather awkwardly into the Uduk vocabulary. So we began new discussions.

"Perhaps we could doctor up their word for spirit," Nick suggested.

"Why don't we just call him *'wadhi gi mis,* the one above'?" Enid added.

Nick and I agreed. We had not dreamed that one day we would be giving God a name. But that was not the end.

Later, when our first Christians began to think for themselves, they said, "*Wadhi* means a person with a human body. You say God is a spirit. We should call Him 'the Spirit above.'"

So God's name was revised for the last time. He became "*Arum gi mis.*"

22

The End of the Rainbow

THE GRASS had crowded in toward our house. Our clearing was small and the grass, eight or ten feet tall, hemmed us in like a wall. We suffered from a kind of claustrophobia but not a soul would help us push back the edge of the clearing. The Uduks were carrying on a major war with the weeds in their fields. In our spare time Nick and I hacked away at the grass. August and September were "the depths of the rains" and days on end the clouds dumped tons of water on us.

One evening late in August, Nick was listening to his radio. "Things don't look very good in Europe," he commented, as he turned it off. As September began, the news only added to our gloom. Germany had marched into Poland and Danzig had been "returned to the Reich." On Sunday, September 3, 1939, we heard Neville Chamberlain's pathetic words, "We are at war with Germany." We seemed far removed from it all but we knew that everything happening in the warring world eventually would affect us.

Local affairs brightened considerably that Sunday, for Enid held her first Sunday school.

"It's a good thing the kids came," Nick said later. "It's hard to tell what this world will be like after the war. We may not have many more years to work with these people."

We tried to get the Uduks to recognize Sunday as the Lord's Day and to come for services then, but they had no names for the days of the week, nor were they aware of the division of time into seven-day periods. The moon was their only time marker, although they had no names for the months each cycle formed. On Sunday afternoons when we visited in homes three or four miles from Chali and invited the people to come the following Sunday, we handed them seven pebbles.

"Each morning when you get up, throw one pebble away," we said.

"When you throw the last one away, hurry to our place. It is Jesus Day."

So a group of children appearing together on that Sunday morning was a major victory.

On Monday, Enid trudged to the village and back again.

"I guess I said the wrong thing today," she sighed, as she scraped the mud from her shoes at the back door.

"What's happened now?"

"Oh, nothing serious." She came in and dropped into a chair, her legs weary from pulling her feet out of the mud. "I was sitting in the village with a group of men and women when I saw a beautiful rainbow in the east. I said, 'Look at that rainbow! Isn't it pretty?' The men all glared at me as though I had insulted them. 'There's nothing pretty about that,' they said. 'It's bad.' They explained that if the end of the rainbow should settle down on the village, the people would get dysentery, so when a rainbow seems to be getting too close, they shoot at it with their bows and arrows to drive it away. The one I saw was too far away for them to worry about, but the way they talked, they seem to think that we, with our careless attitude toward nature, are dangerous people to have around." Her story finished, Enid relaxed.

"I guess that's what the Apostle Paul called changing 'the truth of God into a lie,'" I commented.

With the coming of another dry season, Nick built himself two native-style huts; he decided to live by himself while we built his new brick house. He set up his stove outside one of the huts with a few sheets of iron as a roof and he turned one hut into a dining-living room, the other into a bedroom. For the first time in eighteen months Enid and Leigh and I were alone. We had enjoyed our time with Nick, for the isolation, the illnesses, and our work, especially on the language, had drawn us together. We had had our differences and misunderstandings, but they were soon forgotten.

December came and we strained our ears for the sound of the first truck. When the stove roared, we jumped, and when the wind whistled through the iron roof, we ran to the door. "I was sure I heard a truck," we said over and over. But there was none.

One day we did hear it. There was the familiar whine of second gear, then the roar as it shifted into low. We ran out just as the truck emerged from the grass which in places still lined both sides of the road. Earl Lewis and John Phillips jumped out of the cab and there was general confusion and animated conversation. Enid was excited, even though there were no women in the party. It had been seven months since the last truck had come and gone, seven months since she had talked to a white woman. She peeked through the strings of a sack and Leigh jabbered with her. Then she laughed at herself.

"It seems so silly to get excited about a sack of potatoes," she said apologetically.

We had a good visit and after they left Nick and I began our building, a project that was to take months of sweat and tears before the house was completed for Nick to move in.

One day an Uduk informed us that a "cloth house" had been set up near the trading post. We went down the hill to investigate and there, seated in front of his tent, was an Egyptian who described himself as an anthropologist.

"I'm working on my doctorate for the University of Paris," he informed us. "I've studied many tribes in Africa, taking extensive notes on their culture and thousands of measurements."

He stayed a month, and we often saw him sitting in front of his tent, a tape measure around the head of some wondering Uduk man. If our talk about God was difficult for the Uduks to understand, this measuring of heads made even less sense.

"I've finished my work here and I'll be moving on tomorrow," the anthropologist said one afternoon during tea with us. "I've had an interesting time with these Uduk people. We anthropologists judge the progress of a tribe not by measurements but by the things they do, the implements they produce for themselves, and the extent to which they have to rely on other people. Without doubt, this is one of the most primitive tribes on the continent of Africa."

We agreed with his conclusion about the Uduks and knew Chali was a challenging place for the Lord to show His power.

Before the rains set in again, Enid longed to see the women missionaries nearby. Phyllis had been the last one she had seen, so when Lewis suggested on one of his visits that we go into Melut with him, we jumped at the opportunity and soon were rattling along on the cracked cotton soil, the roar of an overheated truck engine in our ears.

A telegram awaiting Lewis on his arrival at Melut contained the news that Glen Cain would be stopping by with Bob and Claire Grieve, who were on the way to their assignment at Doro. This was exciting news for us, for Bob and Claire were our friends and we were the only people in the Sudan who knew them. Bob had finished medical school at the University of Oregon and had just completed his internship in Spokane. His wife, Claire McClenny, had grown up with me in our church in

Tacoma. Her brother and I had often gone on preaching trips to out-of-the-way mountain towns and had held services together in the Rescue Mission where Claire played and sang for us. She had attended Whitworth College in Spokane and had met Bob there when he was still an undergraduate. And now they were in the Sudan; it would be wonderful to have home folks with us again.

"I feel as if a load has just been lifted from my shoulders," Enid sighed.

"What load have you been carrying?" I asked, surprised at her remark in the midst of our excitement over the news of the Grieves' coming.

"Why, the load we half-consciously carry," she explained, as though I ought to know. "The long rainy season, the isolation, no doctor to call on when one of us gets sick. It's going to be wonderful to have Bob and Claire with us."

I admitted that I, too, felt more relaxed. When finally Glen Cain drove Dorcas to the back door of the mission house, we rushed out to greet Bob and Claire. How young and fresh and eager they looked! There would be much reminiscing and exchanging of views on the work we had come so far to do.

Enid's visit with her women friends was soon over; it was time to return to Chali. Glen took us all to Doro, where we left Bob and Claire, and then went on to Chali. At Doro, the Oglesbys had replaced the Ohmans, and Zillah Walsh was the other member of the staff.

The dry season would soon be ending and already showers could be seen falling across the plain to the west and in the Ethiopian mountains to the east. Early in June the radio brought fresh war news. Italy had entered the war on the side of Germany and now things would really be different. Italian territory, Ethiopia, was only fifteen miles away. In Nick's words, we were "between the two belligerents."

Before long the District Commissioner wrote from Kurmuk, officially notifying us that Italy had entered the war, and stating that he was authorized to inform us that a state of belligerency now existed between the Sudan and Italy along the Ethiopian frontier.

He added as a postscript: "We aren't expecting any trouble."

Our growing apprehension was not allayed by his optimism.

23

Our First Uduk Convert

THE GOSPEL MESSAGE, wrapped up in parables or illustrated by familiar events in their lives, had been heard many times by our neighbors. Yet nobody believed. Other missionaries had told us of people accepting Christ on the very first presentation, but we had not seemed able to reach the Uduks. We put it this way:

"God who made the world and all men is living now. Men are separated from Him because of sin, but He still loves His creatures and sent His Son Jesus to pay the penalty for sin by dying for them. Those who believe and receive His Son are forgiven their sins and have eternal life. Won't you receive this wonderful gift of God?"

When we allowed ourselves to dream a little, we could see hundreds of Uduks, dressed in white, walking to their churches on Lord's Day morning. There would be churches in all the villages and the elders— young married men, we imagined—would have learned to read the Bible and would be teaching the children to read. But it was only a dream, an expression of intense longing to see the Uduk people delivered from all that was sordid in their lives, from that which had them living like animals. Our egos were not fed by a stream of Uduk people coming to hear our words of wisdom. We had to go to the people in their villages and on their farms. Perhaps we did not have the spark to start a spiritual movement.

"I guess we can't expect to have any converts until we get a Sunday service started," Enid said wistfully.

"We'll just have to remember that there are a lot of people praying for us," I replied, looking for something encouraging to say. "It's the Lord's work, we're not in this thing alone."

"Perhaps something is going on in the hearts of the people." A note of hope crept into Enid's voice. "Healing sometimes goes on for a long time before it is outwardly visible."

One morning a man named Mona appeared at the back window. "Jo Li," he said, "I have arrived."

"Very good," I said.

Mona was a typical Uduk, short, with a wide head that was flat on top. Unlike my nose, his had hardly bothered to grow. He differed from most Uduks, however, in that his shoulders were sinewy and broad from throwing many a spear and pulling countless times on a taut bow. His arms were solid muscle from hours spent wielding a hoe or an ax, and his legs were hard from chasing wild gazelle and antelope, as well as from dancing, in which he excelled.

Mona's head and body were covered with the customary dull red mixture of sesame oil and ocher. Only his face, peering out from this greasy makeup, showed how black he was—like the soot in the attic of his hut. Against this black background, his straight teeth shone sparkling white without benefit of toothpaste. Uduk custom had long ago claimed the four incisors at bottom center.

Mona had probably come for medicine, I surmised, since this was the hour we spent every morning treating patients. Therefore, I asked him if he needed medicine.

"No," Mona replied. He saw that I was puzzled. "My wife had a baby last night," he went on.

That still did not explain his presence but by this time Mona had come in through the back door and we snapped fingers.

"Ko Li," he said to Enid, "are you good?" Enid said she was feeling good. "The baby is a boy, so I have come."

We began to understand that Mona's visit had some relation to the birth of his son during the night.

"Are your wife and baby good?" Enid inquired.

"They are good," Mona said, "but I have to sit for five or ten days."

"Why is that?" Enid asked, suddenly realizing that something new was happening.

"If I work when the baby is tiny," Mona explained, "it will make him tired and he might get sick and die."

We could have understood how the activity of the mother might have affected the child but how the father was concerned puzzled us.

"How does that happen?" I asked.

"If I hoe the weeds, the baby will get tired. If I chop a tree down, it will be like chopping the baby."

We were aware that the Uduks did not separate the physical and the spiritual. Now we learned of their fear that any activity of the father during the first few days of the baby's life would be transferred spiritually to the body of the child.

"Since I can't work now," Mona declared, "I thought I would just sit here."

"We'll be happy to have you sit here, Mona," Enid said. "You can help us learn your language."

"I might be able to help you wash clothes," Mona volunteered. "I could wash them but I couldn't wring them. That would be like wringing the baby's neck."

So Mona, with nothing else to do, came to our house every morning. Together we reviewed much of the language material we had gathered and every day we told him about God and His Son "Yesus," who died and rose again to give him life. Mona always listened intently and appeared interested, and soon we thought we detected a change. Perhaps he was beginning to realize that God loved him.

The fifth day he arrived late. "I have been to my field," he explained.

"Can you work now?" I asked.

"No, I was just trying out the work and the baby. I weeded a small space"—his arms described an area about a yard square—"and tonight I'll see if it has harmed the baby. If it has, I'll have to sit for a while longer."

Whatever the reason, we were glad Mona still had some time for us, for each day he seemed to understand a little more. By the end of the week he knew all the simple facts of salvation. Would he receive Christ? On the eighth day we decided to draw all the threads together—God, sinful man, Christ, and Mona.

"This talk is very big," he said.

He was reaching out to understand and he had some points of reference. The fact of spirits having anything to do with human beings was comprehensible but the incarnation of a spirit was hard for him to grasp, though spirits, supposedly, could do anything. Ours were different, however, for they were self-existent. All Uduk spirits came from the dead. The hardest problem for Mona was that of sin, because sin did not punish people, at least not Uduks. It was the spirits that caused all the trouble.

"Mona," I said finally, "you have heard the talk. You need 'Yesus' to help you. Will you receive Him now as your Savior?"

Mona had his elbows on his knees, his head on his hands. He was staring unseeing at the ground, but after an agonizing wait he lifted his head.

"*Nye.*" Mona had said "Yes." He was a Christian! It was as simple as that.

We looked at our first believer, sitting on the dirt floor before us. He did not have a stitch on but, like the lilies of the field, he was clothed inwardly in a beauty we could not see. A guest in our home might have seen nothing significant, but for us the whole scene had a heavenly glow.

With his sitting period safely past, Mona did not revert entirely to his former ways. He appeared at our door almost daily and we watched him come and go—although several years would pass before we would know all that was going on in his heart.

"You say God killed an animal and made clothes for Adam and his wife?" Mona asked one day.

"Yes. God wanted them to be clothed."

"Could I work for you some more?"

Apparently he was changing the subject but actually he was not. Mona worked for a while, took his pay one day, and disappeared. The next day he came back wearing a knee-length shirt he had bought at the local trading post. The shirt was soon soiled. When he had finished washing our clothes—fortunately, he could now wring them out, too—he took off his own shirt and washed it. Then, standing stark naked, he hung it on the line.

A few weeks later, after he had given his shirt its fifth or sixth laundering, he disappeared over the hill. Evidently our message was getting across and he did not want to be seen without clothes on. When he returned, he took the dry shirt off the line and put it on again. Soon Mona had earned enough money for a second shirt and two pairs of trousers. Now when he washed one suit, he wore the other. We were amazed to see how quickly he had solved the clothes problem.

The Sunday after his conversion Mona had brought his brothers and cousins. He wanted the men "to hear the talk," and thus began our first services on our front veranda.

Although Mona came regularly on Sundays, his relatives and neighbors attended irregularly. He had turned himself into a clothes-wearing foreigner and they had no intention of doing likewise. The first talk they had heard, however, proved irresistible. They fought off the desire and stayed away for weeks but they returned. (Mona's brother was to resist for twelve years before the Word, which would not die in his heart, eventually caused him to believe.)

We needed more hymns; Christians have to sing to express themselves. Singing one song through several times at each service, Sunday after Sunday, grew monotonous. How did one write hymns? Get out a hymnal and translate from the English? "I Come to the Garden Alone." What for? To steal fruit? "Out of the Ivory Palaces." Oh, yes, out of the very big chief's house made from the tooth of an elephant.

Translation held out little hope. Native tunes? Yes, by all means, but we had not heard any except those used at dances. When we asked Mona about singing God's words to one of their tunes, he disapproved, emphasizing that the Uduk songs were identified with beer drinking and sex.

We began to look for easy melodies in our hymnals. We had used only one, "We Praise Thee, O God," so there were plenty left. Finally one morning Enid thought she had found just the hymn in "Come Thou Fount of Every Blessing." We decided not to translate the English words but to prepare a simple message. Proper Uduk phrasing did not always fit the original tune, so sometimes we danced on one note and quickly skidded off others.

Soon we wrote words to other tunes, and were amazed at how quickly the people learned to sing them. Unlike some Africans, they seemed to have no trouble with our music, despite the fact that their scale had but five notes. Sometimes we could manage to produce only one verse and a chorus, but hoped to add other verses at a future time. We thought the church would grow out of the morning service but with Mona's conversion the morning service had grown out of the church.

24
Flight

ONE FRIDAY morning in mid-July Nick disappeared into the tall wet grass. He had told us he would not be back until the following Tuesday or later. "We're running out of money," he had added, "and the trader here can't give us any. I think I'll hop on my donkey and go to Kurmuk and see if I can cash a check."

That Sunday was a good day for us. Mona brought his cousins and friends, and some women and children came without being asked. It was the biggest crowd we had yet had.

The last rays of the sun had just faded when we heard a scuffling at the back gate. We went out to see if it were a messenger but instead found Nick.

"What happened?" we asked, alarmed.

"The Italians have taken Kurmuk. Come into the house and I'll tell you about it."

Inside, Nick almost whispered, "There's no telling when the Italians might get here."

"But when did they take Kurmuk?" I wanted to know.

"This morning." That was a shocker.

"When did you leave there?"

"This morning."

"You mean you came from Kurmuk on a donkey in one day!" Enid exclaimed.

"I walked most of the way." We could see Nick was really shaken. "I borrowed a donkey for the last seven miles."

"Tell us about it," we begged.

As he talked, Nick was tense and his anxiety was evident.

"I got up at five-thirty this morning and had just finished dressing when I heard the hum of a plane. The District Commissioner had warned that trouble might come soon, so I ran out and got under that big wild fig tree at the end of the rest house. I could see the plane coming toward the town. It dropped some bombs in an open field and suddenly one exploded right near me." He paused and took a deep breath as he wiped his face.

"The plane had just swung back toward Ethiopia when I heard gunfire. Bullets began going *zing, zing* past my head. I looked down the slope below the town and saw soldiers coming. They were raking everything with machine-gun fire so I decided I'd better get out. I didn't want to be caught by the Italians."

We were listening intently.

"I didn't have my sun helmet with me. It was in the rest house along with the mailbag I got from the postmaster yesterday. I started running down through the ravine away from the rest house, then I circled back to the road to Chali and kept going. I could hear the rattle of the Italian machine guns and the rifle fire from the British post." Another pause, and Nick told the remainder of his story.

"The Italians won't stop in Kurmuk. They could get here by tomorrow if they wanted to. We've got to get out."

Nick had walked three or four miles before noticing a spot of blood on his shirt. He had discovered a small shrapnel wound in his stomach. We were thankful that the Lord had spared him. Nick had been an observer in the front lines during World War I and this fresh experience with bombs and bullets had unnerved him. He had no desire to relive his war experiences and wanted to start west toward the White Nile and our station at Melut. As we had never been bombed or shot at, we did not fully share his anxiety, and since Mona was now coming regularly we hated even to think of leaving.

Nick had supper with us, then went home to clean up. He brought his camp cot and bedding back to our house. He thought we ought to stick together in case anything happened during the night.

The next day Gari came. "You white people are fighting each other," he said. "It will be better for us if we move away from you."

So Gari and his clan built temperary huts a mile away. There was no land ownership in the tribe and people could build wherever they liked. We felt desolate.

Nick became increasingly preoccupied with leaving. He began to sell some of his surplus goods, including empty bottles and cans, his sugar supply, and equipment. He traded his herd of goats for two donkeys and we managed to buy a third. "If we have to leave," Nick had said, "we'll have to use donkeys. None of these people will carry our goods for us."

Enid and I packed an emergency outfit. It was reminiscent of Ethiopia, for once more we were talking about the fascists. Nick spent much time walking up and down in front of our house, his hands clenched tightly behind his back. Finally he reached a decision. He pushed the door open and entered the house.

"I don't want to press you folks to leave," he said, "but if we stay, we should identify ourselves so the Italians will know we are Americans and nonmilitary people. If we don't write and tell them who we are, they'll bomb us or shoot us up and say they didn't know we were here."

"Do you really think we should write to the Italians?" I asked.

"If we stay, I feel we should," Nick replied.

I wrote to the "Commanding Officer, Kurmuk," to describe the stations at Chali and Doro and list the personnel and citizenship at each, and I concluded with the statement that an American flag would be visible at each place. The trader said he would start the letter on its way and somebody else along the line would see that it reached its destination.

We had no flag but we dug a piece of muslin out of our scrap bag, along with some red material, and sewed red stripes on the white cloth. We marked out the forty-eight stars in the upper corner and colored around them with blue ink. Then we placed the flag on Nick's roof, where it could be seen more readily than on ours, and anchored it with stones.

One morning I looked down the path. "That looks like Bob Grieve!" I shouted. "Hi, Bob! Is everything all right at Doro?"

"Yes," he called, "but how is Nick? I came to see about that splinter he's carrying around."

Nick had written to Bob about his wound but had not asked him to come. Yet Bob had decided it would do Nick no good to be carrying a piece of shrapnel around, so he had walked the thirty miles from Doro in a day and a half. Bob was like that.

I asked about his wife, who was pregnant.

"Claire is nauseated all the time," he said. "She's lost a lot of weight and I haven't been able to help her at all." He was plainly worried. "I ought to get back to Doro as soon as possible. I'd better fix Nick up today."

He called Nick in, stretched him out on the bed, and went to work with his alcohol and local anesthetic. "There she is," he said finally, handing the splinter to Nick. It was about an eighth of an inch wide and a quarter of an inch long, and had been deeply embedded in the flesh. "It's good it didn't go in any farther."

The next day Bob mounted one of Nick's donkeys and set out for home.

Tension continued to mount. Down in the village one of the women had a baby and named it Italia. However, Mona and others were coming regularly on Sunday mornings and the weekly service on our front veranda had become an established, if small, feature of Chali life.

"Perhaps it isn't fair to Nick for us to insist on staying," I said to Enid one day.

"I've been wondering about that myself," she agreed.

"We're feeling the strain ourselves," I went on, "and we haven't been through anything. Nick's nerves were upset by the bombing in Kurmuk and he's staying here out of loyalty to us."

It was difficult to know what to do but we prayed for guidance. August came and we were in the worst of the rains when we received a letter from the Italian commander in Kurmuk. He acknowledged my letter and ordered all of us at Doro and Chali to appear in Kurmuk with our passports. "I hope the trip it will like to you," he concluded in his attempt at English.

In my reply I said:

"We do not have animals or carriers for such a trip and Mrs. Grieve is too ill to travel. She is expecting a baby."

We had no more letters from the commander. Enid, Nick, and I talked and prayed again. We could not see any future in going toward the Italian lines. We kept thinking of traveling westward to the Nile, but how would we get there? One hundred and fifty miles of tall grass, swamp, and mud separated us from Melut.

In the meantime, we canned corn for use in the event we decided to stay. The cans were still in the pressure cooker when one afternoon the corporal of police came to the door, a Maban by his side. Both looked distressed.

"This man has just come from Doro," the corporal said.

"Good," I replied. "Did you bring a letter?"

"Letter?" The Maban was surprised. "They were too busy burying the doctor to write a letter."

"Burying the doctor!" I exclaimed. "What do you mean?"

"The planes flew over and dropped bombs. The doctor's wife is dead, too," he added.

Those awful rumors! Yet for some strange reason this one had the ring of truth, much as I hated to believe it. I yelled for Enid and Nick and they came running. I told them what the Maban had said. Then I turned to the man again.

"Why did you come here?" I asked.

"My brother was staying here with the police," he replied. "When I saw what happened at Doro, I thought you must have been bombed, too, so I came to get my brother away from here."

"How about the other people at Doro?" I asked rather frantically.

"The Oglesbys were hurt some but Miss Walsh is all right."

Ken and Blanche Oglesby had recently arrived to take up the work at Doro. We thought they would be able to get a letter to us the next day but no message came. It was Sunday and, as we thought of the tragic turn of events and prayed, we decided we should leave our station and try to go at least as far as Doro. Our missionaries there might need us. If the Italians had bombed Doro, what did they plan to do to us?

"We have decided we should leave," we told the corporal.

"That is best," he agreed. "We don't know what the Italians will do now."

"We have donkeys to carry some of our load," I told him, "but we need carriers for the food we must have for the road."

"I'll send a policeman with you as far as Doro," he offered. "He can get women to take your goods from village to village. When do you want to leave?"

"Tomorrow."

It was hard to prepare for this kind of trip with any enthusiasm, but we had to go. We began our final packing early Monday. Mona was there and others wandered in, among them Elephant Chief. Their hearts were as burdened as ours. We gave away the remainder of our grain and peanuts.

"Ko Li," Elephant Chief said hesitantly as he sat on the floor of the back veranda, apprehensive at our leaving, "could I have just this one thing?" He held up a rubber pig that belonged to Leigh, delighting at its squeak as he squeezed it.

"Of course you may have it," Enid replied.

We had planned to leave right after breakfast but at noon we were still packing.

"We might as well eat lunch before we leave," Nick said.

"And I don't see any reason to do the dishes when we're through," I added.

We had been opening precious cans of fruit and vegetables carelessly and we opened some more for the last meal at Chali. We left the pans on the stove and the unwashed dishes on the table. Things would not look too comfortable for the fascist invaders when they walked in.

Just as we were about to leave, a boy arrived from Doro. He had a long letter from Ken Oglesby telling of the bombing in detail. It was true, both Bob and Claire were dead. We went on our way with heavy hearts.

25

"These Died in Faith . . ."

WE HAD left the house at one o'clock with the women carriers and Mona. It was four before we reached the last Uduk village. We had come only four miles and a swamp lay just ahead of us. I looked it over and waded in to explore its depth. It would be hard going. The next village was in Maban territory and eight miles away, so at the rate we were moving we would get there about midnight.

"There's a road around the swamp," our police escort said. "We'd better spend the night here and start out in the morning."

We paid off the Chali women carriers and they returned home. Mona went with them and our morale dropped to a new low as we said good-by.

It was eight-thirty the next morning before we started again. The road was overgrown with grass that towered to a height of ten feet, so we traveled through an endless tunnel, mile after mile. We sent the loaded donkeys ahead to break trail and to shake the dew from the grass. Only Leigh thoroughly enjoyed the extended donkey ride. It was the first time he had ever had one that was long enough.

"We'll spend the night at Neela and get to Doro tomorrow," I said to Enid, trying to encourage her.

The following day new carriers were rounded up in Neela. This time they were men but they were not accustomed to carrying loads and were distinctly unhappy at the prospect. Then, too, the man who had brought us word of the bombing at Doro lived in this village. The people, after hearing his report, did not want to become involved in our troubles. Finally the bearers came and at nine-thirty our caravan set out. After an hour the sky clouded over.

"It's going to rain," I said to Enid. "Let's get our raincoats on before it comes."

We pinned a square piece of plastic around Leigh and then donned our light plastic coats. The wind struck first and swirled the grass around us, then the rain came.

"We'll just have to keep going," I said.

The bearers grumbled and we did not blame them, for they were cold from the pelting rain. The wind blew the tall grass down across the path and we walked through the tangle, the Mabans showing us the way.

"This donkey can't carry both of us," Enid said, sliding off her mount. "Can you watch Leigh and let him ride?"

I slithered along beside him, the donkeys sinking deeper and deeper into the mud. Nick tried to lighten the loads to help the pack animals but it did no good. "We'll never see this stuff again," Nick groaned, as he rolled the suitcases and bedding bags off into the grass. Most of our carriers had disappeared.

"That donkey is going to fall with Leigh!" Enid cried suddenly.

I lifted Leigh off and carried him. It was almost impossible to stand, let alone walk, yet we staggered on. The pack donkeys were somewhere behind us and most of our baggage was now strung along through the woods, thoroughly soaked, but we did not much care. The rain would not let up. The mud sucked Enid's shoes off and broke the laces in mine, so we carried them. It was a little easier to walk barefoot except when there were thorns.

Leigh refused to be carried by anyone else, and when at last we sighted the drenched roofs of a Maban village among the palms, I had been carrying him for two hours without resting. I knew I could never have done it in my own strength. I did not have that much. Soon after we reached the village the rain stopped. There was a new nicely mudded hut there and the surprised owner invited us in. He lighted a fire and we tried to get dry, but the smoke nearly choked us. We were afraid Leigh might catch pneumonia, so we stripped him and stood him by the fire.

Nick was sitting by the door. "Here comes a boy with the pressure cooker!" he cried.

The night before, the chief at Neela had given us a small goat which Enid had cooked. We had eaten half for supper, and left the other half in the pressure cooker, along with a can of peaches and one of jam— our lunch for the day. We were ravenous and tore the goat limb from limb.

"How are we going to open these cans?" Enid asked.

"One of these spears will do," I replied, and, taking one from its resting place against the wall, pushed the point through the top and cut around with it. We enjoyed the peaches and jam without benefit of plates or spoons.

"Here comes a donkey," Nick called again.

Somebody had kept the tired animal going with its light load. It carried a suitcase of Nick's and one of ours which held clothing of mine and Leigh's. We changed Leigh and I put on some dry garments. Nick did the same. Enid's clothes were nearly dry by this time, which was just as well because her suitcase did not arrive.

Nick pulled a handful of keys from his pocket. "I'll not need these again," he reflected aloud.

He took a long look at them. Some were for his house, some for his cupboards, others were for his trunks and the suitcases he had just left in the swamp. He walked out of the house and threw the keys as far as he could into the tall grass. His gesture was symbolic. It did not look as if we would ever need keys again. Our station was abandoned and the Italians were in Kurmuk. Bob and Claire Grieve were gone, and the few things we had been able to take from Chali were under water somewhere along the road.

The donkeys, their saddles empty, straggled in later. We loaded what was left of our baggage and started down the road toward Doro, Enid and Leigh back on their donkey. The sun was shining as it dropped toward the west.

At five-thirty we came out in the clearing at Doro Station. Ken Oglesby and Zillah Walsh ran to greet us. They looked haggard. Ken told us the story quickly.

When the two planes flew overhead on that fatal morning, Bob had run out of the house with his big American flag streaming after him. They were all running toward the woods when Bob called to Ken to help him hold the flag. They never dreamed the Italians would bomb them, for there were no military targets within hundreds of miles. Yet the planes flew right in their direction. One bomb landed close by and riddled the flag. A fragment hit Bob in the forehead and as he fell Claire fell beside him, hit in the back. Bob never regained consciousness. He was buried in the late afternoon as the sun was setting and as Claire lay dying. She was buried beside Bob the next morning.

"What are you going to do?" I asked Ken.

"We'll just have to stay here. Blanche was hit, too, and she's in no condition to travel."

It was easy to see that evacuation to a safer place was imperative. The Oglesbys were unnerved and the nightmare of nursing Claire in her last hours had shaken Zillah Walsh badly, although she herself had escaped actual injury, as she had been in her house when the bombs fell.

The decision of the Doro staff to stay on revived all the uncertainties Enid and I had faced at Chali. "Shall we go? Shall we stay?" we were again asking ourselves.

We were now the only ones left who had not had the shattering experience of being bombed. We did not want to leave the Doro people behind but Nick's equilibrium had been further disturbed by the Doro bombing. "We ought to get out of here," he said with conviction. He was quite sure the Italians intended to march to the Nile.

Enid and I were not sure about anything. Certainty had come only for Bob and Claire. If we ever reached Khartoum, I would have a headstone made for their graves. It would read: THESE DIED IN FAITH.

But we would have to live in faith.

PART III

The Sudan

. . . the full corn in the ear

26

War Babies

OUR SITUATION improved somewhat when the sergeant of police, at the post located just two miles from Doro, sent men back along the road for our suitcases, boxes, and bed rolls. The contents of the bags were a sorry sight on the line, for most of the colors had run and many of the clothes were mildewed. The Lord seemed to be indicating that we should leave, yet we had no clear plan for crossing the Dinka plain. We did not know how we would cover the long distances between villages.

Our Chali corporal had returned to his post, so we told the sergeant at Doro that we would like carriers. On Labor Day, 1940, we had mixed feelings as we left the Oglesbys and Zillah Walsh. Perhaps, we thought, they were doing the Lord's will for them, and we were doing the Lord's will for us.

Two policemen accompanied us, along with women bearers to carry our loads. We started out at ten o'clock in the morning but traveled only twelve miles. On the second day we had not been on the way long when two policemen approached us from the direction of the Nile. They brought us a letter, which we tore open and read excitedly. It was from the Assistant District Commissioner, John Bowers, who said that he, Davison, Phillips, and McMillan were proceeding to Doro with a contingent of police to evacuate the women and children. He added that he had not heard from Chali and therefore did not know what had happened there.

"They're going to camp tonight at the same place you are," the policemen said.

We felt unutterable relief. It seemed we were doing the right thing after all!

We reached the rest house at two o'clock.

"The District Commissioner and some other men are down on the motor road eating corn," one of the local farmers told us.

I quickly scratched a note to them and, after placing it in a slit stick for the mile journey, the man went off with it. When Bowers read it, he jumped up, shouting, "The Forsbergs and Simponis are up at the rest house!" My note was the first indication they had had since the bombing of Doro that we were alive.

"Praise the Lord!" John Phillips said, also jumping up. He had the presence of mind to grab the last ears of green corn from the fire for us.

We were sitting in the middle of our stuff when the four men appeared. The same emotions flooded all of us, although we struggled to keep calm. We had a lot of information to exchange.

"We came in two trucks as far as the Kidwa swamp," Bowers said. "We'll send one of the trucks back with you and leave the other there in case we need it. We'll have to carry Mrs. Oglesby out to the truck."

We forgot all about the long distances between Dinka villages. How could the men have possibly gotten to the Kidwa swamp in September? They had come ninety miles through the mud.

The following day we began the walk to the truck with a policeman and Laurie Davison. We agreed it was just like old times, for our paths had crossed in the Ethiopian wilderness in another war. We would not reach the truck that night, so we camped and planned to go on the next day.

Enid was beginning to tire. "I know it's been a hard trip," she said, "but I shouldn't be so tired. I'm beginning to wonder if—"

We had separately wondered "if," but this was the first time the subject had come up between us. I had tried to make things as easy as possible for her but I could not remove the mud nor dry up the water. Nor could I shorten the road or the travel hours of the day. The last time we had done this kind of emergency traveling our first born had been on the way. Were we going to have a baby with each war?

Just after nightfall, we reached an abandoned village. We were so worn out we made only a pretense of eating, and went to bed.

Breakfast the next morning was more appealing and fortified us for the journey ahead. After walking for about an hour we arrived at the edge of the swamp. The path was invisible under water but the opening in the grass indicated the way we should go.

"It will take us about half an hour to wade this," Laurie warned us. "The water will be knee deep most of the time and in the stream bed it will probably come up to our hips."

I held Leigh securely and stepped into the water, while Laurie helped Enid. The carriers followed, their loads on their heads. We would not need to hire women again and we were happy for that. Wading through the mud-bottomed stretch of water with no place to rest seemed an eternity. When we finally emerged on the far side, there were the trucks. What a sight they were and what a difference they would make! We hurried to where they were well hidden under the solid foliage of a tamarind tree. The women were paid off. They had received good wages all along the road but that had not made them any more anxious to carry for us. When we parted, we were mutually relieved.

"If it hadn't been for Johnny Phillips, we never would have gotten this far," Laurie explained. "Many times we came to stretches of mud and water we couldn't cross. Bowers wanted to leave the trucks and go on by foot, but John insisted that we scout around some more. We always found a way until we got here. Of course this swamp goes right on to the Nile this time of year and there's no way around it."

We plowed through mud for nearly two days before we finally ground to a stop on our Melut Station. Sometimes we circled miles from the road, searching for dry ground for the truck. More than once we skidded into huge mudholes, but we did get there and could now go on to Khartoum by river steamer.

Before we left Melut, Blanche Oglesby and Zillah Walsh arrived in the truck, followed by Ken Oglesby and Stan McMillan. Our steamer paddled its way to the river port of Kosti, where we transferred, with our goods, to the overnight train to Khartoum. At Khartoum we were greeted by Dr. and Mrs. Lambie and others as though we had returned from the dead. We began to feel that way ourselves.

"When we heard what had happened at Doro," Dr. Lambie said, "and then had no word from you folks, we were afraid you'd been bombed, too."

The day after our arrival, Nick and I went with Dr. Lambie to see the judge of the high court. He helped us prepare our affidavit describing the events at Doro. When Ken Oglesby arrived, he did the same. All the papers were forwarded to the American minister in Cairo. With these documents on record, our government then protested to Italy over the killing of United States citizens at Doro.

The Italian government eventually replied. It denied everything.

27

Back to Chali

WE SETTLED down as best we could at Khartoum. One day Dr. Lambie came to me.

"His Majesty is planning to attend the Unity Service in the Cathedral. Would you like to go?"

We went together to see the Emperor Haile Selassie in the Anglican Cathedral. Greek and Coptic bishops and priests came down the aisle, their luxuriant beards, and the robes and headdresses of the Eastern churches, contrasting sharply with the plain formality of the Anglicans and the simplicity of the Evangelicals. I had learned to be satisfied with the spiritual unity the Apostle Paul spoke of in I Corinthians 12:27: "Now ye are the body of Christ, and members in particular," and in Ephesians 4:25: "For we are members one of another." Anyway, we had come to see the Emperor.

The crowd, too, was obviously waiting for His Majesty, who had become the outstanding symbol of the battle against fascist aggression. Soon he arrived at the back of the church and began his progress down the aisle, accompanied by his aides. As one man, the congregation rose.

These were not days for magnificence or pomp; men were being honored for their courage. The Emperor had fled his country in defeat and in England he had waited, in exile, for the tide to turn. It had been a lonely exile as the guest of the very people who had remained silent when he was in distress. It had taken courage. Now his allies had been forced to return to his side and he had become their symbol of ultimate victory. He was in Khartoum, en route back to his throne in Addis Ababa, and the Italian armies were crumbling.

Already we were planning our eventual return to our station. Also, we now knew that we were to have a baby in this war, too. In the meantime, we would have to find a place to recuperate from the effects of our months of anxiety at Chali. We went south, up the White Nile, to the end of the steamer route at Juba. The next few months in the cool Imatong Mountains overlooking the plains of Uganda were revitalizing. Then we returned to Khartoum to await the birth of our second child.

At Khartoum, Dr. Lambie briefed us on the situation. If our baby did not arrive before April 20, the date we had been given, it might be too late to get back to Chali because of the rains. He told us the area had been under military administration during the war and the Civil Secretary had not yet given the Mission permission to reoccupy Chali and Doro.

We prayed that our baby would arrive early, and that the Civil Secretary would have a change of mind, then went ahead with our preparations to return to Chali. In the middle of our packing, Enid had to go to the hospital. It was April 10. Our prayer had been answered!

I was waiting in the office of the hospital when a nurse came in.

"It's a boy," she said, beaming.

I felt a slight twinge of disappointment. We still had a girl's name and had not planned on another boy. All the way home I tried to think of a boy's name. We settled the matter during visiting hours that first night.

"I'd like to call him Robert for Bob Grieve," I said to Enid. "Would you? We'll need another name to go with it, though."

"I'd like to name him for Bob. What about James?"

"James Robert. That sounds good."

He would be Jimmy of course, but the next day Enid decided she wanted to call him Jayme.

"How did you feed your first baby?" the doctor asked Enid that night.

"With a bottle."

"Well, this one can't be a bottle baby. There isn't any milk in the Sudan suitable for a formula."

Enid protested that she could not nurse him, that the American doctors who attended her first delivery had told her she could not nurse Leigh.

"You can nurse him," the doctor assured her. "Don't think you can't. We'll do all we can to help but you'll have to persevere."

Enid persevered and soon discovered that nursing a baby meant a great deal more than just feeding it. A whole new world of maternal emotion was opened up that far surpassed holding a bottle.

Jayme had done his bit by coming ahead of time. Now it was up to the Civil Secretary to say we could go to Chali. One day, after a business trip to town, Dr. Lambie brought news. The Civil Secretary had said we could all return to our station. So our second prayer was answered.

I brought Enid and Jayme home the next day. It was 117° in the shade. Leigh was delighted with his baby brother. When Jayme was less than a month old, the four of us left Khartoum on the Nile steamer. At Melut we were met by Stan McMillan, a New Zealander who had taken over the truck duties from Earl Lewis.

"We brought a lot of your stuff from Chali to Melut for safekeeping," he informed us. "Now we'll have to take it back, together with the goods you've just bought. We'll have to make two trips, I guess."

"I'm glad you're going to drive us to Chali," Enid told him. She had confidence in his ability to keep the truck going, as she remembered vividly the muddy plain stretching beyond Melut.

Nick was going back, too, and Stan said he would take him in with the first load and then return for us, so Nick could be straightening things out while he waited. In the dry season Chali is a ten-hour run each way. It would take longer this time. Stan was back on the seventh day and then it was our turn. We were looking forward to a visit with Ken Oglesby at Abaiyat. Early in the year his wife Blanche had died of malaria and heart complications, and Ken had taken her body to Doro for burial, the military having given him special permission. Now he was awaiting his eventual return to his station.

We ground our way to Abaiyat. When we reached it, Ken came running out, shouting, "The *Zam Zam* has been sunk!" He had just heard the news on his radio.

The Egyptian ship had left New York with several hundred missionaries who had been prevented by the war from returning to their fields earlier. Out in the South Atlantic the *Zam Zam* had been attacked by a German raider. The passengers and crew had been taken aboard the raider, and thence to occupied France. But we did not know that now, nor that those belonging to neutral nations had been required to proceed homeward through Spain and Portugal, instead of to their original destinations. Mr. and Mrs. Ohman and Mary Beam would not be at Doro for the rains.

We looked at each other blankly, suddenly feeling very much alone. The expected reinforcements would not be coming now.

After lunch we climbed back to our places in the truck and began grinding through the mud again. Two days later, when we were still forty miles from home one of the bearings burned out. We were wondering what to do next when a Belgian Congo military truck which we had passed earlier appeared through the trees.

"You are stuck?" the driver asked.

"Yes, we are," I replied. "Could you take us to Chali?"

He agreed and we piled our suitcases and duffel bags on the load of gasoline cans they were hauling. Stan said if he could fix the truck, he would bring the rest of our things, but that he might have to unload and return to Melut for repairs. We left Stan to his troubles but we did not reach Chali that night. We had to camp once more, and the next day was our fourth on that ten-hour trip. Two miles from Chali the hind wheels of the military truck sank into the mire.

We were not far from an Uduk village and soon two boys appeared, herding their goats. "Is that Ko Li?" one asked, pointing at Enid.

Before long men and women from the village were eying the truck as they approached. They had seen many military vehicles pass but the occupants of this one were different. We had wondered how we would be received. Had the nine months of war and uncertainty made them any more friendly?

"Ko Li, Ko Li," the women called as they recognized Leigh's mother. Nick had told them about Jayme. "Where's the baby?"

Enid lifted him out of his basket.

"What is his name? What does he eat?"

"His name is Jayme and he drinks milk just like your babies."

They were vitally impressed at hearing about his diet. They had always maintained that we were built differently and even claimed that Leigh was not our child. "You got him out of the water," they had said. Perhaps they thought that anyone so white must have come out of a stream. But something had happened, for the Uduks were treating us as though we really belonged! Our fingers were red after snapping them with so many of the people. Enid and I exchanged a long look of happiness. We were home.

"We'll walk the rest of the way," I said to the driver of the truck, and we thanked him for bringing us to the end of our journey.

"Go on, Jo Li," the women chattered, "we'll carry your things."

We could hardly believe our ears. The women picked up our goods and started off. Enid carried Jayme, while I held Leigh. Two miles of mud and one hour later we knocked on Nick's door.

"For goodness' sake!" he exclaimed. "I didn't think you'd make it until after the rains. It's been raining every day." Nick had thought he would be living alone for another six months. "I couldn't get out of washing the dishes we left," he grinned. "They were waiting for me when I got back."

In our nine-month absence practically nothing in our houses had been touched. Nick had cleaned up some of the termite dirt but much still had to be done. Work is hard when hearts are heavy, but with Uduks beating a path to our door to see the baby, the burden somehow lightened. The refrigerator, baby's bed, high chair, and many of our supplies were sitting somewhere along the road where Stan had left them. We had decided to manage without them until after the rains, when one day Stan drove up to our front door with everything.

"How did you ever make it, Stan?" we asked.

"It's the usual June dry spell."

"When did you leave Melut?"

"Last night. The roads have already dried out."

Stan had brought Ken Oglesby in and left him at Doro. He quickly unloaded our goods and headed back toward Melut, for the June dry spell might not last.

We had been most anxious to see Mona again. He had been friendly on our arrival but we detected a certain coolness in his attitude. We reasoned that perhaps he resented keeping the goats for us while we were away, or that he might have taken some of the missing animals and now felt guilty. Mona was seldom at his home when we visited and several months were to pass before I would have a satisfactory talk with him.

"Mona," I then said, "I don't know why you stay away from us and the Sunday services. If you have sinned and are afraid of the Lord, just remember He loves you and is waiting for you to confess your sin and to return to Him."

Mona came back.

28

The Uduks "Do the Paper"

JAYME THRIVED and we found that he was a missionary in his own right.

"I didn't think we'd get through to the people in this way," Enid said one morning.

"In what way?" I asked.

"By our having another baby, of course. We've had more visitors in the month since our return than we had in the previous year and a half. They don't come to see us, they come to see Jayme."

He was fat, the way Uduks like babies to be, and full of the aimless motion and sound they could understand. His dark eyes and hair were in sharp contrast to Leigh's light coloring. The Uduks' interest did not yet carry over to the things of God, however. A few more came to church, but none was really ready to stand with Mona. Although by our standards his Christianity was simple, he was well ahead of his people. It was wonderful to have them coming to us but we continued to visit their villages. Contact with them in their homes was most important, especially since we still had so much to learn about their way of life.

The Uduks had planted their corn during the heavy rains that had made travel difficult for us. When the much-needed rains stopped, they sought a cause for the evil. One afternoon Enid was visiting in a village.

"Go on home. You are stopping the rain," one of the more disagreeable men said.

Enid did go home shortly afterward, and it began to rain hard again. We thought of the man in the village and of how convinced he must be of our culpability.

Our anxiety for the children and young people grew. There was need for them to attend school and be taught that natural events were not to be looked on with dread and suspicion. Our first efforts to interest the children in school were comparable to Elijah's cloud, the size of a man's hand. But as we talked about "the paper," the cloud grew larger over the villages.

"Your children need to learn how to 'do the paper,'" we told the chiefs.

"Yes," they sighed, "we know. The District Commissioner said that you would teach the children to do the paper and that we should help you."

We knew we faced a struggle—educating people who did not want to be educated—but Nick and I finally called on the chiefs to make definite arrangements for a group of boys to start their studies.

"We'll bring the parents of the boys tomorrow to talk," the chiefs promised.

They did not come, so we went to some of the parents themselves.

"Your boy should come and learn to do the paper," we said.

"Will that help him to herd cattle or to grow grain or to get married?" they asked.

We announced the opening of school for the first of August but it was September before we started. Since no boys came to us, we went to them in their villages. When I returned home at seven the morning of the first day, I had had six boys in school.

"I didn't have a soul," Nick said. He had gone to Babu's village and I had had my school in Elephant Chief's village.

Enid was busy making flash cards for us. Every morning at six o'clock, Nick and I plowed our way to our separate villages, flash cards in hand. We sat in the shade of a tree or under a roof set on poles. When it rained hard, we did not meet. In time the boys showed up fairly regularly and they were not slow to learn. They soon knew the flash cards Enid had prepared and she had to make others. Progress with numbers was more difficult.

"How are we going to teach these people any arithmetic above the number twenty?" Nick asked one day. His class had not yet learned to do addition up to twenty, but he was already wondering.

"I don't know how we're going to get around their five-digit system," Enid replied. "I've worked out some lessons based on it but it's very clumsy."

The Uduk people count by fives. They go from one to five, then it becomes "five jump one." At ten it is "ten jump one, ten jump two," until they reach twenty. Twenty is called "one person," meaning all the ten fingers and ten toes.

"When we were building your house," I said to Nick, "I asked an Uduk to count the mud bricks we were making down by the well. There were several hundred of them on the ground. The fellow counted by twenties and fives until he got to eighty. But then he forgot how many 'persons' he had counted, and lost track and gave up."

In the end we adopted the Arabic numerals and the change solved the counting problem in the school. In the villages, though, the people still jumped fingers and raised their feet whenever they needed to add a toe or two.

After we had been teaching for several weeks, Nick and I talked of the school attendance.

"The boys danced again all last night," he said, "and were too tired to stay awake today."

"I had the same trouble. Some of my boys had been asleep only an hour or two when I woke them up. Others came right from the dance."

It was difficult to run a school for boys whose parents preferred them to herd the flocks. We were afraid the pressure we had to exert to keep the boys in school would eventually alienate the people entirely. In spite of opposition and indifference, however, we finally succeeded in having boys from both villages come to us for school on our verandas.

"Now we can really teach them," Nick said, "but we'll have to keep up the pressure."

With the boys coming to us, it was possible to enlarge the curriculum, add physical education, especially dodge ball, and also a class in "general knowledge," which was a catchall. We used round objects to illustrate the relation of the earth to the sun and moon, and described the eclipses. Of course we taught Bible, often using flannelgraph illustrations as we talked.

When I said mosquitoes bred in water, I had to prove it by having the boys fill a jar from a pool and then wait for things to happen. Soon larvae were visible and then, as I had told them, the mosquitoes appeared on top of the water. The boys had to accept what they saw, but when I further stated the mosquitoes carried malaria, they thought this was nonsense. However, I persisted.

We knew that the Uduks were wonderful naturalists. They could identify every track in the forest, whether antelope, warthog, or lion, and whether the tracks had been made that day or three days earlier. They had names for the hundreds of varieties of grasses, weeds, and trees, and most of the adults and children could identify them all. They believed that the Uduk tribe was the center of the universe, that every night the sun went into a hole in the ground and came out again every morning, and that when an eclipse began the moon was dying. Yet when they saw tadpoles and frogs in the water they did not know the relationship between them. I had the boys bring some tadpoles from the stream and put them in a jar which I left in the schoolroom. Jo Li was right, they agreed finally—the tadpoles turned into frogs.

While Nick and I were busy with schoolteaching and language study and visiting in the villages, Enid turned to producing Uduk literature. The school was demanding more and more primer and simple reading material, so with the miscellaneous linguistic information we had jointly gathered she wrote up the customs of these people and typed out the many folk tales we had heard. Foremost in our endeavor was the desire to give the Uduk people spiritual help and a type of education that would lift them up, at the same time retaining the good in their own way of life.

We were glad when a piece of equipment, not too far removed from Uduk capabilities, was announced for Chali. The trader decided to have an oil press. A maker of presses came from Kurmuk, chose the right kind of tree, chopped it down, and from it made an eight-foot length, about eighteen inches in diameter, into a mortar. When I saw the trader, he was in the last stages of hollowing out one end of the log.

The finished oil press was a contraption! Five feet of the eight-foot log were underground and a pestle six inches thick and three feet long was set in the mortar. A shaft was then secured to the pestle, running outward from the mortar. A trained bull was harnessed to the machine and sesame seed, rich in oil, was poured into the mortar. The bull went round and round, turning the pestle, and soon one of the boys began dipping oil out. It worked! In two weeks Chali had moved from the eighth century to the tenth.

"Now we can buy oil to put on ourselves when we get married," Basha said one day. He was only thirteen but Uduk children talk about marriage as soon as they can put words together. Marriage was always a problem for us. How could we cram five or six years of schooling into our boys before it was time for serious courtship?

"But you don't get married," Enid replied. "You just grab your girls and run off with them."

"Yes," Basha said slowly, "but there is more to it than that. Didn't anybody tell you about 'crawling like a weasel'?"

"What do you mean?"

Basha laughed. "We have to crawl like a weasel to get the girl's consent."

There were not many opportunities for the Uduks to explain their customs. All their own people knew about them and we were the only ones they could regale with their doings. Basha was frankly amused and delighted with the chance to tell us about it.

"When a girl is old enough to marry," he explained, "she leaves the family bed and builds one of her own by the wall, away from her parents."

"But I thought the boys and girls lived with their uncles," Enid said.

"When it is time to get married," Basha told her, "the girls go home to their mothers, if their parents are still living together."

"You say the girl makes her own bed," Enid prompted.

"Yes, she makes her own bed and then cuts a hole in the wall just big enough for her boy friend to put his hand through. When the other members of the family are asleep, the boy comes crawling like a weasel up to the side of the house." Basha was intent on his explanation of this important phase of their life. "The boy puts his hand through the hole in the wall and the girl can tell by feeling the rings on his fingers just who he is. If she is interested in him, the two talk through the wall and after some days she may even open the door of the house and go outside to talk to him."

"What if she doesn't like the one who comes?"

"Oh, then the girl talks to him in a loud voice, and the boy is afraid the parents will wake up, so he runs away. He knows he isn't wanted."

"What happens after that?"

"After a few weeks the boy says, 'I want to marry you.' The girl says, 'After I get my beads ready.' If she isn't in any hurry, she keeps telling him she doesn't have her beads ready. If he gets tired of waiting, he may watch until she goes to the river for water and grab her and run off with her. Then they are married."

"How do they get married?" we asked.

"That's it," Basha replied. "When he runs off with her, they are married."

"But sometimes the boys run off with girls without crawling like a weasel," I objected.

"Oh, yes," Basha agreed. "Sometimes a boy wants a certain girl and doesn't bother to go to her home. He meets her on the path and runs off with her. If she doesn't want him, she screams and somebody rescues her. If she doesn't object, she goes with him. Some of those marriages don't last long."

"None of the marriages seems to last very long," Enid remarked drily.

"Well, what are the men to do?" Basha asked, defending his sex. "The women always refuse to cook food or make beer. They nag us all the time and cause trouble."

Little Basha had already had his Uduk education; he was talking like an old man of the tribe. We knew of no other tribe in the whole Sudan whose men married without paying a bride price. We wondered if such a payment would not help to stabilize the tribe's marriages. In the confusion of trying to find a solution to so many problems—early marriage, indiscipline, complete lack of interest in anything outside of their experience—we were thrown back again onto our original premise:

"It will be difficult to help these people unless they come to Christ first. The school should grow out of the church."

29

The Road to Heaven

BEFORE LONG we declared a vacation for the sake of the teachers in the school rather than the pupils.

"I'm going to take a three-day preaching trip to Belilla," I told Enid one morning. Belilla was a section of the Uduk tribe twenty miles west of Chali. Our visits to this village had been infrequent and brief.

"How are you going to get there?"

"On my bike. I'll take Mona and Joygo with me to drive the pack donkeys." Joygo had been a neighbor during all of our time at Chali and considered himself a special friend of mine.

"What do they know about loading and driving donkeys?"

"They've been learning a lot and on this trip they'll learn more."

On a day soon after that, the two of them drove the loaded donkeys down the road. I ate breakfast and then followed on my bicycle. I had to stall often after I caught up to them because the bicycle was too fast, but it was better than walking or riding a donkey.

We arrived at the Belilla rest house toward evening. Mona and Joygo were worn out from the trip; never had they worked so hard at keeping loads on donkeys. I set up my bed in the sprawling house built for the infrequent visits of the District Commissioner and any other travelers who might need shelter. The villagers were home from their fields and soon heard we were there.

"Jo Li and Mona have come," they said. "Mona and Joygo have become foreigners. They have taken to wearing clothes." They snapped fingers. "Mona," they said, in simple greeting. Then they apologized. "We're sorry we don't have any beer. We're out of grain."

"I didn't come to drink beer," Mona told them. "I came to tell you the true word."

"We have heard that you have taken up with the foreigners' talk," they said. "Are you going to tell us now?"

Mona, Joygo, and I sang for them, then I talked and Mona added his word.

"Come back tomorrow afternoon," I said, "and we'll have a big talk."

After the crowd had gone home, Mona, Joygo, and I prayed together. Then we went to bed. The next morning my two companions said they would visit out in the fields about three miles from the village. As they left, the children, most of them with babies saddled to their backs, began to arrive. They snapped my fingers and I snapped theirs.

"Jo Li," they said, "we have come."

The children may have forgotten much about us but they did remember my name was Jo Li. Most of the morning I sang with them and talked to them. I visited some of the women as they spun cotton or ground grain in the shade of their homes. Then I returned to the rest house and ate my rice and sardine lunch.

"The men are coming now," Mona reported a little later. It was beginning to rain and I asked him to invite them inside.

There were about forty of them and I watched as they came in. They were almost indescribable. They wore no clothing and there were gray spots on their knees where they had crawled through their grain fields, weeding. The red oil had formed dirty little balls on their heads. I realized that they needed God more than any other people I had seen.

The men listened as I talked, undaunted by the fact that I was a white man. They would judge the talk on its merits but the message had to be simple and fundamental. They would have to be told that sin was not breaking a taboo, such as imitating the call of a bird; that God and not the spirits of the dead—who they believed lived in the air above a nearby hill—was the central fact in the universe; that salvation was God's work, not ours; and that they, poor as they were, could possess the God of the universe and eternal life by believing that Yesus had died for their sins. I talked to them as carefully as I could.

"This is the way to heaven," I finished.

Mona gave his testimony. He had received considerable teaching by this time and it was good to have one of their own people say what God meant to him. In the early days when he had spoken to them about God, Mona always concluded with "They say this." Now he based his belief on something more substantial. "God's paper says so," he told them. "And this is the way to heaven."

When Mona had finished, an old man who sat just in front of us lifted his hands and smiled with full comprehension.

"That is just like Birapinya," he said. "Our people used to go to heaven. It was much nearer in those days. Birapinya was an enormous tree and it reached all the way to heaven."

Mona knew the story well and was about to stop the old man when I shook my head.

"Let him go on," I said.

"The people used to climb the tree to heaven to drink beer and dance," the old man began with enthusiasm. He went on to tell how, after having a good time, the people would return to earth to work. There was an old woman who lived in a hut near the foot of the tree and one day, when the girls and boys came by to climb the tree to heaven, she asked one to stop and grind her dry okra for her. The girl refused, so the old woman asked each girl as she passed but none was willing to help.

The old man warmed up to his subject and began to act out the story.

"Finally a girl came along with her brother. The woman asked again, 'Come and grind my okra for me.' By this time she was angry and when the girl refused, her brother ordered her to do it, for he was afraid of the old woman.

"Most unwillingly the girl knelt at the stone and ground the okra. 'You may go on up now,' the woman told her, 'but dance only a little. Then you come down,' and she wagged her head threateningly. She was still angry at the girls who had refused to help her. When at last the brother and sister returned to earth, the old woman set fire to the tree. The people up in heaven saw the smoke rising and scrambled down through the branches."

The old man was so absorbed in his story that he climbed onto the person next to him. "Some of the old folks couldn't travel fast enough," he said, "so they climbed on the backs of the strong people." He swayed from side to side as he demonstrated the dangerous ride down the tree. "Before the people could reach the ground, the tree fell. The tall people broke into pieces when they hit the ground but the short people were not hurt."

I smiled as I recalled that the Uduks were the short people.

"So you don't have any way to heaven now?" I asked.

"No," the old man said wistfully. "Heaven's a long way off."

"That is just why we have come—to tell you about the true way to heaven." I made no attempt to discredit his story. "Jesus is the way. Just as the sin of the girls in refusing to grind for the old woman brought separation from heaven, so our sin separates us from God. Jesus came to open the way for us to return to Him."

I thought of the words of Scripture, "I am the way, the truth, and the life: no man cometh unto the Father, but by me." The Uduk story showed the intense longing of the people for a way to heaven. They tried to reconcile heaven at the top of the tree and the Christian heaven of sinlessness, beauty, and peace. They were being asked to make a commitment to a new and strange God, a God who did not threaten them with immediate disaster if they refused to placate Him.

Before the three days were over, there were several men who were deeply moved by the message of salvation. Too, they were just as deeply impressed with the profound change in Mona. They had thought God was the white man's affair but Mona had taken up with it and was sitting there, talking convincingly about it and not even taking a sip of beer!

"What is it like to be a Christian?" they asked themselves. "To be a Christian is to be like Mona," they concluded. They were offended by Mona's conversion, but intrigued, too. He had set a high standard of Christian conduct and they were not ready for it yet.

"When we leave tomorrow," I said to Mona and Joygo, "I'll go ahead on my 'little one foot' and you can drive the donkeys." "Little one foot" was my bicycle, which left only one track.

At six the next morning I said good-by to Mona and Joygo and pedaled fast. Rain was threatening and at seven it hit me hard. By seven-thirty I had struggled to a halt; when mud clogs a bicycle's wheels, there is nothing to do but walk. I left the bicycle leaning against a tree and set out. The rain came down in sheets and I was still twelve miles from home. At twelve-thirty I staggered into the house, soaked through and mud-spattered.

After a short rest I discussed my impressions of the trip with Enid. We wished some of the children, who had been quite friendly, would come here to school. When Mona and Joygo arrived at six o'clock, after having spent the whole day in the mud and rain, we had a further talk. Mona slumped to the floor, tired but happy that the people thought his message interesting enough to ask that he return.

For a week there was no more rain, so I decided to do something about the bicycle. I called a boy.

"Tomorrow morning early you go and bring my little one foot back," I said. "You'll find it leaning against a tree just beyond that rocky mountain," and I pointed westward to the hill I had crossed.

The boy started out the next morning, and as he was walking through a village six miles away he met two Uduk men pushing the bicycle.

"Did Jo Li tell you to bring the one foot?" he asked.

"No," the men replied. "After Jo Li left his little one foot out in the woods, we had no more rain. Village people blamed little one foot so they sent us to get it and take it to Jo Li so it could rain." They looked at the sky. "We'd better hurry, it's coming now."

Our boy went with them to their village, and sat inside a hut all afternoon, watching the rain. All afternoon, too, he listened to the sage remarks of the people. No sooner had they moved Jo Li's little one foot out of the woods than the rain came! When next morning he arrived home with the bicycle, there was considerable awe in his voice as he told us how the Uduks had caused the rain to return. Mona, who had been listening intently, spoke up.

"Did the Uduks carry little one foot into the village because it was stopping the rain?"

"That's what they said."

Suddenly Mona looked disgusted. Then he smiled, and we were heartened in the realization that he had come a long way in the Christian faith. Someday, like Mona, most of the Uduks would recognize the tree to heaven for what it was—a fable—and they would know that bicycles do not stop rain.

June came and with it Leigh's birthday. We wondered what present we could give him. A hobby horse or rocking dog would take too much of my valuable time, so I finally decided to make him a kite. I nailed some pieces of bamboo together, tied a string around their ends, and pasted a piece of paper over the frame. We had a ball of string with which to fly it.

On Leigh's birthday I took the kite out and he followed, excited in anticipation of what was going to happen. I gave him the kite but held the string.

"Let it go, Leigh," I called.

He did so and the kite went straight up. There was a good breeze and it rode bravely, so Leigh came over to where I was standing and helped hold the string.

Suddenly a crowd appeared from a nearby beer drink. "What is that thing?" they all asked at once.

"Pull it down," Amat said. "It will stop the rain."

I groaned inwardly. I should have known better, and as I looked at the Uduks they seemed so unfriendly, almost menacing.

"It's just a thing for Leigh to play with," I explained.

"What's it made of?" Amat asked. He seemed to be the speaker for the group. Perhaps he had had the most beer.

"It's just a piece of paper and some bamboo sticks." I shrugged carelessly, trying to minimize the kite's significance.

"Paper?" the Uduks chorused. "Of course it will stop the rain!"

An old man stepped up to me and took my arm. He drew me aside from the rest. In a low voice he spoke to me confidentially.

"That paper is from your country and the rain doesn't know anything about it. The bamboo is from our country. You just pull it down and sacrifice a chicken by it. Then you can fly it all you want."

By this time Enid had joined us and wanted to know what the trouble was. I told her what had happened, and then, over Leigh's protests, decided to pull down the kite and store it in the attic. There was no point in offending the people just to fly a kite, I thought somewhat grimly.

The kite never flew again.

"What have you got there?" Enid asked several days later, as I stood at the door kicking mud off my shoes.

"The skin of a lion the police shot last month."

"Did they give it to you or did you buy it?" she pursued relentlessly.

"I bought it," I replied loftily. I felt quite smug about it. It had cost me fifty cents. The skin had been locally treated and was fairly soft.

"We can use it as a rug in the living room," suggested Enid as she accepted the skin.

"The men can sit on it when they help with the translation work," I agreed. "It will protect them from the hard cement floor." I was happy that Enid had not asked me to take it back to the lion.

Proudly we spread the skin near the desk in the living room. When Mona, Joygo, and another helper, Dirgo, came the next day, we thought they would appreciate this addition for their comfort. Instead, they carefully avoided stepping on the skin.

"We don't mind if you walk on it," Enid said. "You can sit on it, too."

The three looked at Enid in surprise as they carefully pushed the lion skin away and sat on the floor.

"Go ahead and sit on it," I urged. We thought they were being polite.

"Oh, no," Dirgo replied.

"Jo Li," Joygo said, "if we step on that skin or sit on it, the next time we go to the forest we will probably be killed by a lion."

"You mean it's taboo to sit on a lion skin?"

"Of course," Dirgo said.

"I wonder," Enid said later, "how long it's going to take us to get to the end of these taboos and spirits?"

We could see then, however, and at other sessions, that Mona was thinking. Whenever he propped his head on his knees, we knew he was lost in thought. For a year and a half his "theology," the beliefs he had been trained in, had been badly shaken. He no longer attributed the rain to the magic of the rainmakers and he had come to believe that after death his spirit would go to heaven, not to the rocky hill nearby. Nor was it sinful to imitate the call of a bird or allow twins to live. But what of this suggestion that he sit on the lion skin?

We left the skin where it was and each time they came our three helpers stepped over it and sat on the floor.

"Did you notice that Mona walked across the lion skin this morning?" I said to Enid one day.

"I didn't see him when he came in."

"He's probably thinking about it. He'll have to think the matter through and then he'll have a good laugh at himself when he realizes how foolish he was to connect lions in the forest with the skin on the floor."

Each day Mona sat nearer the skin, and finally he sat right on it. Dirgo and Joygo soon joined him and one day, as they were sitting together on the skin, they burst out laughing. It suddenly appeared ludicrous to them.

"How would a lion out in the forest know whether we had sat on a lion skin," Joygo said, "and what could he do about it?"

They had begun to reason but they still had a long way to go.

Death posed even more problems for the Uduks than did a mere lion skin. When one of their number, Kalmanya, had died, her people were worried, for she had been a character. We went to watch the burial and to sympathize with the bereaved.

"We'll have to be careful," the old burying women said. "She loved her granddaughter and she'll be back to get her."

The burying women had to be careful but they also had to be kind. Two female goats were brought into the house and stretched full length beside the corpse. Then big male hands closed over the goats' muzzles to shut off the breath, for when the goats died in this manner, their spirits joined the spirit of the dead. Thus Kalmanya would have milk to drink.

The men slowly dug the grave with their straight picks and hoes. They dug a manhole two feet in diameter down to a depth of one foot, then down another foot a second hole was dug only eighteen inches wide. They next hollowed out an underground chamber, the men taking turns sweating in the hole. Meanwhile, the village herd of cattle was driven by and Kalmanya's nephews picked out a bull and a cow, which they crept up to and speared. The two animals were skinned and the meat cut up and spread out on the roofs of the huts and on the forked poles that stood in the yard. Some of it, along with the intestines and stomach, was put in large earthenware pots to cook. Nothing was wasted, and the dogs snarled as they fought for scraps.

In the hut the villagers wailed. The women, whose job it was to prepare and bury the body, sat around the corpse. It was rubbed with red oil. There were beads around the head, neck, and waist, rings adorned the fingers, anklets the legs, and the arms were covered with bracelets. Kalmanya was more decorated in death than in life. When the mourners came out of the hut they were so exhausted and hoarse they could scarcely speak. They were glistening with perspiration and breathing heavily as they sat in the shade of the hut. No children were present and even some adults, who feared to expose themselves to this new spirit, stayed away. It was bad enough for those who had to be there.

The mourners would be hungry after the burial so women were busy at the grindstones. There would be food for everybody, the meat the most attractive item. The Uduks never killed an animal just to eat its meat. They killed only for funerals and sacrifices.

When the digging was finally completed the women took one of the hides and spread it, complete with head, on the bottom of the grave. As the body was brought out of the house there was a loud cry from the women. Two or three men grabbed spears and danced in front of the corpse, the spears swinging in circles to ward off other spirits. The little cortege walked around the grave three times while the crowd screamed and the men danced. Then the women lowered the body into the grave. They laid it on the hide, the head resting between the horns and pointing in the direction of the hill to which the spirit had gone or would soon go.

The Uduks believed that the spirits of their dead made forays into the villages periodically. Were they not responsible for the sickness or death of a person, or some calamity such as drought or insect pest invasion?

"Bring the things," an old woman called.

A gourd of oil, beads, a pipe, and some small gourds which the dead woman would need in the spirit world were placed beside her. Then one of the old women sat on the edge of the yawning hole and began to address the corpse reproachfully.

"We know you. You have been a tongue wagger and have spent your time running from village to village with your talk. Now when you clear out of here don't you dare come back! You leave your granddaughter alone! You go out to the hill and stay there!"

"She's a bad one," the other women agreed. "She is sure to come back. We ought to do her with cherries."

So they removed the stones from some wild yellow cherries and crushed the pits. Then, taking the paste, one of the women climbed down into the grave and carefully smeared it over both eyes.

"Now you can't find your way back!" she shrieked triumphantly, and, picking up some dirt in each hand, clambered out and threw it on the ground. All the men and women who had worked in the grave had taken the same precaution. This was part of the superstitious ritual.

Then it was time for the final ululation and weeping. The men gathered around, their backs toward the grave, and began pushing the dirt into it. Not even the smallest chip or straw was allowed to fall in. When the grave was covered, one of the women brought a gourd of water for the men. They placed it on top of the fresh earth, then they washed their hands in it, pressing the gourd until it broke. The hoes and picks used in the digging were placed on the grave, to be left there until cleansed by the sacrifice of a chicken. The gravediggers all bathed from gourds of water brought to them, and the women smeared them with red oil. The mourners ate the grain and meat and went home. Spirits of the dead were particularly troublesome at a new gravesite.

We too went home, heavyhearted. We had gone to the funeral to watch and weep. Now we hoped the day was not far distant when the Uduk people would no longer sorrow as those who have no hope.

Two months later we heard wailing again.

"Who has died?" we asked Mona.

"Nobody," he said. "They're fixing Kalmanya's grave."

Again we went down. The body had disintegrated and the ground had settled with the heavy rain. Fixing the grave meant packing the dirt down again. The women were wailing as they had at the funeral. The men pounded the earth, then sacrificed several chickens on the grave and had a hearty meal. They had more to eat at funerals than at any other time.

Death was no more discriminating at Chali than it was elsewhere. The witch doctors had to go as well as their patients. When we heard that a certain witch doctor had died, we showed Babu a picture we had taken of him standing. Babu held the snapshot in his hand and, after studying it, nodded knowingly.

"And now he is dead," he said. "If he had been sitting down when his picture was taken, he wouldn't have died."

30

Furlough at Last

FOR NINE months during the war Nick had been in Khartoum doing the work that originally sent him to Ethiopia and the Sudan—helping his own Greek people. At Chali, the first year after his return, he became restless.

"I would like to go back to the work in Khartoum," he said one day. His restlessness increased and we knew we would lose him. He left us not long after that.

Our stone house was falling down piece by piece, so we added another room to Nick's house and moved in. Right after that we had our first visitor. He was a clean-cut Sudanese official, who stood erect in his full khaki shorts and well-tailored bush coat, the typical dress of British and Sudanese government administrators. His pith helmet was decorated with a metal replica of a crane, the emblem of Blue Nile Province in which he served.

"I am Meccawi, Effendi, the sub-Mamur from Kurmuk," he said modestly.

Meccawi was young, almost boyish looking. His face radiated kindness as though it were saying, "I hope above everything else that we can be friends." He was not officious in his new position. He spoke humbly, as though wanting to make sure that he did not say the wrong thing. His hair was close cropped, Sudanese style, and his cheeks bore the marks of his Arab tribe. His light color confirmed history's record of the mixture of Arab and indigenous blood in the northern Sudan.

A sub-Mamur was at the bottom of the administrative ladder, a sort of county deputy sheriff. Meccawi had just completed his course in administration at Gordon Memorial College in Khartoum and Kurmuk was his first appointment. I introduced myself and invited him in for a cup of tea.

"You have two children here," he said. "Will they be staying with you through the rains?"

"We will all be staying," I replied, "but we have no doctor now."

"Yes, I remember. I am sorry. It was too bad." His expression of regret was so genuine it almost embarrassed him. He was deeply concerned for us and for his own people who had been deprived of a doctor's help. If some disease should spread among the tribes, many would die.

"I'll be in Kurmuk for another month," Meccawi continued. "If I can do anything to help you at any time, do let me know." He spoke pleasant English.

After he gave us the latest war news and drank his tea, he departed. He had no local problems to discuss with us for we were not in his district.

"He seems like a fine young man," Enid said, as she watched his truck disappear down the road in a cloud of dust.

"I like him very much," I replied.

We were favorably impressed with our first contact with this young Sudanese official. We thought Meccawi was the kind of man who would go far in the Sudan administration. As we walked slowly back to the house, we talked of this and that. Would there ever be an independent Sudan? Would the demands for self-government arising around the world be heard here too? Would there someday be a "last" governor-general of the Sudan? Would there be a "first" president? Perhaps.

Enid returned to her desk which as usual was covered with the books and papers that inevitably accumulate wherever translation work is undertaken. There were now several Uduks who called themselves Christian and more than anything else they needed some part of the Scriptures to read.

"John is certainly the richest gospel for preaching material," Enid said, as she puzzled over her myriad language notes.

"I seem to use it oftener than any of the other gospels," I replied.

"We've got a lot of material on hand as a result of our translation of parts of John for our messages. Why don't we start translating the gospel from the beginning?" she asked.

"All the instructions on translation work say to begin with Mark," I reminded her.

"I know. Mark is shorter and is written in a more direct narrative style without John's complicated vocabulary. Still, we've done quite a bit of John and we could translate the sections that are easy and usable. We don't have to get it printed."

Translation work among the Uduks was a great change from our original way of working in the tribe. Since we could not do much sitting in the villages we had to turn to concentrated study at home. Mona was Enid's mainstay and the two of them plugged along; they puzzled, they searched, they made pleasant discoveries. Often they were stalled for days on end on a verse or two. Week after week, month after month, Greek lexicons, English versions, and many other reference works were piled high on Enid's desk. Finally the work was finished and instead of doing just the easy parts, Enid and Mona ended up with a complete translation of the Gospel of John.

After the arrival of a party of missionaries in Khartoum, the Field Council met to arrange for the staffing of the stations. We wondered if anybody would be available to join us at Chali and were therefore overjoyed when Mary Beam was sent to Chali on transfer from Doro, where she had been before her furlough. Betty Cridland was assigned to our station also. I was to have a new house built for them. Mary would remain at Doro and Betty at Khartoum until it was finished.

We had met Mary only once in Ethiopia, then again, briefly, in the Sudan, where she had gone directly from Ethiopia. She was a hard worker and never spared herself. Her lean, freckled face was surmounted by a tangle of red hair. When Mary was in a hurry, which was most of the time, her hair had to hang on as best it could. It received little attention from Mary. Betty had been carefully brought up in one of Philadelphia's better suburbs and had grown up in the Episcopal Church on *The Book of Common Prayer*. She was about five feet two inches tall and people often asked if she were Enid's sister. She was well built and her dark hair was rarely out of place. She hurried through her many tasks and knew how to break up an hour into twenty-minute periods that could be used to start and finish three jobs.

Mary and Betty had met at Columbia Bible College in Columbia, South Carolina. It was there that the Christ of the prayerbook came alive for Betty. Following graduation, Mary went to Ethiopia and Betty remained at the Bible College as secretary to the president. She also taught several courses. When Mary had returned to the Sudan she brought Betty with her. They complemented each other. Betty was the student and linguist. Mary eventually handled the workmen, the car, travel equipment, and helped in the school discipline and boarding matters.

The two reached Chali in 1943. As I led them through the front door of their new home, I realized things were going to be different for Enid and me. Enid had been the only woman on the station; now I was to be the only man.

Enid began a regular class for Mary and Betty and taught them what she knew about the Uduk language. Our notes by then were fairly ample and we had a growing vocabulary. Some points of grammar still eluded us but that was minor.

Leigh was six that year and Enid borrowed some school books from Peg Phillips and began to teach him. It was not easy for Leigh to concentrate. Such rigid discipline was unknown to his little Uduk friends, who played outside while waiting for him to finish doing the paper. In spite of this, by the end of the rains Leigh was ready for second grade. By then, too, Mary and Betty were able to undertake a heavy schedule of work on the station—a schedule that would be heavier than we thought, for we were to go home on furlough. Our term of service was supposed to be four years and already we had been in the Sudan well over five. Because of the war and the impossibility of overseas travel, furlough had been forgotten. But now in the spring of 1944, the enemy was on the run and allied ships in convoy were moving back and forth through the Mediterranean.

For some time the Uduk women had been pointing out that "Jayme's little follower" was long overdue. They were relieved to learn that his little sister—surely it would be a girl this time—was to be born in early September. We would need to be near a doctor at least by the first week of August.

"We might as well try to get home," I said to Enid.

But what about Mary and Betty? We did not want to leave them without help, and wondered if the Ohmans could come to Chali for a while. Ever since Ethiopia had been reopened to missionary work, following the return of the Emperor, the Ohmans had felt the urge to return to their old post at Soddu. The Christians in the Walamo tribe would need help and very few of the missionaries who had been in Ethiopia in pre-Italian days were able to go back. They had become involved in other things.

"Permits haven't been issued for the reoccupation of Soddu Station yet," Walter Ohman told us. "We'll be glad to spend the rains at Chali to help keep the work going until we can return to Soddu."

We were glad that Mary and Betty would not be alone. Betty had done well with the Uduk language and Mary, too, had made good progress. She was able to handle the clinic and the maintenance of the station, and they had Mona, with others who were following along. He would make a big difference to the work.

We looked back over the past five years. They had been broken by war, sorrow, travel, building, and sickness. The illnesses of our two children filled pages of our diary. Over and over were the same entries—*croup, sore throat, malaria, dysentery.* We had lost many hours of study and work as we nursed the little boys back to health. It had been a never-ending battle. The children would benefit by a trip to America where they could be built up with good food in a temperate climate. And it would also be good to remove them from the downward drag of Uduk life.

Yet in the years at Chali our roots had gone deep. We had been in the Sudan longer than we were in Ethiopia, so that we did not feel we should eventually follow the Ohmans there. We thought of our days in Ethiopia —the luscious vegetables from our garden, the green grass, the clear spring just a few feet over the hill, the cool air, and the relatively civilized people. It was a pleasant place. But the Sudan needed us, and we were not prepared to change unless the Lord clearly showed us that He wanted us in Ethiopia.

We said good-by to Mary and Betty and the Ohmans, snapped fingers with Mona and our neighbors, and drove off down the road.

31

A School for Our Children

HOME WAS many miles away. Leigh had malaria and we carried him in a cot in the back of Dorcas. By the time we reached Melut, his temperature was normal, so we traveled by boat and train to Khartoum and on to Cairo, where we had arranged to stay with members of the Egypt General Mission.

"We'll be here for about two weeks until we can get passage home," I said to Betty McGalliard as she welcomed us to her home in suburban Zeitoun, where she carried on a work with women. She was a tall, attractive woman who spoke Arabic well, but when she spoke English she was right out of northern Ireland.

Betty made us feel at home at once. It was a good thing she was that kind of person, for our two weeks in Egypt turned out to be four months. The invasion of Normandy began and shipping was diverted, pending the outcome of events there. Finally it was too late for Enid to risk going, so we sent Leigh home to America with John and Peg Phillips.

Our third child arrived in Tanta, Egypt, at the American United Presbyterian Hospital on September 6, 1944. We did not think it could happen again but it did—our daughter was a son. Jayme and I went to see Enid the day after the baby arrived.

"I've run out of boys' names," I said to her.

"We'll have to call this one Malcolm, Jr.," Enid declared. I demurred for a while but finally gave in.

When one of the teachers in the mission school visited Enid she suggested that we call him Kimmie.

"How do you get Kimmie out of Malcolm?" Enid asked in surprise.

"Why your husband is Mal and the baby Kim—Malkim." The name stuck.

When Kimmie was three weeks old, we boarded a ship which joined a convoy of more than seventy freighters as we sailed out of Port Said for home. We spent four weeks on the water. Early on the last day of our voyage I took Jayme up to the deck. The coast line was just visible through the haze and I turned his head toward the shore.

"That's America!" I said.

We made for Milwaukee as fast as we could to rejoin Leigh. Enid was returning to a changed home. Her father had died and her mother was waiting for us to help fill the empty place he had left, so we settled down with her in Milwaukee. The war was still on and it was not the same America we had left six years before.

"With gas rationing we can't get to church as much as we used to," our friends told us.

We were disappointed; that was just the way we would use our ration.

The Christmas season came. It was a happy time for our boys who would have this Christmas in America with their grandmother. Next Christmas they probably would be in Africa again. An announcement that Handel's *Messiah* was to be sung on a Sunday afternoon by the Arion Musical Club found us making our way to the Milwaukee Auditorium. When the music began, we did more than listen—we lived it.

"He shall feed His flock like a shepherd." Our minds were back in Africa, full of questions. Shall we go? Shall we stay?

"And He shall . . . gently lead those that are with young." He had indeed led us. How soothing and reassuring were the words and music against the background of our last five years in the Sudan.

"Come unto Him, all ye that labour and are heavy laden, and He will give you rest." It did not matter that there had been turmoil, apprehension, almost despair. As the soloist sang and the orchestra played softly, we knew we had had this kind of rest.

"He shall speak peace unto the heathen." How appropriate! The surfeit of fear and the absence of peace were the cause of all of the woes of the heathen.

"Hallelujah!" The audience was swept to its feet in the tribute given by everyone since the first performance of this greatest of oratorios. "Hallelujah!" It echoed in our hearts, the perfect word of praise. "And He shall reign forever and ever!"

Then the fanfare of trumpets broke loose. "For the trumpet shall sound and the dead shall be raised incorruptible!" We had seen so much corruption. Mona, at least, would someday be raised incorruptible—if he were not caught up alive into the air, according to the promise in

First Thessalonians. We knew many more in Ethiopia and the Sudan who would be with Mona on that great day.

When the last "Amen" of the great chorus faded, Enid and I self-consciously exchanged glances. Our handkerchiefs were damp. Our smiles were a trifle wan. It was a rare experience. I gripped Enid's hand wordlessly as we walked toward the exit.

We began to look anew at the churches in every city we visited, and we read their advertisements in the Saturday newspapers, designed to entice people to attend. Religious radio broadcasts, local and national, seemed to compete with one another. For thousands of languid people Christianity was only a comfortable way of life. Africa kept pulling at us—our talents, our strength, our devotion—and we were inextricably caught in the web of her need. We could not stay in America and live with ourselves.

Enid and I had been silently wondering about our children's future. I felt Leigh should go to a school in Africa rather than in America, and thus be near us during our next four-year assignment. He could spend his vacations with us in Chali. We had heard that our Mission was considering the possibility of starting a school in Addis Ababa for the children of staff members. No doubt, I thought, this project would take two or three years to complete, so without much faith I wrote to our secretary for information. His reply made me realize just how small my faith had been. He wrote that the Mission was planning to send Mr. and Mrs. Graham Hay to Addis Ababa right away to start the school, and that they should be ready to accept Leigh by the time he arrived there.

It was easier now to face both the future and our friends. We went from church to church, telling of what the Lord had done for us in our five years in the Sudan. There was considerable interest as we tried to paint a vivid picture of the fear and superstition of the Uduks, of their detrimental tribal customs, and of our efforts to help them. We had laid foundations; we had reduced the Uduk language to writing and had begun translation work; we had established friendly relations with the people and many of them were coming regularly to services.

We said: "Though this was their way of life, God saved Mona out of it." We were announcing a great victory but had difficulty in making it sound that way. "Five years, one believer!" we could hear the unspoken—and sometimes spoken—comment. We tried to explain: "Only one, yes, but he set such a high standard of Christian living that the rest of the people weren't yet ready to follow him. To be a Christian meant to be like Mona. Think what the church will be when they do believe!"

We were telling only what the Lord had begun to do; the job was not finished by any means. But our furlough was and we had much packing to do, for when we shipped our goods to the Sudan, Leigh's things would go separately. We addressed them to The School for Missionaries' Children, Addis Ababa, Ethiopia. Later, it would be renamed Bingham Academy, for the founder of our Mission.

We sailed for Port Said in December of 1945. Kimmie was fifteen months old and he learned to walk on the freighter as it tossed its way across the Atlantic. He was the picture of blond health as he took a few steps, stumbled, fell, and tried again. His four dimples were often visible.

After a short stay in Egypt, we were back in Khartoum, where we met Graham Hay. Mrs. Hay had already flown to Addis Ababa with their younger daughter, Virginia; the older girl, Betty, had remained behind to travel overland with her father. We were glad to meet the man who would be Leigh's "father" during the next year. He would need one; he was eight years old.

Hay was in his forties, and lean and active. A former businessman from Waterloo, Iowa, he had been appointed secretary of the Toronto office of the Mission. But children's work had been the Hays' first love and when the call came for a couple to open up, and become the parents in, a proposed school for our missionaries' children in Addis Ababa, the Hays volunteered and their offer was accepted. While we were together in Khartoum, Graham spent much time getting acquainted with Leigh, in order to make it easier for the boy to break from his family. He took Leigh around town and was always asking questions and discussing little matters with him.

Howard and Ruth Borlase were newcomers to Khartoum, too. Dr. Lambie had been forced to return to the United States because of ill health and Glen Cain had gone back to Ethiopia to supervise the reopening of the Mission's work there. Because of the acute shortage in administrative personnel caused by these changes, Howard had been sent to Khartoum from Nigeria to serve as field director. He made the arrangements for Graham and his daughter and Leigh to travel from Khartoum to Eritrea by train.

"We're planning to leave January first," Graham said one day.

That left us three days. We tried to make the most of them with Leigh but we discovered there was no special way to act. Above all we wanted him to know that we loved him, and that we were sending him away from us because we really did love him. We hoped and prayed he would believe with us that if we put the Lord first in our plans, He would put us first in His. Kimmie was too small to know what was going on, but Jayme had become very much attached to his big brother and did not look forward to the farewells.

January first came. I purchased Leigh's ticket and checked his trunk.

"We'd better get to the station," Howard Borlase called.

Taxis were waiting and the baggage was being carried out. It was a typical missionary departure, with tropical hats on the chair waiting to be picked up. There were well-scratched trunks and battered suitcases. Lines had been painted through *New York, U.S.A.,* and *Addis Ababa, Ethiopia* written in, and the paint had run a little. There were blankets, bags of cookies and sandwiches, and an array of odds and ends. African trains are slow and one must take extra things along for comfort and entertainment.

East was indeed East, and West certainly was West, but the twain frequently met on the platform of the Khartoum railway station. Porters arranged the luggage in the compartment. One of us led in prayer. Our feelings had infected the others and several nonrelatives had tears in their eyes. The station bell rang and the train whistle blew. We hugged Leigh and kissed him, and probably said "Be a good boy" just to fill in a big empty space. What does one say?

The train was moving. Leigh and Graham leaned out of the window and waved. Many others were leaning out, waving, but we hardly noticed. It was, in fact, hard to see anything now that the train was gone. I turned away from the crowd.

"What are you crying about, Ruth?" I heard Howard ask his wife. "He's not your boy."

Perhaps nobody could see Howard's tears; they may have been running down his throat like mine. Leigh would come back in eleven and a half months, but it seemed as if we were looking into eternity itself.

The train would follow the Blue Nile for nearly two hundred miles before turning east toward Eritrea. Graham later wrote from Asmara, describing Leigh's trip. "If left to himself," the letter ran, "his heart was back home and the tears came readily. He asked several times how long a year was and how many days it had and did the days go by more quickly in Africa than at home." The second day there were a few more tears, then he began to take an interest in beating Graham and Betty at checkers. Travel now meant something more to him than the distance it took him away from us. He settled down to his new independent life.

32

A School for Our African Children

IN A FEW days it was our turn to appear at the railway station with baggage, bundles, baskets, and typewriter. A portable duplicating machine came later by freight. The Borlases saw us off and we would spare them emotion this time. It must be difficult, I thought, to have to be so often with tearful people at the railway station.

"I can hardly wait to get back to Chali," Enid said as the train pulled out of Khartoum, and I echoed her words.

With considerable nostalgia we retraced our steps south, left the river steamer at Melut, and crossed the familiar Dinka plain. It was the dry season. We passed through the Maban country and crossed the invisible line into Uduk tribal territory. Soon we saw huts and people, and the children and old folks waved to us. We waved back and drove on up the hill.

Mary and Betty were waiting. They had been waiting a long time, for the year of our furlough had turned out to be twenty months. It was wonderful to be home and there was much snapping of fingers. Mona was there and he seemed to have matured a great deal. How good it was to see him!

"These are the men who have been learning to read," Betty said, pointing to the group that had turned out to welcome us.

We knew them all by name. They had shown some interest before our departure; now Mary and Betty had had them studying for several months.

We went to our house, which was pleasantly familiar. The termites had eaten away some of the front door but that could be replaced or patched up. The old folding rocking chairs were there and so were the old pressure lanterns. We had hoped something would happen to them in our absence, for we had not had the heart to throw them away. Across the living room a number of papers were hanging from a string. They were letters—written in Uduk—from the men in the class. How well they had done! It was just like Mary and Betty to arrange something like this to welcome us.

"You really do know the paper," we said to the men who had followed us inside. They were proud of their accomplishments; doing the paper was at last gaining respect in the community.

It did not take long to settle down to the heat, the incessant demands of the work, the translation, the village visitation, the church, and the letters. We had always been mailbag watchers and now, with Leigh in Addis Ababa, we would be even more diligent. Shortly after we arrived, our station staff met to discuss affairs.

"With the men learning to read and more people attending the church services, perhaps it's time to try to get the school going again," I suggested.

"We can't go on using the same primer," Enid said. "We'll have to prepare a new one. The old one is out of date."

Enid and Betty agreed to work out a new primer based on the findings of the Summer Institute of Linguistics, held at the University of Oklahoma, where Betty had studied. Mary promised to do the duplicating.

"As soon as you have finished a few pages of the primer," I told them, "I'll try to start the school."

I visited the two local chiefs and the parents of prospective students, and met with less opposition than in the early days. They seemed to sense the inevitability of it, and realized that Jo Li would not give up until their children learned to do the paper.

"If you can send me fifteen boys from this neighborhood, we can have a good school," I said to the chiefs.

"No, no," they protested. "If our children have to do the paper, the children from the other villages have to do it, too."

So in self-defense they got after the other chiefs and when school opened I had twenty-five boys and girls. Those from outlying districts stayed with relatives, but living was difficult for them because these relatives were not their uncles. One by one they returned to their homes and I was left with the local boys and a few girls. These pupils made good progress and we soon caught up with the production of the primer. By working fast the three women managed to keep just ahead of us.

"We're nearly through with the primer," I told Enid one day. "You'll have to give us something else to read soon."

We had received a copy of simple Bible stories published in America, so we wrote to the publishers and received permission to translate and duplicate their book. As each page was finished, we used it in the school. At last the books were ready! We made cardboard covers and stapled the pages together. The books were attractive, but I could not use them —the children had already read them!

"We're just making trouble for ourselves having a school," Enid said, looking at the neat pile of books. "But I guess the only thing to do is to go ahead. We might as well revise and duplicate that translation of the Gospel of John." The portable duplicating machine we had brought back was turning out to be one of our most valuable pieces of equipment.

Although the children settled down to regular attendance at school, there were still difficulties. It was not easy for them to exist on the one meal a day their mothers cooked for them. We kept them busy all morning and they had no time to hunt for supplementary food.

One day, all of them waited on me. "Are you our father?" their spokesman asked.

"Of course not," I replied.

"Then why do you not let us go to the dance?"

"Well, at this school I'm a sort of father to you."

"Then why don't you feed us?"

They had laid their plans carefully and I was trapped, although I had seen it coming.

"We'll never have a good school," I told my co-workers, "until we board the children."

Without a boarding department there was no way to keep the boys from wearing themselves out at the all-night dances, and they needed to be better fed. They were really progressing with their reading and there was a growing appreciation of reading, writing, arithmetic, health, and general knowledge. Doing the paper was beginning to take root.

One of the children discovered that doing the paper gave him a prestige that he could not have had any other way. He was being shown his place by a member of the superior Berta tribe when suddenly he turned on the Berta. "Can you do the paper?" he asked. The Berta, who had not expected a blow from that direction, was stunned. Of course he could not do the paper. He walked away, ashamed that the lowly Uduks were surpassing him.

With the primer finished and the school going ahead, Mary and Betty began to talk about the work that all of us hoped to see done, namely, to start trekking out to the distant villages.

It was the rainy season and travel was difficult. However, it was also the best time of the year to visit the people, for each afternoon they would be returning to their homes from the fields. Thus Mary and Betty, in their fresh, clean clothes, started out on the first of a number of ten-day trips. They returned disheveled, tired, and caked with mud from head to foot, but remained only long enough to pick up clean clothes and fresh outfits. Then they trekked out to another section of the tribe.

Mary, who had been occupied much of the time with the Chali medical work, had been released for the trekking by the recent arrival of our first nurse, Bea Noffsinger. While in New York during our furlough we had met Bea, who was then a candidate for service. After having been graduated from Moody Bible Institute she had completed her nurse's training.

"We need a nurse at Chali," I had told her. "If you come out, I'll build you a house." A promise that sounded larger than it really was!

Bea had been accepted by the Mission and had been sent to Chali. I kept my promise and built her a little one-room brick house in back of the one occupied by Mary and Betty, with whom she boarded. Under Bea, the medical work became a full-time job.

With the rains over, it was time for our Mission leaders to gather in Khartoum for the December Field Council meeting. I made my way north with Enid, who had a serious nutritional disorder and needed medical care. I knew the Borlases were due for furlough and supposed some couple would be brought from Ethiopia or Nigeria to take their place. I was totally unprepared for what happened. When I returned to our room at noon on our second day in Khartoum, Enid took one look at me.

"Are you sick?" she asked anxiously.

"Not sick," I replied, "just scared. They've asked us to move to Khartoum to take over the office and home during the year the Borlases will be on furlough."

"If they want us to, you know we can," Enid said quietly. I looked at her gratefully.

"This year we're supposed to put up the new buildings for a boarding school at Chali," I reminded her. "Somebody will have to run it when it's finished. The children will have to be clothed, fed, disciplined, and there are the adult classes, the preparation of school materials, and the translation work. I don't see how we can leave Chali now."

But the decision was not ours, so we returned to our station, depressed rather than elated. I put up four classrooms and two two-room dormitories, as well as two brick houses for the Uduk staff. Mona would have one of the huts. He was to be the "father" of the school. The responsibility of starting a boarding school among such hitherto uninterested people as the Uduks was great and now we were leaving. We felt like quitters.

Mary and Betty knew what awaited them. They would have to spend days in the villages getting the consent of the parents for the boys and girls to come to school. They would have to go to Kurmuk to buy blankets, onions, peanuts, salt, and soap, hire a man to make mosquito nets, clothe every boy and girl who came, find and buy pans big enough for cooking the food, and employ women to do the cooking. The problem of finding women willing to work was enough to wreck the school before it started.

Nothing seemed right. I was going to a job I was downright afraid of. I was leaving Mary, Betty, and Bea with duties far too heavy for them. The schoolwork would halt their trekking and the translation of the Scriptures would be at a standstill. There would not be enough time to visit the local villages, and still less time to help the growing church. Although we disliked leaving our co-workers with this heavy burden, we at least knew they were in good hands and had no fear that they would be molested. We had never felt animosity from the people, apart from the incident of the kite when their own fears had so thoroughly confused them. And now a Christian community was coming into being. Only those of us who knew the Uduks could realize how safe our friends would be.

33

Our Daughter Is Born

AT KHARTOUM our family had become smaller, since Jayme was sent to join Leigh in Addis Ababa. Kimmie, who remained with us, attended the Clergy House School at the Anglican Cathedral, thus sparing Enid from teaching him his first-grade lessons. She took up her duties as housekeeper in the Mission home and I began my work in the office. Many new problems confronted us but there were rewards, too. Long letters from Chali kept us in touch with events there. The year would soon pass, we told ourselves, and we would be returning to our station.

But the Borlases did not come back. They were sent to Addis Ababa and we stayed on in Khartoum in charge of the Mission. We continued to live on the Chali letters: "Mona's wife has become a Christian and has been baptized . . . Kithgo has become a Christian . . . The schoolboys have settled down after a rash of runaways . . ."

While we were still in Chali the women had been constantly remind-ing Enid of her responsibility as a wife and mother. Kimmie was growing up, they frequently observed. When Jayme had followed Leigh, and Kimmie had followed Jayme, the Uduk women had been reasonably satisfied, but four years between children? That was much too long!

Our next furlough was to be in December, 1950, and it began to appear certain that we would present our parents with a new grandchild —a granddaughter, we hoped. It was not going to be easy for Enid. The nutritional disorder, the unavoidable disorganization of life that war brings, the anxiety for children far away, the long days and nights of exacting toil, interruptions, and frustrations—all had taken their toll. She had paid a price; her hair was nearly white.

October came.

"I think you'd better take me to the hospital before you go to the office," Enid said one morning. I did so, leaving her in care of the nurses.

During the morning I was half busy, half thoughtful. In a determination not to get my hopes up, I reminded myself that in some families there were eight boys and no girls. I planned to stop at the hospital on my way home at one o'clock, but just before one the phone rang. It was the British nurse, saying that I had a daughter. My heart soared!

"You'd better come right over," she added. My heart sank as she continued. "It's not visiting hours, but you can see your wife and daughter. I think you'd better get here as fast as you can."

Her tone was elaborately casual but there was a note of urgency that I did not miss. I was at the hospital in a few minutes and at the foot of the stairs met the doctor, who was just leaving. He congratulated me on the birth of my first daughter, then hesitated, his face grave.

"There's a bit of disappointment for you, I'm afraid." His tone was kind but it bewildered me. The buried fears that many parents have as they await the birth of a child were released and raced through my mind. "The baby was born without a left hand."

He had said it and I felt sorry for him, not myself. He had had to give me bad news and it hurt him. "We don't know why these things happen," he went on. "I haven't told your wife. I thought it would be better for you to do it." He wrung my hand again and left.

It took me at least a minute to climb the stairs and walk down the corridor to Enid's room. My mind churned. What should I say? How could I say it? What could I *do*? I stopped at the door, my heart pounding. I looked at the crib, then at Enid.

Her face was flushed and bore an expression of utter weariness. I crossed the floor to the bed and knelt beside her. "We have our little girl." I tried to sound cheerful but it was useless, so I blurted out, "No left hand."

Tears came, Enid's first, then mine. It felt good to cry. I had been on my knees, I had said the words. A long minute elapsed, one that separated itself from time and floated away into eternity. Then something happened. Unexpectedly peace came over me, inexplicable peace. I returned to the moment when I met the presence of the Lord, the moment that had headed me for Africa. Now my feelings were deeper, more complex, but He was near, even nearer than on that day so many years past. The Lord had followed me up the stairs and down the corridor. It seemed as though He had paused and let me go into the room alone. But as we met, Enid and I, in our deep unspoken spiritual love, we knew He had walked in with me. We both felt it.

The anguish disappeared. Some disappointment remained and does still, though perhaps that is not the word. It is more our great concern for our little daughter, who brought us a new kind of responsibility, but it began with a benediction beside that hospital bed.

"I thought something might be wrong," Enid said. "I asked the nurse if the baby was all right and she seemed rather evasive."

In time, two minutes had passed. It was an eon compressed into one hundred and twenty seconds. I had not seen my baby daughter, who lay in the crib at my back. I walked over and looked down. At last, after many years of waiting, I was looking at my daughter. A bright-eyed, alert little girl peered up at me. She was well-oiled and tightly blanketed. She needed to be kept warm, I thought, amused, although probably it had not gone under 100° that day.

"We don't have to worry about a name this time," I said lightly, managing a smile. It was October but we were not going to change the name now, so Dorothy June it was.

I went home. Our friends there knew we had a daughter but that was all. I would have to tell them and I fell back on the doctor's words again. A telegram had to go to Leigh and Jayme in Addis Ababa, and a letter to the Hays, asking them to explain the details to the boys.

That evening I returned to the hospital. Normally the babies were removed from the room during visiting hours but the doctor knew there was more at stake than our baby's health, so the nurse had been told to let us have her. For half an hour we were alone, the three of us. Enid and I were self-conscious, each wondering what the other was thinking. She spoke first.

"Ever since you left I've thought of only one verse of Scripture, 'In every thing give thanks: for this is the will of God in Christ Jesus concerning you.' "

"I've had just one verse in mind all afternoon, too," I said. " 'Who comforteth us in all our tribulation, that we may be able to comfort them which are in any trouble, by the comfort wherewith we ourselves are comforted of God.' "

As senior missionaries—the change had come so gradually that we were hardly aware of it—many of the younger workers turned to us for help in their sorrow and disappointment. Now we would be better able to help them.

About the time our daughter was born, we were learning a new hymn in our services in Khartoum.

> It passeth knowledge that dear love of Thine,
> My Jesus, Saviour, yet this soul of mine,
> Would of Thy love in all its height and depth,
> Its breadth, its length, its everlasting strength,
>   Know more and more.

That was what we had felt, not His anger nor His chastisement, but His love.

34

"And Children in This Life"

IN DECEMBER, 1950, we went to America with Dorothy. Leigh and Jayme flew down from Addis Ababa and traveled with us, so our family of six was together for the first time. Our furlough passed quickly. On our return to the Sudan, Mary and Betty would take theirs.

We had raised our children in Africa, but Leigh had outgrown that continent. He had finished the eight grades offered by our Mission school in Addis Ababa, so we returned to Africa without him. By our next furlough, he would be in college or ready for it. We remembered the heartbreaking scene at the railway station in Khartoum when he left us the first time as an eight-year-old. Leaving him behind as a teen-ager seemed even more difficult. There was not much outward emotion in the parting but the anxiety concerning his spiritual growth and welfare persisted all through the separation, although we knew he was in good hands.

When we reached Khartoum, there were more farewells. It was time for Kimmie to leave us. We put him on the plane for Addis Ababa, accompanied by Jayme, who now had assumed the role of big brother. If parting from the children was difficult, the Lord knew how to assuage our grief, for soon we returned to Chali to spend a year during Mary and Betty's furlough. It was dark when we arrived but a great crowd of our "brothers and sisters and children in this life" welcomed us. They had been waiting all day and we snapped fingers until there was no more snap left. I was quite sure some of the children were repeaters. What a contrast to the day the roof blew off our house and no one had shown the slightest concern!

We had not thought that Dorothy would spend any of her life at Chali but we were happy that she, too, could do a little growing up where her brothers had lived. She quickly became the center of interest;

221

Jo Li and Ko Li had actually produced a daughter, and her blonde curls fascinated the Uduks.

Mona came with his wife and little Kona, whose birth had brought Mona to us in the first place. The child, too, was a Christian. "Jo Li, Ko Li, you have arrived?" Mona asked. It seemed superfluous but it was his best manner of greeting. We agreed that we had arrived.

Kwaat, the little girl who had ground the grain and fed the children during the year of the famine, our first at Chali, was on hand, too. There had been a long lapse when she had not been near the church, but now she and her husband were two of its most earnest members. Indeed, she had been the first Uduk woman to be baptized and admitted to the church. The seemingly futile seed-sowing of our early years had borne fruit.

It took us several days to absorb all that Mary and Betty had to tell us about the work we were to take over. Then they climbed into their jeep and headed for Khartoum and America.

The Egyptian anthropologist, who had measured heads while declaring the Uduk people among the most primitive in Africa, would have been amazed. He had rightly said that the Uduks had almost no crafts of their own. Now there were various sizes and shapes of neatly decorated and properly fired pottery around the girls' dormitory. Grace Carter and Rosemary Russell, who had joined the Chali staff as teachers, had taught the girls this and other skills. Afternoons, the schoolgirls sat in the shade of their workshop, weaving attractive palm-leaf baskets. Many of their dresses they had made themselves, some of them on the sewing machine. Their love for clothes and sewing surpassed their former indifference, and they now sewed for the entire school of seventy boys and girls. Tidiness and cleanliness were stressed, and they had long since come to appreciate their mosquito nets.

Nor were they allowed to forget their tribal skills. They helped cook the food, and it was village food prepared and served village style, but there were additions of meat and oil they would have had less frequently at home.

The schoolboys were not far behind. They made their own bedsteads and tables, planted crops, and went hunting and fishing. In their arithmetic classes they learned about paying taxes and were taught that it was not a fine but a reasonable way for them to support their government. And they learned how to buy and sell without losing money.

As before, Mona was the "father" of the school. For this position he received a small salary. He saw to it that the boys were where they should be at night and helped with the discipline. When the boys went astray, Mona spent hours leading them to repentance. Mona was "father" to the adults, too, who wore a path to his door with their troubles and joys. The sick came from distant villages and they went to Mona's house first, where he fed them or gave them coffee. Village people sought his help; they drank his tea and found relief in talk.

The tribal economy had never called for any expenditure on clothing. Beads and red oil were inexpensive; now Mona had to buy clothing for himself, his wife, and his family. An Uduk Christian had more than spiritual problems! Although he did not spend much money on clothes, Mona always appeared neatly dressed when he led the church services, which was often. Offerings were taken in the church but they were not for him; that money paid the expenses of the conferences held on the station. It also helped build a new church in some other tribe or paid for Bibles sent to needy people in another part of Africa.

Since it was no longer necessary for the missionaries to do all the preaching in the church, they devoted more time to teaching the Christians in afternoon classes. Here the new converts learned to read and write—illiteracy and Christianity are incompatible—and to study the Bible. They now had the Gospels of John and Mark in their own language. Enid and Betty had translated them, Betty continuing with the translation where Enid had left off.

Each Saturday morning I met with the elders to discuss church affairs and to assign speakers for the following week's meetings. Mona was always happy to take his turn as preacher in the Sunday morning services. Matters of discipline were also dealt with in the elders' meetings. Occasionally young people, and older ones, too, fell into sin. Ordinary village life did not encourage Christian living. It was like trying to keep dry while sitting in water.

"What are we going to do?" Mona asked at the end of one of these long discussions.

"You should all move together and build a Christian village," I said, "as Miss Beam and Miss Betty have so often told you."

This idea had been suggested many times before but it had not seemed attractive. The clan had always been the basic unit in the tribe and there was an intense loyalty between brothers and sisters, more intense, we had early discovered, than that in the marital relationship. Wives frequently went back to their own villages to cook for their deserted brothers, their deserted husbands being left to shift for themselves.

Eventually the idea took hold, so that when some of the young Christians were ready to marry, they asked the older ones what they intended to do about the Christian village. The older people were hesitant, and it was not until two young couples settled in a place apart that they made the break. Then the Christian village began to grow. It had been a struggle for us. At first we had thought the Christians should continue to live with their own unconverted people in order to win them to Christ. Now we saw that this arrangement was unfair to the children, for family life was not lived behind closed doors. There was little that was hidden, even from the toddlers. The Christian village became a reality but the believers did not isolate themselves. They continued to farm with the village people.

When the church matters were settled, there were those of the school to consider.

"Jo Li," Mona said one day, "the school children are doing it with the paper."

"Doing what with the paper?" I asked.

"They are making love with it," he replied.

Some of the boys and girls in the school were exchanging letters that could lead to suggestions of marriage. In the village they heard marriage talk from infancy but we had banned it in the school.

"If there is talk of marriage in the school," Mona said, "the parents will object and take their children away."

It had taken a long time to interest the Uduk people in writing. Now we found ourselves having to discourage this interest, at least in one direction. But the paper had helped in another way. Slight misunderstandings among children or adults often led to sulks that lasted for days. When husbands and wives broke up over some trifle, neither would make a move toward the other and the rifts often became permanent separations. Now the church was having an influence even in non-Christian homes. Separations and polygamy were not as popular as they had been.

Where the schoolboys were concerned, Mary had found a solution. Before she left, she told us how to handle them. "Give them a pencil and paper and tell them to write their complaints and their confessions." The paper did wonders and smiles quickly returned to little faces.

For several years the missionaries had sponsored gatherings that would bring in as many Uduks as possible from the outlying villages. Recent conferences had been held by the Chali Christians themselves, and they had invited people from the Koma and Maban tribes as well. Enid and I reminded each other happily that great strides had been made, and recalled the early difficult years.

Before conference time came, the believers began their preparations to feed seventy-five guests. The Christians brought their offerings of grain and money to the church, then the men went out two by two to the distant villages, inviting the people to come.

The meetings began.

"Our stomachs are good that we can gather in this way," Mona said as he stood before the crowd of two hundred people.

Our stomachs were good, too. The Uduks spoke and we spoke, and the messages were interpreted into Maban, Koma, and Arabic. I remembered the British official who had told us they planned to organize a native administration for the Maban tribe. "But we have no plans for the Uduks," he had added. "We may just tack them onto the Mabans."

Now, at least where the church was concerned, the Mabans were tacking themselves onto the Uduks.

Mona was speaking again. "We used to say that we couldn't walk through the Maban villages because we were afraid of the people. Now we are brothers and meeting together and we are not afraid. All this is because of what Yesus has done for us."

From bright Chali the people took the Light of the World back to their dark villages.

35

"The Power That Worketh"

MARY AND BETTY returned from furlough and we went back to our work in Khartoum. If Chali had changed during our years there, so had Khartoum. The British, who had been so secure in their administration of the Sudan when we first knew them in 1939, were now, in 1953, talking about evacuation.

The typhoon of nationalism had swept India and Indonesia, Syria, Lebanon, and Palestine. It would eventually bring anxiety to the ruling powers in Kenya and the Gold Coast, and in North and South Africa. It did not matter that many of the earth's peoples were well off under their foreign governments. They were willing to accept a lower standard of living if that was the price of their freedom. The Sudanese wanted their freedom. This independence tide, hardly a trickle on the desert sands when we first saw the Sudan, was now running like the Nile. The vocabulary of the Sudanese was full of new words—*independence, union* (with Egypt), *self-government, elections, parliament, evacuation, colonizers*. On her end of the river, Egypt was coining new phrases—*one God, one Nile, one king*.

The Egyptians and the British could not agree on a formula for Sudanese independence. Egypt insisted that the only change in the status of the Sudan to which she would agree was one that would link the country to Egypt. The Unionist party in the Sudan took this proposal as the main plank in its platform. Britain and the Independence Front parties in the Sudan insisted that the Sudan should decide its own political future. The Farouk-Neguib-Nasser succession eventually led to an agreement between the two countries, granting the Sudanese the right of self-determination.

The agreement signed at Cairo on February 12, 1953, provided for a transitional period during which Egyptian and British influence would be neutralized. The British Governor-General's influence was modified by the appointment of an international commission to advise him. Neutrality in the elections for the new parliament was assured by the setting up of an international electoral commission.

In government, the free and neutral atmosphere was to be guaranteed by the appointment of Sudanese to all positions held by British and Egyptians in administration, police, and the Sudan Defense Force. A committee was set up to supervise this Sudanization. Finally, all Egyptian and British troops were to be withdrawn and a constituent assembly elected. This assembly would meet to decide whether the Sudan was to be independent or linked to Egypt, after which it would draw up a constitution in conformity with the decision made.

The elections took place in November and December, 1953. In the northern cities, voting was by ballot. In other northern areas, populated by less literate people, the men voted by lining up behind the one who displayed the emblem of the candidate they wished to vote for. In the tribal areas, the representatives of the electoral commission set up hastily made boards which showed the names and emblems of the candidates. Not even this much was done for the bewildered swamp and bush dwellers. They wandered up to a voting booth, which consisted of four poles set in the ground and covered on three sides with palm matting, and entered it. Before the voter were two five-gallon gasoline cans, one marked with a spear (the emblem, for voting purposes only, of the Independence candidate), the other with an elephant (for the Unity-with-Egypt party). Only the emblems were clear. What they represented to the tribesman was the shadow of a shadow. Where was Egypt? For that matter, where was Khartoum? The voter picked up a token and dropped it into one of the cans. He had voted.

When the votes throughout the country were counted, the Union-with-Egypt party had a majority in Parliament. The elections had been as honest and as efficient as conditions permitted. The Sudanese were ready to run their own government.

But toward the end of 1953 the Union-with-Egypt demand had subsided to a whisper while the one for independence had swelled to a roar. By 1954 the people could not wait to go through the weary process of the election of a constituent assembly. On August 16, 1955, Parliament met in an unusual session and voted the Sudan independent. It was the dawn of a new day for the Sudanese. Out in Kordofan Province, one of the Sudan's largest and most important areas, the first Sudanese governor of that province was installed. He was Meccawi Suleiman, now Sayed (His

Excellency) Meccawi, who had visited us years before at Chali. After he had served a short time as governor, he was called to fill one of the most important positions in the Khartoum government—Permanent Undersecretary to the Ministry of the Interior.

With the departure of the British, the ghost of General Gordon himself had to accept demotion and Gordon Memorial College became Khartoum University College. For the Sudanese, independence did not mean reverting to the pre-Gordon days. They wanted to take over the running of their affairs from the British but they wanted to run those affairs in as British a manner as possible. Their constitution would have to guarantee freedom of speech, of the press, and of religion.

We thought of the many ways freedom of religion had been interpreted in the countries of the world. We hoped there would be real freedom for the non-Moslem citizens of the new Sudan to believe and propagate their faith. And we hoped there would be a freedom that would allow Moslems who desired to become Christians to do so safely.

My duties in Khartoum included an annual trip to Addis Ababa on Mission business. There was time on one of these trips for a visit with Nick, who was now working with his own Greek people in Ethiopia.

"Dejazmatch Abeba is in the hospital here," he said. "Would you like to visit him?"

We were shown to his room and Abeba raised himself on his elbow and peered at us. A decade or more had passed since I had seen him. They had been hard years for him—and for me.

"I was in Gofa when you left for the war," I said.

The bitter war years had almost blotted out the idyllic ones he had spent as governor of that province. Suddenly the picture came clear.

"Ah, but you were just a boy then," he said.

We spent half an hour reminiscing about the old days and about the goodness of the Lord. Abeba had spent the years of the Italian occupation in exile abroad. He had returned when his Emperor was restored to his throne, but it was already twilight for him. Not long after we saw him, he was carried from the hospital and laid to rest in his own native soil.

The Ethiopia I visited was a new country. In our early days, the governors of the provinces traveled between their capitals and Addis Ababa on mule back, sometimes accompanied by hundreds of retainers and servants. Now these same governors made the journey by plane or car, and with only a secretary or two. Wherever possible mule travel was supplanted by motor and plane transportation.

Most impressive of all was the change in administration. The provincial governors and their followers no longer collected their taxes in kind or in services from the governed. Taxes were collected in cash and the officials received their salaries in cash. In the changeover, though, not all the inequalities and excesses had disappeared. A visitor to Ethiopia in the early nineteen-fifties might have been impressed with its backwardness, but to those of us who had seen Ethiopia in the early nineteen-thirties, the country seemed to have made a tremendous surge forward.

Walter Ohman was back at Soddu with his Walamo people. When the Italians forced him out, he and his fellow workers had left fewer than forty-eight church members there. Although the Italians had tried to stamp out the young church, there were soon more than ten thousand believers. Following the return of the missionaries to the southern part of the country, the number of believers quickly passed fifty thousand. The Ethiopians were doing the evangelizing. Actually, the function of the missionaries now was to teach the believers and to help and advise the church.

The Walamos told their story. No prophet or evangelist had arisen to stir the country, but as the number of believers and churches increased, they sent simple but literate members to the various sections of the tribe where they settled with their families as members of the community and farmed and preached. The Lord used these men to move the people to repentance. Church after church sprang up wherever they went.

Norman Couser had returned to a similar situation among his Kambatta people. With the help of Walamo evangelists, the church in Gamo had grown large and strong.

The gates of hell had not prevailed in Gofa, either. We had said good-by to a handful of believers; now there were several churches. "Sleepy" Hailu, who had served us coffee made from leaves of coffee trees, was one of their leaders. We had not forecast this role for him.

The church of Dafarsha and Dabalki had grown strong, too. The believers were no longer worried about taboos, such as the one that had forced them to send their wives out to miserable huts to bear children.

I returned from the green hills of Addis Ababa to the dry sands of Khartoum. How wonderful, I thought, if the power that is working in Ethiopia would begin to work in the Sudan.

Then I realized it *was* working. Enid and I revisited Chali, too, where Mary Beam and Betty Cridland were now in charge.

"We had two German doctors here recently," Mary said. "They were interested in applying some psychological tests to the Uduk people."

"They said that some of the Uduks have very high I.Q.'s," Betty added. "Rasha, one of your early schoolboys, rated at the top."

"But that isn't all they learned," Mary continued. "They said that fear is the basic emotion in primitive people like the Uduks. Then one day they said they had found a group of people here in whom the absence of fear was phenomenal. They were the believers!"

Nurse Bea Noffsinger took us to see Praise and Prayer, Doatgay's twins. They were thriving, quite unaware of the importance that was attached to them. As we looked at the attractive children we remembered the words we had once heard, "Twins have the evil eye."

"But you must see the new twins," Betty said, and she led us to the hut where Rasha lived. Proudly he showed us his twin sons. His wife, though, had almost lost her mind at the taunts of her unconverted relatives. The curse would not die easily.

There was now a place, too, for unwanted twins. Chali Station had built an orphanage. First to be admitted were Praise and Prayer, long cared for in Bea's home, followed in quick succession by several sets of twins. We could only imagine the number of twins that had been destroyed before the people began to bring them to the missionaries. In the orphanage were not only unwanted twins but orphans as well. Doatgay had died in a subsequent childbirth but the baby had survived and it was being cared for with her twins.

The surrounding villages were overrun with children. Mothers no longer waited until death closed in before bringing their babies to the clinic. Bea's child welfare work was having spectacular results. She had been able to do much in cutting the death rate in the cerebrospinal meningitis epidemics, too, and had herself come through a serious attack. Marriage had also become more meaningful to the believers. Hence, Bea had been able to curb considerably the spread of syphilis, as well as to cure many of her patients.

Believers were having a strong influence on unbelievers, and the marriages of the latter were becoming more settled and the children were brought regularly to the clinic. We knew that what we saw at Chali was not the result of mere teaching or helping.

"The fear of the Lord is the beginning of wisdom." The Uduk believers had begun well.

And there was the church. We had not come to Chali to enroll Africans in our religion. What we believed allowed for no such program; we could only tell them about Christ. The new birth had to take place within them and without it we could claim no adherent.

School was not a place for gaining followers. The boys and girls were taught the Scriptures but we did not want them to become "schoolboy Christians." They, too, had to be born again. With the disappearance of their heathen lethargy, the believers begged for more instruction than the missionaries could give them in the afternoon adult school. In our early Chali days we had often wondered if we could ever get these people to want to do the paper. Now Mary and Betty were saying, "How can we possibly teach all these people?" Those who had studied long taught the newcomers reading, writing, and arithmetic. Missionaries taught the Bible. One day several of the Uduks asked Mary and Betty to teach them Arabic, since they wanted to tell the Arabs what the Lord had done for them. So Arabic studies began.

The first Sunday of the month was Communion Sunday. Betty had given the church a form of service in the Uduk language. Mona led. The believers sang "All for Jesus," the only hymn I had personally translated. They had chosen it as their communion hymn!

Mona held a list of the church members and read out the names. Every member was expected to be there and to answer to his name. The Africans had a genuine concern for their church. Then the communion service followed.

My head was bowed. Two African hands holding a dish were stretched out to me. I took the bread and ate with thanksgiving, and when the same African hands were extended to me again, I took the cup and drank. The bread and the cup were memorials to the Savior who died for me, but the hands that served me were Mona's.

I remembered the communion service when I first served the bread and the cup to him. Then he was surrounded by missionaries. Now he had served me and I was surrounded by Uduk Christians. Many books have been written about unity and brotherhood. Our only source was the Bible, and we had found unity with some of earth's most unlikely people. We had found that unity at the cross.

Mona had first come to us because the birth of his son had made work taboo for a while. He had sat on the floor of our house while we gave him the bread of life, the Word of God. He had reached out to understand. Now I was sitting low on the bamboo slats, the pews in Chali Church. Mona was bending over me and I was reaching out to understand. But I could not really comprehend—"it passeth knowledge."

Mona was standing before the congregation, pronouncing the benediction: " 'Now the God of peace, that brought again from the dead our Lord Jesus, that great shepherd of the sheep . . .' "

As we left the church, I was scarcely able to greet my friends after that emotion-packed hour. I reviewed mentally our real goals for the Africans. What were they? Education? Social and moral well-being? Technological progress? Freedom from fear? How could these goals be reached?

The communion service had brought it all into focus. As we had fellowship together, our eyes fixed upon the Lord in His death, everything fell into place. Throughout our lives we had sought to make God Himself our goal and He had embraced all our need. We wanted for the Africans what we had wanted for ourselves. It was as simple as that!

It was already written in that portion of Scripture that always moved me more than any other. I knew it by heart—Ephesians 3:14-21. As I walked away from the church, I said it aloud to myself:

For this cause I bow my knees unto the Father of our Lord Jesus Christ, of whom the whole family in heaven and earth is named. That he would grant you, according to the riches of his glory, to be strengthened with might by his Spirit in the inner man: That Christ may dwell in your hearts by faith: that ye, being rooted and grounded in love, May be able to comprehend with all saints what is the breadth, and length, and depth, and height: And to know the love of Christ, which passeth knowledge, that ye might be filled with all the fulness of God.

It was all clear now; we were one family—our needs, desires, and aspirations one. There remained only the benediction:

Now unto him that is able to do exceeding abundantly above all that we ask or think, according to the power that worketh in us. Unto him be glory in the church by Christ Jesus throughout all ages, world without end. Amen.

19353